BEYOND THE FAR HORIZON:

WHY EARTH ENERGY DOWSING WORKS

THE LIFE AND WORK
OF
BILLY GAWN

Compiled and narrated by

Nigel Twinn

First published in 2012 by:

Penwith Press
Cornwall
UK
www.penwithpress.co.uk

ISBN   978-0-9533316-4-2

Printed by TJ International Ltd.
Trecenus Industrial Estate
Padstow, Cornwall
PL28 8RW

Contents

New Frontiers

Making Sense of the Seriously Spiritual

Appendices

List of Photographs and Illustrations

Preface

Our vision is restricted by the horizons around us. Some of these are close by, others further away, but there is a far horizon beyond which we cannot see. With optical enhancing tools such as telescopes or binoculars we can see more clearly, but even these do not allow us to see any further.

In all other aspects of life we tend to have horizons, usually self constructed, which limit our ability to observe or experience beyond those limits. They are put in place at an early age through our upbringing, education, and general life experiences. There is a great feeling of comfort and safety in not going outside our box and that is where we tend to stay.

Even those who have entered into the world of dowsing are no exception. There too, barriers are erected that keep us within our comfort zone. I believe that these barriers are constructs of our belief systems and that they prevent us from seeing or experiencing anything that lies over and beyond that forbidden horizon.

Some years ago, whilst sitting on a park bench in Glasgow during an interval at a BSD Congress, I was introduced to the concept of visualisation dowsing by the renowned American dowser Terry Ross. This allowed me to add to my deviceless dowsing skills, to further develop my ability and to see glimpses of what may lie beyond that far horizon. These glimpses may lack clarity, but they are perhaps enough to allow us to seriously look and challenge the various theories concerning the creation of the universe. They may also allow us to gain a better understanding of our place within it.

For those entering into the field of Earth Energy dowsing for the first time, it is hoped that this book will encourage, inspire and guide you through the confusion that exists and to allow you to progress well beyond that far horizon.

As yet there is no recognised 'Bible' or rulebook relating to what we now term 'Earth Energies'. What we have are opinions - and diverse opinions at that. The main thrust of my dowsing career was, and still is, to examine these subtle radiations, to see if any sense can be made of them and to determine if there are any general rules that apply.

For the last thirty years I have observed earth energies as they appear naturally, and also those I have contrived as the result of the many experiments I carried out. From these observations, I have attempted to move on to suggest a premise from which certain logical conclusions could be drawn, and to establish principles or sets of laws that those observations obey.

Much of this book is built upon simple basic observations that I have repeatedly made - and these provide the foundation for the consideration of certain possibilities that are examined in the subsequent chapters.

I had been asked on many occasions by some of my friends to put in print my dowsing experiences and views, but I could never decide where to begin or where to finish, never mind what to put in the middle, so I allowed time to go on without taking action.

It was in the spring of 2011 that I got an email from Nigel Twinn enquiring if I would allow him to produce a book based on my life experiences. Nigel is one of the few people that I would allow to take on such a task, so I agreed. I want to thank him for reading through the many articles and papers that I have written down through the years - some published, many not - as well as involving me in conversation on several occasions, and bringing all this disjointed material together into a coherent book.

I would like to emphasise that, whilst some of my views differ greatly from many of those who are at present in the mainstream of dowsing, I respect those views and do not in any way suggest that they are incorrect. They are the views of where people stand at this particular time. I may be looking at things from a slightly different perspective, because that is where my life experiences have led me. I express my opinions based on my life's journey, and on what dowsing has revealed to me. I hope that they will be accepted as such, and considered with the same respect that I give to others.

W A (BILLY) GAWN

Introduction

Warning! This book could change your life - I
kid you not.

There are ideas in these pages that will be
quite unexpected - and possible conclusions
that you could find both uplifting and unsettling.

On the surface, this appears to be the lively life
-story of a genial gentleman from Northern
Ireland - a seemingly quite ordinary farmer and
builder, who has chanced upon a whole string
of really exciting, and seriously unconventional,
aspects of the world around us.

If that were all it was, this book would still be a riveting read.

However, there is a sub-text. The concepts and ideas that flow from Billy Gawn's
discoveries are profound. They question the very way we view reality - albeit in a
gentle and gradual manner.

Unlike some of the wilder and more confrontational authors at the cutting edge of
21st Century thought, Billy takes a calm and very grounded - if slightly maverick -
approach to the nature of man and his relationship to the cosmos.

His toolkit is simple - dowsing, research, evidence, practice. Everything he does,
he does himself - meticulously. Only then does he examine the implications and
consider the possible consequences.

Like many of the more important thinkers of modern times, Billy has no interest in
inflating his own part in the great dramas that unfold in this book. He is someone
who just feels he was in the right place at the right time - perhaps even the
intended time - to discover a few missing pieces of an infinitely large jigsaw.

However, even being just part of a process propels the participant, perhaps rather
unwillingly, into the public arena. In years to come, I feel Billy will take his place
on the podium with others who have influenced the emergence of this new thread

of thought - but he will still no doubt be ducking away from the fierce focus of fame.

For my own part, I had been dowsing for a decade or more, when I went to an event, held by the British Society of Dowsers, in Cambridge in 2002.

It was my first venture to such a gathering and I felt I might be a bit out of my depth. I needn't have worried.

The speakers were excellent and, even if I didn't understand it all, at least I felt the long trip up from Devon had been worthwhile. Then this tall, nicely-spoken chap with an Ulster accent took the stage with a trademark smile, and the whole show slipped into another gear - well, more like another warp-drive.

I've never met anyone who's been hit by an asteroid, but I can empathise with their plight. One minute you are quietly shuffling your papers and minding your own business - and the next moment your world has been catapulted into a parallel universe.

As Billy was talking in his endearing lilt, it dawned on me that the things he was talking about were either ridiculous or remarkable. He was describing how he had carried out zillions of practical experiments with painstaking attention to detail - and, in so doing, he had discovered unseen aspects of the world around us, and about the world within us.

He was either a visionary or a charlatan. Having been a Personnel Manager for many years previously, I felt I knew a charlatan when I heard one. Billy was for real.

In the years that followed, I attended several of his talks and courses - and I came to appreciate and to respect his work. He always had the same measured delivery; the same self-effacing answers to those tricky questions about life, the universe and everything. There was no side to him; no promotion of the ego, even when it would have been fully justified. Just dowsing, research, evidence, practice, suggested conclusions.

Nothing more, nothing less.

Billy is an accomplished author in his own right. He has published a book and a string of articles about elements of his work. However, he never seemed to get the time, or to be in the right space, to summarise his exciting and varied life - to draw the threads together to his own satisfaction. Despite a fair bit of gentle prompting from various quarters, it was beginning to look as if he would never get around to it.

In the Spring of 2011, having had some modest success with a biography of one of his fellow mould-breakers, I asked Billy if I could help him with the authorship of his story.

To my immense pleasure he agreed.

This book may meander from the mundane to the metaphysical, in a way that I trust you will find both captivating and challenging - but it is all completely factual, exactly as he experienced it. None of it is faked; none of it is supposition; none of it is a flight of fancy.

This is the story of Billy's life and his experiences, exactly as it is - but it also says a lot about your life, too.

Sit tight, read on - and watch out for asteroids!

NIGEL TWINN

FROM GENETICS

TO REVELATION

The Reluctant Revolutionary

Dowsing works!

If I had been compiling this book a decade ago, the whole of this first piece would have been devoted to a screed of evidence showing that dowsing delivers - for most people, at least some of the time.

For centuries, experienced water diviners, hard-nosed mineral prospectors, senior military officers, trained archaeologists and respected health professionals have used dowsing to great effect. But that's all history now - and anyway there are plenty of good books on that subject already. Just two words will suffice to introduce this story - Dowsing Works.

How dowsing works

So, if we have reached base camp, where next? This book deals with how earth energy dowsing works - or at least it explains one man's research into the mechanics and techniques of the skill.

In the second decade of the 21st Century, even the 'How' of dowsing is becoming mainstream with the growth of awareness of the subject. There are still several schools of thought, and doubtless the debate about precisely 'How' will rage for decades to come. A description of various points of view is included towards the end of this book, in the section entitled Dowsing, Science and Spirituality.

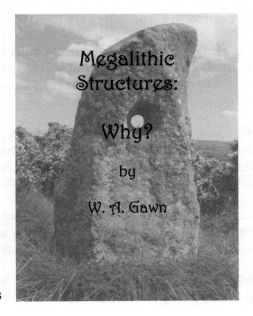

Megalithic Structures:

Why?

by

W. A. Gawn

However, for those new to the subject, at Appendix A there is also a description of Billy's own explanation of the mechanics of earth energy dowsing. This is an updated précis of the description to be found in his previous book *Megalithic Structures: Why?*, first published in 2000 and now in its third (2009) edition.

As far as this work is concerned, we clearly state a detailed and reasoned position on 'How' - and this story unfolds from there, based on that platform.

Why dowsing works

This book goes right to the heart of matter:

- **<u>Why</u> does dowsing work?**

- **<u>Why</u> can we dowse?**

- **<u>Why</u> should we dowse?**

This story of 'Why' is told through an analysis of the life and work of farmer, builder and dowser from Northern Ireland - William A (Billy) Gawn.

Outside of his immediate group of contacts, few will have heard of him. This is understandable. Nevertheless, it is a pity, because he has carried out a quite exceptional amount of painstaking research, over a long period. This has led him, by sheer logic and personal experience, to some profound insights.

The universe, fate, synchronicity - call it what you like - has made Billy's place in time and space unique. On one level, he is just a quiet and self-effacing gentle-man, who has been drawn, a little reluctantly, into the limelight - simply because he wanted to know 'Why?'.

Yet, while seeking to avoid personal fame, he is nonetheless very keen to get his groundbreaking research out into the mainstream of debate. As you read about his work, and hear the reasoning that flows from it, I am sure you too will see 'Why!'.

His first attempt at doing this - through *Megalithic Structures: Why?* - resulted in much animated interest in the niche world of dowsers, but raised little awareness elsewhere. Now in his late 70's, Billy wants to encapsulate several decades of largely solitary investigation into a work that will open doors and cross boundaries.

You don't have to be a dowser to appreciate the importance of what Billy has discovered - and you don't have to be terribly academic to understand what he has to say. What you do need is an open mind, and a thirst for knowledge.

While Billy's name is well known and, perhaps to his own surprise, quietly revered in the dowsing community, as an individual he has chosen to keep himself to himself. However, to understand why any man's work can be so significant, we have first to appreciate why he looks at life the way he does - and to do that, we must leaf back through the pages of his recent family history, and put some perspective to the person.

An Ulster Upbringing

Two factors in Billy's life immediately set him apart, quite literally, from any other dowser I have met. Firstly, he has lived all of his long life in a small rural area in Ulster, physically separated from mainland Britain by the Irish Sea. Secondly, he comes from, and belongs to, a traditional family - and a traditional community - of Northern Irish Presbyterians.

However, as we shall see, his views and his outlook have certainly not been constricted by this closely-knit way of life - quite the reverse, in fact!

Billy may be keen not to elevate his own part in this story too far, but he is a consummate raconteur in his own right, and he is more than capable of telling his own life story:

'The Gawns came into Ireland in the mid 1750's and lived just a few miles down the road from where I live now. They moved up to this land, near the hamlet of Donegore in County Antrim, around 1800. That was when my great-great-grandfather was the head of the family. We've always been farmers, and I don't think many family members moved on to other professions until quite recent times.

In my grandfather's time, there were three farms here, run by three brothers. Now, the three farms have all been brought together. Originally, they were small farms, only about 30 acres each, but that was sufficient in those days to maintain a family of up to 10 children. It was more or less subsistence farming.

The Second World War revolutionised farming around here, and encouraged the introduction of more progressive methods, which meant investing more money in the farm. To make that investment worth-while you had to have larger acreages, which required yet more investment - so we were drawn on to a kind of financial roundabout. To have a viable farm holding now you would need about 300 - 400 acres. Farmers today have a very different way of life, but they have just as many worries, because they probably owe the bank a lot more money!

I went to the local primary school. From the age of four, I had to walk the two miles to school in the morning - and back again in the evening. There was no concern about whether it was raining or snowing - you just had to wrap up and walk! At 11 years old, I moved up to the local grammar school in Ballyclare, which is about 6 or 7 miles away. I cycled to school every day. In the last couple of years there was a school bus, which took us about half of the way - so we rode our bicycles to Parkgate and caught the bus from there. I

Billy on the left with his brother Dick

stopped formal education shortly after I reached 14 years of age. In those days education wasn't free - fees had to be paid for a grammar school education. There was no thought of going to university, as it could not have been afforded. Only the privileged few went there in those days - just a few per cent of the population.

It meant that when I started dowsing, I wasn't hamstrung by some of the things that were taught at university - about concepts that can't be true. Consequently, I wasn't aware of some of the mental boundaries that restrict a lot of other people. Whether that was a good thing or not, I don't know, but maybe it enabled my mind to wander a bit further than most!

After finishing secondary school, I came home to work on the farm, and I worked for my father until I was 18 or19 years old - but I soon began to realise that there wasn't much of a future in it. However, my father kindly gave my brother and I the opportunity to farm on our own. We both took it up, and we went into poultry, pig and arable farming - and the farms were expanded.

We were one of the first families in the district to have a combine harvester, and we grew between 200 and 300 acres of grain, which was unheard of in those days. However, in the harvest season, we worked very long hours - maybe a hundred hours per week - and sometimes even more. There was one particularly bad harvest when I didn't get to lie down in a bed for six weeks. The most I got was two hours on the sofa - then it was up and about and at it again.   That was the ethic I was brought up on - work just had to be done. If there's a job to do, you do it - you don't look at the clock.

I was in partnership with my brother for a while, but eventually he moved on, and I tended the farm on my own for a number of years. I then went into poultry farming in a sizeable way, for those days, and also extended the pig farming business. However, I started to develop a bit of arthritis, which still affects me now, and I found that tractor work wasn't very suitable - so I began to look for other ways to earn a living.

I decided to buy some earthmoving equipment - diggers and excavators - and to employ others to drive them. From that, there was then a sort of natural progression into building and construction, as I had been preparing building sites for some time. I started winning contracts to build small factories, warehouses and school extensions. I was progressing reasonably well until Mrs. Thatcher came to power in 1979. She brought in a moratorium on public spending, which meant that my business turnover collapsed. I dropped down from employing 40 to 50 men to just 4 or 5 men. Work just couldn't be acquired at a profitable level.

So, rather than bankrupt myself, I sought out another opportunity. I took a job in a local factory that installed insulation, and I managed the everyday work of their home insulation business at a supervisory level. The business progressed well - and they started to get into a line called 'low energy structures'. For the rest of my working life, I was involved in training and supervising people to construct houses that required very little energy input. Even most dwellings being built today do not measure up to the efficiency of those buildings. A lot of that work took me over to England - and we built projects throughout the Midlands and beyond. I stayed in that line of work until I retired at 65.

However, shortly after that, my youngest son bought a Victorian house in Belfast - and I did most of the physical work involved in renovating it, including building an extension and laying out the grounds around it.

Almost immediately after that, I built the house we now live in, which is situated in about an acre of ground. It's built over an old quarry on a rocky outcrop. It took about a year and a half to build the house, and another three years to landscape the gardens, which were designed by my wife.

I got married in 1960 - and we have three children and several grandchildren.'

Billy's personal background is one of a typical rural twentieth century family making intermittent progress in a current of growing national prosperity. His father's life - which was the backcloth to Billy's own development - was very different.

'Although my father gave us a lot of freedom to pursue what we wanted to do, work was the only thing that really mattered to him. You can understand it, as his father died, during the international flu pandemic of 1919.

My father had to take over the farm at the tender age of 19. Although he had an older brother, he was studying at college in Dublin. My father had a younger brother, a sister and a grandmother to support. As there was no money in the bank to pay the expenses of running the farm, my father had to go into debt to make ends meet. Therefore, he had to work very hard for about 20 years to get that debt paid off. During that period there was the great depression, and there was no money to be had. Due to the circumstances of the time his income was low, and he had to live accordingly.

It was only in the 1940's, when he began to keep cows and to produce milk, that he started to get a steady income. By today's standards, we lived in poverty. But everyone was in poverty, so it didn't matter quite so much. We had darns on our socks and pullovers - but everyone had that, so it wasn't a stigma. Nobody called you names because you didn't have the right designer label on your jacket!

The vast majority of the food we ate was produced on the farm, so we didn't starve. However, it meant that we learnt to respect money - and even today, we still respect money.

My father was mechanically minded, and if he had been able to pursue a career outside farming it would have been in mechanical engineering. However, he still exercised this side of his ambition by building home made tractors for himself and some neighbours. They were made up from parts of conventional vehicles, cars, lorries etc. suitably modified. His last endeavour was a tractor with hydraulic lift. He used parts that came from the undercarriage of an aircraft that was being scrapped after the war. Although crude looking, it had about twice the capacity of those being manufactured by Ferguson and others at that time. It was capable of speeds of up to forty miles per hour, something that modern tractors only achieved in recent times.'

It can be difficult for those of us who have been brought up in the relative comfort and security of post-war southern England to appreciate that life, life expectancy, and the outlook on life was subtly different for the generations that preceded us - particularly for those living away from the mainland mainstream. Add to that the relative isolation of British rural communities in the era before television, let alone the Internet, and psychologically you are standing in a very different place indeed.

David Gawn, Billy's father, driving his home made tractor with hydraulic lift

Billy's upbringing may have been pretty well-defined by modern standards, but there are aspects of his outlook that predate his career as a serious dowser, which indicate he may have had a rather more holistic view of life than some of his contemporaries.

When we started out on the grand undertaking of committing Billy's life to print, I did wonder how a life-long vegetarian like myself would hit it off with a professional pig and poultry farmer. But life is full of little surprises . . .

'Long before the organic movement really got going, I never liked the idea of consuming large quantities of chemicals. When we were growing grain, I became very aware of the quantity of chemicals that we were pumping into the ground - and spraying on to the crops too. You came to appreciate that a lot of it was ending up in the watercourses and the reservoirs.

When you taste food that's grown organically, compared to food that's grown chemically - there's no comparison whatsoever. The one tastes as it should, the other tastes as it shouldn't!   Some of it is almost inedible.

Although I'm not a vegetarian, I eat very little meat. I think that chefs tend to destroy the flavour of vegetarian dishes. They seem to think you have to spice it up, whereas I like my vegetables picked fresh, cooked well and served, maybe, with a little butter, or a tiny pinch of salt or pepper. That way, you get the true flavour of the vegetables and you are getting all the vitamins that are in them.'

Community and Commitment

A Presbyterian background

While dowsers are drawn from across the religious spectrum, and many from way beyond it, to my knowledge Billy is the only practising Presbyterian dowser that I have come across. No doubt, someone reading this book will tell me of others - and I look forward to talking to them!

As dowsing inevitably leads the researcher beyond the five gross senses, it can reach into fields that some might consider spiritual, and we will discuss that issue, later in the book. However, Billy has found that, far from demolishing his faith - as Richard Dawkins might have predicted - his belief in the divine has, if anything, been reinforced. At the end of a long day, we are all part of the same tapestry, which we view from different angles. What you experience depends partly on where you cast on to your journey, and partly on where the thread takes you.

Not only has Billy remained an active member of his local congregation, but he has produced an excellent hardback history of his local church - Second Donegore. This erudite tome, in addition to cataloguing the progress of the congregation over the last century or so, also includes a preamble on the development of Presbyterianism.

He has compiled and edited the parish magazine three times a year for the last 11 years. It is interestingly named *Dunnamuggy News* - Dunnamuggy translates as 'the fort on the hill' in Gaelic - the townland on which the church is located. In addition, Billy was a teacher at the Sunday School there for 30 years, and its Superintendent for 25 of those years.

When I was baptized, as an infant in to the C of E, it was little more than a formality. My family were classic English agnostics who just liked to keep their heads down. In the generation before my own, it was the default stance. It broached no awkward questions.

Billy, however, comes from a long and continuing tradition of active and committed involvement in the church. It has great meaning for him and his family - and it's an interesting place to start out on an epic dowsing journey.

'I think coming from a Presbyterian background tends to make you look at things from a more scientific viewpoint, in the sense that I have a cause and effect approach to the world around me. I feel there's a reason for everything.

Over the years, I have tried to find out <u>why</u> things are as they are - <u>why</u> they change, and what makes that change happen. Where-as, if I had been coming from a more spiritual background, I probably wouldn't have started to ask those questions in quite the same manner. I might just have accepted that everything came from God, and that was that. That's why I approached my research in the way that I did.

When you're young you tend to take things on board at face value; they're just facts. It's only when you get older that you start to question them a bit more.

Often, you find that it's not that the message is difficult to understand, but it's the descriptions and the terminology that are used that make it seem so confusing. If you can put your ideas into a different form of words, they can become more under-standable to someone from a different background. That's a common point of reference between my own heritage and the main body of dowsing researchers - the more scientifically minded and the more spiritually minded tend to use different ways of describing the same concepts. This can make a conversation between the two groups quite difficult.'

One of the consequences of coming from the non-conformist fold, which I had not appreciated at the outset, is that there seems to be a fair bit of common ground between the philosophy and approach of the earliest Irish Christians and that of the modern protestants - both having cause to be wary of certain aspects of the line taken by the centralised church based in Rome.

'People in the southwest corner of Ireland are very open-minded, which is why I've done quite a lot of my work there.

St Patrick brought Christianity to Ireland, but he didn't bring it through Rome - he came by another route. When he was alive, he didn't bow his head to Rome. However, he did Christianise Ireland very rapidly. He did this, not by fighting against the old Celtic religion, but by working with it - and by adopting an 'if you can't beat them, join them, and then infiltrate them and gradually take them over' approach!

He was credited with doing away with the snake in Ireland, but as there never were any snakes in Ireland, that wasn't too difficult! I think the snake he was referring to was the witchcraft and belief in earthly spirits that he largely suppressed. However, he only succeeded in part.

On the west coast of Ireland the old magical traditions, the faery traditions, remain deep in the psyche to this day. Even the priests that operate in the churches and the chapels there can be quite open to talking about it. I have spoken with some of them, who do spirit clearing, house clearing and that type of work, themselves. In England, I think this would be a strict no-no. It's regarded as pagan and you shouldn't touch it, but there's a different attitude down the west coast of Ireland.

There was a farm in the west, where I did some work for an English lady from the North East. She had a couple of fields, which had big boulders in them. She asked an old farmer, who had worked the ground previously, why he hadn't removed the boulders. He replied that the stones had special purposes, and when he was going to sow seed in the spring, he would place the seed on top of one of the stones for a period, as this improved germination. He was totally convinced it worked - it was a rational experience, not just a half - remembered superstition. The farmer was annoyed that more modern agriculturalists were clearing all the stones from their fields for ease of cultivation, and he felt it was having an adverse effect on the health of the livestock in the area. These beliefs have been handed down for hundreds, if not thousands, of years in the west of Ireland.

A lot of the early Christian churches in Ireland were built on ancient sites. If a site was already in existence, which people revered and collected at, then that would have been an obvious place to establish your church. Just as if Marks and Spencer was going to open a new store, they would put it where people would congregate. That's what the hierarchy that followed St Patrick did, when they were building their early churches.

I don't think those early wandering 'saints' were aware of earth energies as such, but the people who lived in Ireland before them certainly knew. Those who used the Iron Age sites, and sites dating back before that, were certainly aware of earth energies. However, it is believed that St. Patrick ordered that a stone be erected to block the energies coming from Uisneach, the Navel Stone of Ireland, and preventing it from flowing to other regions of the land - so maybe he had an inkling about the existence of earth energies!'

Billy is part of a long and honorable tradition that finds no conflict between the exploration of science and the acknowledgement of the divine. In one sense, his view could be considered to be more rational than those who have cast the remaindered God into the dustbin of history in the absence of evidence for His retention.

Philosophy and science have achieved a great deal in the centuries since the enlightenment, but they haven't yet - and perhaps never will - come up with a Theory of Everything.

For scientists and theologians alike, at the cutting edge of seeking to understand where we ultimately come from - and why we are who we are - there is a very clear fork in the road.

There are those who propose that our cosmos is infinite - that it just goes on forever, or maybe curls back on itself somehow uniting the beginning with the end. Both philosophers and scientists abhor the use of the vehicle of infinity, as it smacks of a cop-out. It implies that the whole scenario is all too big and too difficult to comprehend - so we'll just study the bit we can see or make sense of, and assume it continues like that ad infinitum. However you wrap it up in fine words, this is not an entirely satisfactory treatise.

The other school proposes that the cosmos is finite. It may be circular, incredibly convoluted through multiple planes and dimensions, or incomprehensibly big, but at the end of space and time it is still a definable entity in an even bigger void. This line of reasoning begs the questions 'What lies beyond the cosmos?' and 'Who started it off?' For those of a religious persuasion, this latter line of reasoning reopens the door to the existence of the Great Creator - although it still leaves the question 'Who created the Creator?' unanswered.

Billy's view is that the whole of existence (or of creation, if you prefer) - including anything that you can sense by dowsing - invites rational investigation. For him, all of it could be explained scientifically, if we had the courage to expand our scientific paradigm far enough. But beyond that, or maybe within it, lies the realm of God - if we define God as the controlling and organising force behind all existence. In this scenario, the divine and the diviner can comfortably co-exist. Regardless of whether you or I agree with this stance, it is a firm platform from which to view the cosmos in all its wondrous diversity.

An aspect of Billy's work that highlighted to me the significance of this religious inheritance for him, was his response to a question of mine about the sources of detrimental energy. Billy's work on the elimination of naturally occurring detrimental energy is seminal, as we shall see shortly. However, when I asked him about his feelings concerning the potentially harmful negativity in the non-physical environment, for example that found at former sites of battles or murders, his comments were, as ever, very straightforward.

> 'I am aware of this, but I've not investigated it myself. I have very briefly looked for entities, and I am aware of energy forms that might fit that description, but I have never looked to see if they are different from normal earth energies.
>
> Although it isn't my area of experience, I could venture to say that spirits are probably a bit like thought forms. It's not the thought form that's out there, but the disruption that the thought form has caused to the energy environment. If you are dowsing for a spirit, it may not be the spirit you find that's still out there, but just the disturbance that it has created in the ether - like the ripples on the pond, rather than the stone that's been thrown to create them.

17

To be honest, I have kept away from that aspect of dowsing as I have never felt comfortable working with it. I suppose, it's part of my Presbyterian upbringing.'

We shall revisit some of these issues later in this book.

Forging an Alliance

Billy's everyday life also has another interesting strand that you don't often find displayed very prominently amongst the dowsing fraternity - an interest in party politics. While most diviners tend to be a rather apolitical lot - at least when it comes to being active party members - over the years, Billy has been willing to play his part in the 'invigorating' mêlée of political debate in Northern Ireland.

In a region dominated by highly polarised groupings, in the main based on traditional religious affiliations, the emergence of a viable centre party in the 1970's was something of a surprise to the outside world. Its founders were as brave as they were visionary - and those who chose to throw in their lot with them risked alienation from friend and foe alike.

'I had a neighbour who was a founder member of the Alliance Party. He approached various people to see if they would be willing to become members - and knowing my political outlook, he asked me if I was willing to join them. So, I went to a meeting, to see what they were all about. I found that they were talking a lot of sense, as they were trying to get away from conflict, and to move towards compromise. However, in those days, 'compromise' was a dirty word - and it still is in some quarters. For two years I was the chairman of the local branch of the party.

A couple of years after I joined the party, they were preparing for council elections. There were also attempts to put together a power-sharing assembly around that time. I stood as a prospective councillor for the Antrim Town area. I got a fair number of votes, but not enough.

The voting system here is Proportional Representation (PR). If you get about half the votes you need, and then a lot of transfers of second preferences from voters supporting candidates who have been eliminated, you have a chance of getting elected. But in those days, the Alliance Party wasn't attracting too many transfers. It was looked upon as a treacherous group by both of the sectarian communities - neither supporting a united Ireland nor over-emphasising the link with Britain.

The next election was for the MLA (the devolved Parliament in Northern Ireland). There were three Alliance candidates, one of whom got elected. I got about two thirds of the way to being elected. I only got eliminated at about the sixth count. However, it was a very exhausting time, fighting two elections within about a month of each other, back to back.

I was also very busy in the building trade at that time, and it was getting very competitive too. So, although I remain a party member, I've stopped being quite so active in it. I suppose, I was active in the party for about four or five years.

After about 40 years they are beginning to catch people's awareness. In the more moderate areas, Alliance is becoming a dominant political force - to the extent that it is now the second largest political grouping in the Belfast City area. However, in the country areas they are still struggling.'

Given the remarkable outputs of Billy's research, one has to draw the conclusion that Stormont's loss was the gain of the world of dowsing.

Discovering Dowsing

In an era of mass communication and instant internet access to a whole universe of information, it is important to remember that not too long ago, most people living away from the main centres of population had very little access to written research work.

Most of those who were born in the post-war era, and spent their formative years living in the heart of the UK mainland, have been exposed to a whole raft of novel concepts - some strictly scientific, some decidedly New Age. Most have read or at least heard about them, even if they haven't taken them all on board.

Growing up in rural Northern Ireland, before, during and after WWII, Billy would only have come to hear about these subtly developing ideas by chance encounters - or by synchronicity, as it is sometimes known.

Dowsing was one of these ideas.

Working with water

'In my late teens, I came across a couple of people who professed to be able to divine (as it was called then). I observed one slightly eccentric fellow cut a twig in the shape of a Y out of the hedge, walk across a field and announce that there was underground water there. I just observed and smiled inwardly, and I did not argue with him one way or the other. However, as he walked away I saw he had thrown the twig down. I kept my eye very closely on where he had thrown it. After everybody was out of the way, I picked it up and walked across the same field with it held as he had held it - and to my great surprise I got some responses, even though I didn't really know what I was looking for. I held on to the twig and tried in other fields too - and got responses there as well. So that was my introduction to dowsing.

Another old chap not far from where I live in the countryside used a fob watch on a chain for what he called divining. He held it like we would hold a pendulum today. On one occasion he used it in his kitchen - the watch swung around madly, and he declared that there was underground water beneath his house. As he did his stuff, I again had a bit of a smile behind his back, but at least it introduced me to the concept.

From time to time after that, I used to cut a twig out of the hedge, mainly just to amuse myself - but I did find a few shallow wells successfully. When they were dug down, water was found at a depth of 10 to 15 feet under the surface of the ground, which was quite reassuring for someone who was essentially self-taught.'

Beyond divining

'In those days, I had no idea that you could find anything other than water. But one day I was experimenting with a Y rod cut from the hedge in a field where a long section of barbed wire had been pulled out of an old fence. It was tangled in the ground, with grass growing over some sections of it.

When I was dowsing in that part of the field, I got a positive reaction, which I naturally assumed was underground water. However, when I looked more closely, I saw that it was where this rusty old wire was embedded in the ground. I was surprised to find that I was getting my response exactly where this wire was lying. Suddenly I realised that in this instance the dowsing action was not related to underground water - it was the presence of the wire that had triggered it off.

I was not aware until then of the necessity of the 'dowsing question' in order to focus my intent. That raised my curiosity - could I use dowsing for things other than underground water? As time went by I found I could, and a new strand of my life, as a dowser, was underway.

On another occasion, we needed to find an underground drain on my farm. I dowsed across the field where I knew the drain was located, and I got a reaction close to where I believed it to be. I had cut two twigs from the hedge and I used one of them, whilst keeping the other in my pocket. When I thought I had found the drain, I put the spare one down on the ground with the main stock of it in line with the drain - but naturally with the Y's of the twig pointing to the left and to the right. I went upstream, as it were, and walked across the position of the drain again to see where it lined up. I walked across the alignment a couple of times and I did not get any reaction at all, which was puzzling. Then I walked across it again continuing for a greater distance, and I did get a reaction. When I looked back, I saw that the new reaction was directly in line with one of the outstretched arms of the twig lying on the ground. This was very confusing, so I turned around and walked in the other direction again going a little bit further - I got another reaction, this time in line with the other arm of the twig. The 'energy line' directly over the drain, where the first reaction occurred, seemed to split into two streams, this being caused by the twig placed over it. I was intrigued by now, so I walked further up the field, and found that the two streams of energy emanating from the arms of the Y-shaped stick joined up again. This resulted in a sort of egg-shaped pattern of energy in the field.

Later, I tried it with other pieces of stick - and I found that you could pick up a line running out of the end of just about any stick for quite a distance. That got me really interested, although I was at something of a loss to know what I was actually dowsing. In Northern Ireland at that time, no one else had ever mentioned this sort of thing - and in retrospect, I doubt if anyone had even thought to look for it.

In the mid-1980s, I saw something on television about dowsing for reactions around standing stones. As I was travelling to and from work each day I used to pass a standing stone, called the Holestone, which was quite close to the side of the road. One day, I quietly put a dowsing rod into the back of my car, and on the way home I jumped over the gate into the field and wandered around the Holestone. Lo and behold, I started to get reactions there too.

I came home and I thought about it. I knew that some people considered standing stones to be 'magical'. I was pretty sceptical about that. So, I just took an ordinary small stone, with nothing special about it, set it up in the yard and walked around it - and I found I got some reactions from that stone fairly similar to that at the Holestone.

I took it one stage further and wandered around the yard, where I got a whole load of reactions of one kind and another. I monitored these carefully for a period of a couple of weeks, but it began to get so confusing because they kept changing a little every day. When in the house one evening I said to myself 'I'm going mad - I don't want any more of this!'

After a week or so, I began to think things over more carefully. I realised that instead of trying to take on the big picture all at once, I should work with one thing at a time - like individual stones. So, I studied the energy field around one stone for quite a while, until I had got quite familiar with it. Then I placed a second and a third stone close by - to see what changes took place. It was a long slow process, but gradually I started to build up my knowledge of this strange phenomenon - and to gain confidence in my own dowsing ability. It was during this period that I first observed there was an interaction at these subtle levels between objects.'

Having no experienced local dowsers to talk to or work with, Billy's early work was, of necessity, built up from first principles. He recalls reading some general popular esoteric hardbacks, such as Ward's *Mysterious Britain*, and a few books that were dowsing-related, such as John Steele's *Earth Mind* and Francis Hitchings' *Earth Magic*, which he found inspiring. But it is telling, that for a man with an excellent memory he doesn't recall the content of those books, other than the fact that they gave him leads to other authors. He found it reassuring that other people, somewhere, seemed to be finding something similar to himself - but that seems to be about all.

One person who did inspire him was the renowned American Dowser, Terry Ross, whom Billy felt was someone who thought outside of the box. He had the opportunity on one occasion to spend some time with him in Glasgow at a British Society of Dowsers Congress. Terry taught him that dowsers should allow their minds to go beyond the visible horizon. He said that most tended to see up to the horizon, but did not dare to go beyond it.

The two men discussed the diverting of underground streams of water and the success, or otherwise, of the various methods used. Billy told him of an unsuccessful attempt he had made on his farm back in Northern Ireland. Terry closed his eyes and after a few moments informed Billy about the availability of a large underground stream on his Antrim farm, into which an offending stream could be diverted. At that time the water in it was gushing out of the ground and water logging the field so badly that it was unfit for farming use. Terry only knew about this opportunity by remote dowsing, Billy had not gone into any detail as to the location of his farm or the field concerned. Billy was aware of the location of the large stream, but had not mentioned it to Terry - and Terry had no means of reference, not even a map, to assist him with his dowsing. For Billy, it was a solid demonstration of Ross's ability to undertake remote dowsing in a credible and verifiable way. On a few occasions Billy had attempted to physically divert the stream and thus dry up the ground but without

Terry Ross

success. After his encounter with Terry Ross he carried out the procedure as described and - to Billy's amazement - the water stopped gushing out of the ground in a few days. Interestingly, after about two years it began to flow again. He did not repeat the procedure, and draining work was carried out soon after which permanently stopped the water flowing over the ground.

Terry was a well-known water dowser and healer, with a radical approach to his subject, but the main influence he had on Billy was that he showed him what was possible. It encouraged him to look beyond the far horizon.

I often write that, in terms of personal development, we all stand on the shoulders of giants - but in Billy's case, I feel that during his formative dowsing years he was standing firmly on uncultivated ground.

On joining the British Society of Dowsers

'In those first few years when I was working in isolation, I felt that what I was doing was totally unique - and that possibly nobody else in the world had discovered this idea of inter-connected energies.

However, I went to the Belfast City Library, where one of the librarians was a neighbour of mine. I enquired if there were any books concerning the things I was discovering. There was no specific section relating to dowsing, but there were about a dozen books about it, or books that at least mentioned dowsing - categorised under the heading of 'paranormal phenomena'.

The first one I looked at was by Henri Mager (who invented the Mager Rosette colour disc to assess the quality of water). He had carried out experiments very similar to the ones I had carried out on the inter-relationship of ordinary objects. This was very encouraging. More exciting still was that in the back of some of the books there were references to a mystical organisation called the British Society of Dowsers - the BSD.

In an effort to put on record what I had observed from the research I had undertaken up to that point, I wrote down some of my findings - at some length. I sent a copy of my script to the BSD, and also to another couple of organisations, whose addresses I had found in the back of a book. One was called RILKO, (Research Into Lost Knowledge Organisation), the other was the ASD - the American Society of Dowsers. RILKO was the only one willing to print my work more or less in its entirety. The ASD reduced my 8 or 9 pages down to 2 or 3, which in retrospect I don't blame them for! The member of the BSD who edited the BSD Journal later told me she was so puzzled by my work that she didn't know what to do with it!

The ASD, in its wisdom, sent the full transcript to Sig Lonegren, an ASD member, who was then in charge of their Earth Mysteries Group. Sig, who now lives in England, remains a good friend of mine. He gave me a lot of help with running the BSD's Earth Energies Group in its early days.

He very kindly responded to me, and we corresponded for several years. I used to send him great, long hand-written screeds, not knowing that he suffers from dyslexia, which makes reading handwritten material difficult for him. But he bravely struggled through them and, to his eternal credit, he answered every letter that I sent to him. He gave me his views on what I had sent and he gave me a lot of encouragement.

Despite his reputation as being a cutting-edge thinker and researcher himself, he once remarked to me 'Hey, you're way out there! You're way out further than the New Age boys'.

It was a great comfort to know that there were other people, who were just as mad as myself - even if many of them lived in the US! I was a member of the ASD for a number of years and they published some of my articles, for which I was very grateful. However, when the editor changed he wouldn't print anything that I sent to him. After four or five failed attempts to get

Sig Lonegren

things printed, I stopped trying and I eventually stopped subscribing to the ASD.

Their magazine seemed to become more interested in quite trivial things - and overall, I felt that the BSD had more to offer that was of interest to me. I was moving on to a different type of research, and I really needed to find people who were on a similar wavelength.

So it was that I turned to the British Society of Dowsers.'

The BSD was formed in 1933 (the year Billy was born), and mainly consisted of retired military officers, led by the BSD's redoubtable founder, Colonel Bell. They had found that dowsing worked for them under operational conditions, and their fascination with this strange phenomenon developed into a group of hobbyists, who met from time to time to exchange ideas.

I doubt if any of them had the slightest inkling that, seven decades later, their homogenous clique would develop into an international research group that welcomes all-comers and delves into the darkest corners of human consciousness.

When I became part of the BSD myself, around the turn of the millennium, there was still a feeling that you were joining a rather secret Gentleman's Club. Your application to join had to be considered by The Council. People I subsequently met told me that they had once been to Congress, only once, and found that it was all very formal, to the extent that you were expected to wear a dinner jacket to the evening meal. Not wanting to incur a trip to Moss Bros, I gave it a miss for several years. If the prospect of that first encounter with the powers-that-be was less than inviting for an accountant from Devon, it must have seemed a very alien environment indeed for the farmer from Co. Antrim.

The last decade has seen a revolution within the BSD, both in terms of scale and in the diversity of the membership. Formality has been replaced by friendliness; conversation and collaboration are the order of the day. It wasn't quite so free and easy in the mid-1990s.

The emergence of the Earth Energies Group

'When you read through the BSD magazine at the time when I first joined, there was very little in it about, what we would now call, Earth Energies. At that time, the person within the BSD who carried the banner for Earth Energy interests was Bob Sephton, but there was no formal group. I corresponded with Bob on one or two occasions, and he was very helpful to me. He is still a stalwart in the earth energy field, and he is still very active within the BSD's Dowsing Research Group.

However, being both geographically and academically separated from the mainstream, I felt genuinely lonely - very much on my own. At the first Congress (now called Annual Conference) that I attended, Members of The Council asked how they could improve the Society. I expressed a view that, as an earth energy dowser, I felt very isolated and on my own - and that it would be good to be able to correspond with others of like mind.

I wanted to ask the membership if there were any others present who had similar interests to my own. After some discussion, it was agreed to put a sheet of paper on a table, where like-minded souls in the room could write their names. About 20 people signed it - and the nucleus of the Earth Energies Group was conceived that day. Michael Guest, then a member of the Council and Vice President of the BSD, and myself met on a few occasions. Eventually, an ad hoc committee was formed and a programme of events was formulated.

The EEG was formally created in 1995 and I went on to chair it for the first 10 years. I had intended that its main aim would be to carry out research into earth energies - to see if we could make any sense of them, or even to draw any rational conclusions from the evidence in front of us. Even now, I'm not sure quite what we have achieved on that front, but we certainly got a lot of discussion going.

I was very anxious that the EEG should provide a platform for anyone who had any opinion whatsoever relating to Earth Energy matters - somewhere that they could get up and express their opinions freely, without fear of being ridiculed.

We decided to produce our own magazine, eventually called 'Earth Energy Matters', to give people an added opportunity to make their voice heard. We published most of what was offered to us, but there were one or two articles that even we turned down, because we felt they were too far removed from reality!

I was sorry when Earth Energy Matters stopped being published as a separate journal and was re-absorbed into the main magazine

Earth Energy
Matters

Newsletter
of the
British Society of Dowsers
Earth Energies Group

Volume 9   Issue 34   June 2004

(Dowsing Today), because I don't feel the subject gets as much page-space as it used to. I am not blaming the present editorship, as they can only consider for publication the material that is sent to them. When it was a separate publication there was a greater onus and responsibility on members to contribute articles, which perhaps is not so great now.

The EEG membership rose very quickly, from 30 members to having 300-400. Being the only Special Interest Group within the BSD, the EEG strayed into many fields other than earth energies, including health related matters and archaeology. It was thought that there had to be some sort of realignment to take account of this sudden upsurge in interest in earth energies - and other groups were subsequently created to cater for water, health, archaeology and research.

In due course, this brought the EEG back into the body of the BSD. In some ways, it has been a good thing, but I also feel it has taken some of the excitement out of the EEG.

Under its present leadership, I have become more optimistic that the group is getting back some of its vitality, and the numbers now attending events is a good measure of that. However, it needs to be remembered that when the EEG only had about 100 paid-up members, attendances at meetings were sometimes up to 70 or more.'

It is very much the legacy of Billy's generation of dowsers that the BSD is able to achieve what it does today. There are still young lions eager to push back the boundaries of dowsing, but they are able to express their enthusiasm so openly only because they stand on the platform created by those who sought to reshape the mould a couple of decades ago.

An unlikely media star

Billy is one of just a handful of BSD members to have appeared on television to demonstrate the skill. He also has the rare distinction of being treated both seriously and courteously. Perhaps what you send out really does come back to you.

'I appeared in an independent television production by Brian Black, who is very much into environmental issues. He produces his own

A frame from the programme demonstrating muscle testing over an edgeline of underground water

programmes and then sells them on to the broadcasters. He produced a couple of series for Ulster Television entitled Hidden Heritage. One of the programmes concerned ancient sites around Ireland.

I was approached to see if I would like to be involved with a piece that concerned stone circles. I explained on camera why I felt they were built the way they were, what they did to the earth energies around them and, by muscle testing, to show how the stones seemed to work.

In the end, I got a five-minute slot, and I was able to get the message across quite clearly. I was treated courteously and there were no aspersions about the use of dowsing - it was taken very straight and portrayed sensibly.'

We will discuss Billy's remarkable research into how megaliths work, his use of muscle testing to determine the location of detrimental energy, and the results of stone circle building projects at home and in various locations elsewhere in Ireland, in subsequent chapters.

Dowsing Without a Device

One of the most intriguing features of Billy's dowsing, and the one that picks him out from the crowd, is his ability to 'see' his dowsing target, almost regardless of distance and obstacles.

Whilst a growing number of dowsers are discarding their devices, as the discipline matures with the passage of time, Billy's technique is very much of his own making.

But how would anyone - especially someone with little contact and interaction with other dowsers - come to abandon the rods, in favour of just looking and walking?

An addiction with attitude

'When I was first smitten with the dowsing bug, I was badly smitten. I practised dowsing day in and day out - and I thought about dowsing day in and night out. In any spare moment that I had, it was in the forefront of my mind - and I went out and practised dowsing.

A lot of the dowsing is of an experimental nature - asking questions such as What if I do this? What if the situation changed to that? I was always looking for new angles to try out. I wasn't just going out into a field, finding an energy line and being satisfied with that. I wanted to know where it came from, and why it wasn't in exactly the same place from one day to the next. It was a highly repetitive process - going over similar ground time and time again, with subtle variations. In some ways, I'd liken it to photography - instead of going out with the stills camera and taking a single snapshot now and again, I was running a dowsing video camera more or less 24 hours a day.

My style of deviceless dowsing developed out of my practice of middle -distance dowsing. At that time I used a Y rod. If I went out into a field, I was able to determine where I had to go to find my target by holding the rod with both of my arms up - more or less at eye level. When I turned round and asked the Dowsing Question, let's say, 'Where is the best supply of underground water?', gradually the rod would turn me around to look at that part of the field. After some time, I began to realise that my eyes had picked out the spot before the point of the rod had indicated it. My eyes were getting there first.

Then I tried just allowing my eyes to select the spot, kept them focused on that location, walked to it and put down a marker of some descript-tion. I walked back away from it for about 20 paces or so, picked up the rod and walked towards it again, with the same question in my mind - but this time with my eyes closed. When I reached a point where I got a response I opened my eyes to check how near I was to the marker that I had put down. I generally found that I was close beside it.

The situation really came to a head one day, when I was going away somewhere to do some dowsing. When I arrived, I looked for my tools in the back seat of the car - and there was no rod! So, I just decided, there and then, that I wasn't going to waste the journey - I just got on with it deviceless.'

Other ways without tools

'Anyone who has been to one of my talks will also have seen me using my hands and arms as dowsing tools. When I get close to the target, I can feel my arms being pushed apart. It's a real sensation, just like coming up against a brick wall. At first, to enable this to happen, you have to assist things a little bit, by re-programming your automatic responses - your default settings as it were. Along with the Dowsing Question, you need to ask when the target is reached that your arms should respond accordingly and be pushed apart.

We are all taught that dowsing works when you hold a tool of some kind in your hand - and, because of that, there are involuntary movements that take place in the muscles of the hands that cause the tool to respond in a predictable manner. I consciously reprogrammed that involuntary reaction away from the muscles that would make the rod turn to the muscles that control the movements of my neck and my eyes - so that my head is turned and my eyes focused on the target. When wanting to use my arms in the way described above then the muscles that control the necessary movement are programmed accordingly.

I do quite a bit of dowsing when I'm driving the car - where it's safe and appropriate to do so, of course! I can ask Dowsing Questions, and my head will turn involuntarily to look at that position. Where it is necessary to be particularly careful is if the target is behind me. My head will be forced to look over my shoulder, and I have to fight against it - or I could end up in the hedge! However, this allows me to follow an energy line over a long distance in a shorter period of time than any other method.

The movement of the muscles is really strong. It's almost as if someone is holding my head between their hands, and turning it around. It's a matter of building up that sensitivity - and allowing it to happen. Normally, we'd fight against the involuntary movement and not be aware of it.

It wasn't something I actively sought to do, it just developed. I'm not alone in employing deviceless dowsing by any means. If you talk to any of the more experienced practising water dowsers - people who are outside dowsing day in and day out - most of them will admit that when they get to the gate of the field, they know where the water source is, before they even get a rod out of their pocket. I remember the legendary Cornish diviner, Donovan Wilkins, telling us at one of his talks 'I know where it is, but if I just walked straight to it without using a rod, the farmers wouldn't believe me. I have to go through a performance'.

The big advantage in using the 'eyes' technique with earth energy dowsing is that it allows you to dowse three-dimensionally. The energies always display themselves in a three-dimensional manner. Therefore you do not need to be on top of the target and you can see it much more clearly by standing well back. You can also dowse for things 100ft above the ground or 100ft below it, although clearly it's hard to be accurate with regard to the actual position of the target at that distance. You can also look across the countryside as far as the eye can see - and you can see approximately where your target is, which is a great advantage. It also allows me to follow the twists and turns that some lines follow - and to see the shapes and forms that the energy takes.

Sometimes when I am in a plane, and there are no distractions, I can look out of the window on a clear day, and I can dowse the landscape beneath me for answers to all sorts of questions. It gives me a much better view of a much bigger picture.

When dowsing on the ground, you can usually only see a small area around you, but if you're a mile up in the air looking down, you can see over, perhaps, a thousand square miles of countryside, just by glancing around. You can see how things are inter-connected. You can see the major flows of underground water; how energy moves from one place to another; how all these relate to the topography of the earth beneath - and you can appreciate the effect of the hills and mountains on these energies.'

Dowsing by sight

'That brings me on to the central question of what I actually see - and the answer is absolutely nothing in the normal sense of the word! That is very difficult to get across. I don't see what it is, but I can see where it is and I can follow the course it takes, whether it be water or energy. I know what it is because of the Dowsing Question that I formed in my mind.

I can see the direction of the location of the energy just as well with my eyes closed as I can with my eyes open, which convinces me that dowsing takes place within the brain and does not need an outside stimulus to activate it other than the Dowsing Question. My head will turn in the correct direction - and when I open my eyes what I am searching for will be before me - exactly on the target. I don't need to have my eyes open. In fact, I do quite a lot of checking out with my eyes closed, as it helps to take away a lot of the distractions. But you do have to do that on level ground, or you'll find yourself flat on your nose!

It also allows me to follow the contours or outlines of whatever is out there. By following the contours, I can determine the shape and form that it takes. If I need more detail, I resort to using my hands - and I can feel around it, just as if I was feeling around a solid object. It's not unlike a blind man feeling around something to determine what it is.

Alternatively, I can mark it out two-dimensionally on the ground. Even if an image is 100ft up in the air, you can project that image on to the ground through dowsing. If I am in a sandy area, I can take a pointed stick and draw the outline on the ground. Alternatively, I can mark it out using powdered chalk or builder's sand - or even by walking in dewy grass or in snow.'

One of the important features of Billy's dowsing technique is that it enables him to quickly locate significant elements in a landscape that the rest of us would never even consider.

There are clearly occasions when he discovers aspects of his search quite unintentionally - they just happen to present themselves as a byproduct of his technique. There are numerous examples in this book of where Billy has come across completely unexpected features and phenomena - and it indicates the scale of the advantage that this method provides over more conventional ways of dowsing.

'At times you have to assist the dowsing process by loosening up the Dowsing Question a bit - by asking 'Are there other important things here that I haven't yet observed?' Quite often the answer is yes, which can lead me on to finding other energy shapes. I look where my eyes are pointing and then I try to decipher the shape that is there.

It's not really that unusual, if you consider how normal vision actually works - because what I am doing is very similar to that. Dowsing happens inside our minds. We first sense something through dowsing, and then we can project that on to the ground. Vision works a bit like that - you get the bounce-back of the reflected frequencies of radiation from the object that it does not absorb into that part of the brain that deals with vision. You visualise the picture inside your brain, and project it out again. What we 'see' is not actually what's out there, it's a projection of what's out there. It's our personal interpretation of it, and we all see things slightly differently.

To take the analogy one stage further, if we send 100 artists out to paint a scene, while there will be some similarities in the pictures they paint, they will all be subtly different. This reflects what they each have seen, and then how they have interpreted it. So, why should it be any different with dowsing? Why should we be dismissive of dowsing because there are differences in what we find and in our interpretation of it? This line of reasoning would actually predict that dowsers would get subtly different responses, which is indeed the case.

In my opinion, all that people need to become deviceless dowsers is the confidence to go ahead and do it - which is true for just about any other ability in life. A lot of people have a knee-jerk reaction of 'Oh, I could never do that'. If you have that attitude, you are blanking your mind and ensuring that you never will. Your subconscious, where dowsing takes place, will never go beyond what your conscious mind believes and allows, and therefore you will never be able to do it.

There are two reasons why I would like to encourage deviceless dowsing; firstly it allows the dowser to access information in a fraction of the time that it takes with rods or other devices, and secondly it is much more discreet and less intrusive when dowsing in public places.

Quite frankly, I feel what I do is well within the reach of others, and it's the one criticism I have of the BSD's training programme. They refer briefly to deviceless dowsing, but there's no real effort to encourage trainee dowsers to take it up at an early stage.

I find that it's easier to get people who have never dowsed before to be successful at deviceless dowsing than those with years of experience, simply because they have not had the time to construct barriers within their mind.

I accept that you have to start small to get it off the ground. But if I could teach maybe a dozen experienced dowsers to become proficient in it, they could then train another half a dozen each - and so on.

I would compare it to Roger Bannister breaking the four-minute mile barrier back in 1954. At the time, it seemed virtually impossible, but five years later even many club athletes were doing it - because he had shown everyone that it could be done. He had broken through that mental barrier.'

Billy is quite insistent that he doesn't 'see' anything pictorially that is different from what you or I would see, but he does see the location and the shape of energy forms. Given the speed and accuracy of his work, it is difficult not to feel there is an element of clairvoyance involved - but without having the gift myself, it is hard to tell how much of his ability is natural intuitive talent and how much is the result of sheer dedication.

In seeking to explain in words a concept that can really only be grasped by demonstration, perhaps the analogy with the other senses, such as visual sight, is very pertinent. Dowsing is forever being dismissed by the scientific hardcore for its failure to provide identical, repeatable results.

There are various reasons for this shortcoming, some of which we will touch upon in another section. However, as one sense among many, it should be expected that intuition would give results that vary from person to person, from place to place and from time to time. Anyone required to be a witness at a road accident, or to give an account of a football match they have attended, could testify to that scenario.

This may make it frustratingly difficult to reduce intuitive dowsing to its constituent parts in the lab - but it doesn't invalidate its usefulness in the hands of an experienced practitioner.

Not dowsing, but drowning

One of the things that struck me quite early on my own dowsing journey was that if I could see everything that I could dowse, I would have such a massive information overload, I'd never be able to cross the road, let alone do a day's work. So how can someone like Billy, who can visualise energy patterns, lines and effects in great detail, cope with such a situation?

'The same thing applies with any form of dowsing including visual dowsing. I only see what I ask for. When I was starting to dowse, I discovered lines everywhere. I couldn't make much sense of it; there was just too much to take in. But once I learnt to refine the dowsing question and focus on one thing at a time and ask for a specific type of line or energy, the whole process became clearer.

If the Dowsing Question is clear, your subconscious mind will select what you are looking for out of the thousands of other possibilities. It won't confuse you - it will only show you one thing at a time. If you want to find something else, you have to ask for it.

If your dowsing question is unclear and imprecise, your dowsing rod will be bobbing and turning every inch, and you won't be able to understand anything at all. If you want to make any sense of the patterns, you have to learn to sift your way through what is out there bit by bit - by adapting the Dowsing Question accordingly.'

While we are talking, Billy picks out the energy lines in the room that we are sitting in as an example - but he finds a myriad in just a couple of feet, and then repeats the process covering the same ground, but coming at it from various angles. Although they each have individual characteristics and flow in various directions, they are so dense that they seem to form almost a solid sheet of energy.

'The only reason I could discern what type of line they are, and where they come from, is because I ask a specific question. I don't 'see' the lines, as such, I just see where they are.

I need to understand what the wording of the Dowsing Question means to me - and if you asked the same question, those words may mean something slightly different to you. Consequently, your subconscious mind will translate that slightly differently, and you will get a slightly different result. This is one of the basic reasons why we get so many subtly different results in dowsing for earth energies - and therefore why it is so hard to repeat it consistently. It doesn't mean to say that any of us is technically 'wrong'. We just all see the world from a slightly different standpoint.

It's a bit easier when you are looking for, say, underground water, because we are all familiar with what water is. You can phrase your question specifically, and you can exclude all other sources.'

Whilst those of us who have dowsed for many years have become used to the ability to do so as a natural phenomenon, there are still many serious sceptics. Some of these are genuinely inquisitive; others are just concerned that their own worldview could be under threat. Not many people enjoy the unanticipated change to their tried and trusted reality that dowsing can unleash on that sort of scale.

Dowsing in the dock

One of the big issues associated with the investigation of dowsing from a scientific angle is that dowsers, perhaps rather naively, tend to allow others to set the parameters of their experimental inquisition - parameters that are often quite alien to them. Under those circumstances, there is absolutely no chance that something as subjective as dowsing could be demonstrated successfully.

'In this context I was invited to give a lecture at a seminar at Cambridge University, to a group of open minded scientists from all over the world, including some in the forefront of modern physics. The lecture was titled 'The effect of Subtle Earth Radiations on the Neurological and Biological System'.

Before my lecture, a chap was explaining how 'chi' energy had been recorded on to audio tapes. Although he was using a normal audio tape, it did not make any sound. However, he did play one of these audio tapes to the group, and I watched how the auras changed. There was a significant change to the energy environment taking place. So I certainly felt there was something on the tape that caused this to happen, but at frequencies beyond the audio spectrum.

His test, for all of us to participate in, was that he had three tapes, in three brown paper parcels. Two of the tapes were unopened, still in their factory wrapping. The third had this 'chi' energy recorded on to it. There were 30 - 40 of us at the seminar, and we each had to hold the parcels in our hands to see if we could tell which was the tape with 'chi' energy on it.

The criteria that I used to determine my decision was the same as I use when examining the energy field of any object. I looked to see the lines of detrimental energy coming from each object. Most objects have a short tail of detrimental energy coming from them. Of the three parcels, one of them had no tail of detrimental energy - it was all contained within the parcel. So, I reckoned that it was the most likely contender.

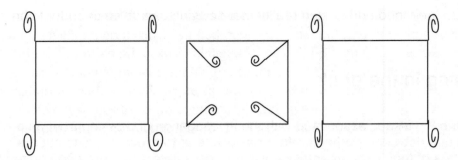

Diagram showing the way that detrimental energy displayed itself from each of the parcels

It was a proper double-blind experiment, in that the presenter himself didn't know which was which either.

I was asked to demonstrate to the assembled group the process I had used to come to my conclusion. I could only explain that one parcel had a different energy display to the others. I was able to point it out with my finger, but that was all. To my pleasure, when the packages were opened I had picked the right one. Very few of the others got it right. As I was giving my talk immediately after that, I think they paid a bit more attention to what I was saying!

However, most dowsing to destruction experiments fail - and the dowser ends up looking pretty silly, and often quite angry. You cannot understand dowsing by reductionism, nor does it respond to vivisection. Dowsing is a much more subtle craft, and it is no party trick.

My advice is that if you are asked to dowse under test conditions, only do it if you can set the parameters yourself - and even then only do it in a field of work in which you already have considerable experience. If you can do that, there is a chance that you may succeed, whereas if you allow others to set the ground rules, you have no chance.

Finding a £10 note hidden in one of several envelopes is something you should never attempt to do in public. Inevitably, you will be wrong - unless you have practised it time and time again and you are comfortable that you can do it without feeling them. Maybe then you could take it on, but not otherwise.

When you start dowsing, it is easy to get too cocky - and you set yourself up for a fall. People want you to fail. They want to prove you are wrong, so they can tell you it is all a lot of nonsense.

With the example of the hidden tapes, I could have asked for which one was which, but that would have been akin to finding lost objects. I did not have much experience of that, but I did have a lot of experience of seeing changes in energy patterns, such as the change that occurred when a tape had the "chi" energy recorded on it. I was correct, because I could see the difference between the one tape and the other two.

The chap who was running the experiment was an American physicist, and he tried to involve me in the marketing of the tapes as a relaxation aid. He was also trying to design, what you might call, psychedelic wallpaper to remove detrimental energy from within a room, which actually seemed quite an interesting concept. However, my computer got a virus from something he sent me. I took that as a warning and I lost interest in the idea!'

DOWSING

IN

THEORY

AND

PRACTICE

Underground Water

Ask a member of the general public what dowsing is all about, and the most common response (other than a shrug of the shoulders) is finding water. This is not surprising. For 400 years the gentle art of using your intuition was an illegal act, having been banned under the 15th Century Witchcraft Acts. During the suppression, it was only the vital role of the local water diviner in finding safe and accessible sources of water, for humans and stock alike, that kept the skill alive - at least in public.

Like most dowsers of his generation, Billy was introduced to dowsing through the need to find water, in his native County Antrim. As we shall see, although he has moved on to investigate many other fields through his use of dowsing, his experience and research into the impact of water lines on the surface of the earth - and more importantly on the people that inhabit it - is as individual as it is astonishing.

To understand the significance of his hypotheses, we must first appreciate the mindset that developed them. Again, Billy takes up the story:

Water is precious

'Water is probably the earth's most valuable natural resource. About 71% of the planet's surface is covered by seawater, which is constantly evaporating - and eventually falling again as rain or snow.

When water from rainfall or snowmelt reaches the ground, some or all of it will soak into the soil. The rate of infiltration depends on the intensity of the input, the moisture already in the ground and the hydraulic characteristics of the soil. The rain that falls on land soaks into the earth and collects beneath the surface in porous areas of the substratum. The movement of this water through the upper layers of the earth's surface is of great importance when we come to study the behaviour of the subtle energies that emanate from the earth. It is important, therefore, that we have some knowledge of how this happens.'

Water in motion

'Geologists and dowsers tend to take rather different approaches from one another when it comes to explaining the movement of underground water.

Geologists regard underground water reserves primarily as reservoirs formed in porous layers beneath the earth's surface. Where the rocks are permeable (i.e. when they allow water to pass through them), they can provide considerable storage capacity - and act as major sources for water supplies. These underground 'reservoirs' are known as aquifers. Aquifers are more common in areas of sandstone and limestone. In some confined aquifers, pressure alone can be strong enough to bring this water to the surface without additional pumping. These are called artesian aquifers. A well drilled into such an aquifer will cause water to gush to the surface - sometimes with considerable force.

However, some rock types allow little or no water to pass through. These are known as impermeable rocks, or aquicludes. Where this rock type exists water can still be found - not in the rock itself, but in the fissures and crevices between the rocks. These fissures were mainly formed when the rock first cooled, but some fractures have occurred within the rock at a later date. Earthquakes and volcanic action can be the major cause of this fracturing - and can create voids within the geological structure. This provides the opportunity for water to accumulate. Due to plate movement, the folding of rock layers, particularly in mountainous areas, can also create vertical fissures. These can allow water to be pushed upwards, forming natural springs on the surface.

While dowsers agree with this view in the main, there are some important differences. The main issue is that the dowser would consider underground water to be primarily a moving force. Diviners sense that water seems to flow like underground streams, rather than merely residing in static underground reservoirs, fed by water slowly percolating down from the surface. This movement sensed by the dowser can be downward, upward or on a horizontal plane.

While geologists accept that this type of movement does take place, they would consider it to be a very slow process, largely dependent on the hydraulic pressure created by the volume of water in the underground reservoirs.

The dowser would consider the movement to be generally more active - and possibly to have an extra force of motivation, in addition to rainwater percolation alone. It is not possible to say for certain which view is a more accurate description of underground water movement at this stage, although doubtless both have a part to play.'

New water

'Many water dowsers hold the view that there is such a thing as 'virgin' or 'new' water. That is, water other than surface water. It is considered a possibility that certain chemical reactions take place, deep within the earth, which cause 'new' water to be formed. This water can be forced upward, under pressure, until it reaches the upper layers of the earth's crust - where some of it actually bursts through to the surface, to emerge as springs.

This scenario is well documented in *The Divining Hand* by Christopher Bird. In it, he describes the life and work of Stephan Riess, a Bavarian born mining engineer, who emigrated to the United States in 1923. Riess was not a dowser in the conventional sense, in that he did not use dowsing tools. However, it would appear that he used his intuition (albeit without admitting to it!) to find large volumes of underground water, in places that the conventional hydrologist would have considered impossible. He developed a theory about the origin of water that supports the view held by many dowsers. The temperature and chemical analysis of some sources of water convinced him that these came from somewhere other than surface water.

Riess discovered an important clue to solving the mystery, when he heard a hissing sound accompanied by a trickle of water. He tracked the noise down to a ball mill - an enormous cylinder that rotates and pulverizes ore to mud, using the tumbling action of steel balls and the water contained within the ore. The water trickling out of the ball mill should normally have been found above the mud in the motionless cylinder - but Riess saw that it lay under a newly formed arch of mud, through which bubbles of gas were rising.   Holding a match over one of the bubbles he caused a small explosion. He believed he was observing 'virgin water' being liberated from the rock by crystallization processes, taking place within the rock itself. Riess later duplicated this water-producing process in a laboratory.

I have some sympathy with this view of the origin of virgin water. However, I feel that virgin water, or perhaps a better description would be 'new sources of fresh water', may be available to us from a different natural process. It is known that faults exist at certain locations in the ocean floor, which allow seawater to penetrate to great depths. If this water reaches a sufficient depth, it would heat up to boiling point and be turned into steam at high pressure. Recent deep-sea exploration has observed this phenomenon occurring, and jets of hot water have been seen rising out of the ocean floor.

It is possible that where this phenomenon occurs close to a landmass, some of the fissures would direct the steam into the landmass itself. This steam, as it cools, condenses into a new source of fresh water - which eventually mingles with water percolating down from the surface. Additional volumes of water being introduced into the aquifers in this manner would add to the movement of the water within them - which would support the view held by many dowsers that the water beneath the ground is far from static.

Regardless of the existence (or otherwise) of virgin water, I believe the way that underground water moves through the earth's crust can cause disturbances in the earth's energy field - with which we interact. There is no disagreement that water flows downward from the surface of the earth to greater depths. This flow through the soil is in the form of percolation, and is fairly evenly distributed across the globe except, of course, in deserts.

When water reaches the bedrock, the pattern of flow changes, depending on the type of rock it encounters. If the rock is permeable, the water continues to filter down and is well distributed. However, quite often in permeable rocks, caverns can be found, created by the water dissolving and washing away sections of rock over long periods of time. These caverns can fill, partly or totally, with water. This is particularly true where the underlying rock is limestone.

Where the rock is impermeable, water does not filter through, but flows across the surface of the rock until it comes into contact with vertical fissures - into which it runs. The frequency of fissuring dictates the volume of flow. Small fissures join with larger fissures, and the scale and force of the flows increase. Horizontal fissures also occur, enabling water that has flowed vertically downward to subsequently flow laterally.

It is a more difficult concept to appreciate that underground water can also flow upward. However, as mentioned above, evidence of this is provided by the presence of artesian wells. Natural springs, where water comes out of the ground under its own force, and is often crystal-clear and ice-cold, also demonstrate that water can flow in an upward direction from a great depth.'

Blind springs

'Whilst we are all familiar with springs, the term 'blind spring' is less well known. It is mainly used by water dowsers to describe where a column of water rises vertically, and disperses through horizontal fissures before reaching the surface of the earth. In the US these features are termed 'water domes'.

When a dowser marks out the water lines at ground level it usually looks like the spokes of a wheel coming from a central hub. (see diagram opposite)

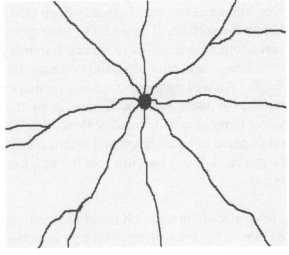

Plan view of a Blind Spring

However, if we consider how this same blind spring would appear when viewed from the side, it is more like a tree in wintertime - with a central trunk and branches coming away from the stem at different levels. These branches may subdivide as the water continues to flow away from the central ascending shaft. (see diagram on right)

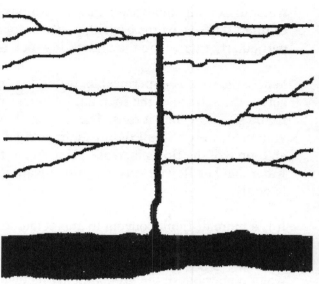

Cross section of a Blind Spring

When we examine, through dowsing, a water source that rises vertically, it is usually found to derive from a larger and wider underground flow. The depth in the earth's crust at which water is present has yet to be fully determined, but in Russia water has been found at a depth of around nine kilometres. Drilling in the British Isles has discovered water over four kilometres down. I classify deep flows as being over 300 metres below the surface. The width of underground streams can vary from just a few metres across to several hundred metres. This does not mean that there is a continuous band of underground water of this constant width. An underground stream or aquifer of this type is made up of a number of interconnected fissures or faults, which have filled with water to make a wide band or flow. The extent of the flow that actually takes place in an underground watercourse such as this, is unknown - however, dowsers are firmly of the opinion that some movement does occur.

I have already mentioned water that can descend down a vertical fissure. The dowsing term for that is a downshaft. It is different from a blind spring in that, instead of dividing up into numerous smaller flows, it usually flows on at a greater depth as a single flow. Sometimes, it joins into an existing deeper flow and becomes part of it. With some others, the vertical fissure is not large enough to take all the water and some of it continues to flow onward at the same depth as the original underground stream. The diagram on the right shows a typical example of this.

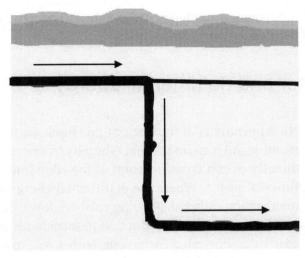

Cross section of downshaft

There are two other important ways that underground water behaves, which are less common than the blind spring and the downshaft. I call them 'a circulating loop' and a 'siphon'. The circulating loop can occur where there is a blind spring and a downshaft in close proximity to each other. The water rises up the blind spring and runs out of one of the branches, where it

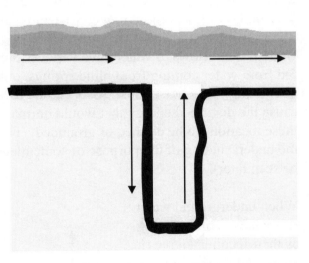

Cross section of a siphon

meets up with a downshaft close by. It descends again to a lower level and then re-circulates. The siphon is very similar to a downshaft in that water descends down a vertical fissure to a greater depth, but there is no horizontal fissure at that level to allow the water to flow onward. It then rises again up a nearby vertical fissure, until it disperses near to the surface in one or, in some cases, two flows.

The significance of being able to identify these different patterns in the movement of underground water will become clearer when we discuss their effect on earth energies.'

Water and detrimental energy

'In Appendix A at the back of this book we describe a simple experiment, using muscle testing, whereby the person under test stands directly over a crossing point of the edge lines of two underground flows of water. Where the detrimental energy rises vertically from the intersection rather than being earthed down into the ground, this can result in a significant reduction in muscle resistance. While this can be easily demonstrated by anyone with a will to do so, as with most dowsing-related activities, it is not quite as simple as that. There are many potential circumstances that could affect the result. It is only when we become familiar with the rules that apply in each situation that we can be confident of getting consistent results.

Underground flows of water have various sources. Some streams are fed from water coming from blind springs, others from downshafts, circulating loops or siphons. Also, certain local circumstances will cause the disturbed energy that would normally rise vertically from these locations to be earthed or grounded. This also provides a clue to the understanding of the purpose of some megalithic structures (as will be seen later).

When underground water flows have a blind spring as their feeding source (ie an ascending shaft of water), disturbed, or detrimental, energy can rise from the edges of those lines. Without any external interference, this disturbed energy will rise vertically from both edge lines, perhaps up to

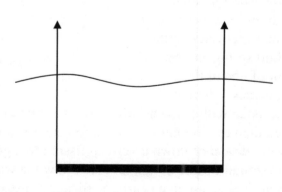

Detrimental energy from edgelines

several hundred feet, or more, above the surface of the ground. It does not seem to be deflected by objects - even those with the mass of a building - and it can be dowsed on the top floor of high-rise apartments or office blocks.

When the brain of a person, or the muscles involved in holding their arm aloft, are exposed to this vertical band of disturbed energy, a greatly reduced muscle resistance will occur. If the underground water flow is wide enough for the test to be undertaken with the person standing at its centre, and not in contact with either edge line, then the muscle resistance will be enhanced and near to optimum strength.

However, where an underground flow is fed from a downshaft a very different muscle-testing outcome will result. When standing over the edge line, instead of a lowering of the muscle resistance, a normal response will be observed with muscle testing resistance demonstrating full strength. It is when the person under test stands at the centre line of the underground flow that a weakening will occur. The disturbed energy coming from the edgelines is drawn to the centre of the underground flow and rises vertically there.

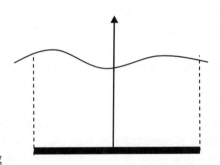

Detrimental energy from centre line

Above a circulating loop of underground water, a weakening of the muscle will occur at both the edge lines and at the centre. The disturbed energy will rise from the edge lines of the upper flow, which comes from the ascending shaft. When the water descends, it forms a stream directly beneath the upper flow. It is from the centre line of this stream that more disturbed energy rises - giving three bands ascending into the air above the circulating loop.

When an underground flow is fed from a siphon, the disturbed energy again rises vertically from the edge lines.

However, for some distance away from the siphon, some of the detrimental energy swirls back and forth between the edge lines, lowering the muscle resistance at any location over the water.

Certain local circumstances will cause the disturbed energy that would normally rise vertically from these locations, to be earthed or grounded. It is useful to look at what causes this to happen. In areas of undisturbed landscape, where there are hillsides and slopes on which there are scattered random boulders of substantial size, or natural woodland, little or no disturbed, or detrimental, energy will be found to rise above the surface of the ground. One of many such places where I observed this is on the island of Harris, in the Outer Hebrides off the west coast of Scotland, where the hillside remains scattered with natural boulders. Another was in Spain, in an area of natural pine forest. It also occurs where the topography of the ground is quite undulating with natural and regular shaped banks surrounding small flat areas.

Therefore, if muscle testing is carried out randomly, without the assistance of dowsing to select the test locations, it may not be possible, in some areas, to observe the weakening effect on the arm muscle - as the locations where detrimental energy rises may be a long distance apart. It may take hundreds of random tests before one would be fortunate enough to test directly above where detrimental energy rises.'

Relocating water

'Many dowsers, myself included, have made the observation that the course and direction of some underground flows of water can be changed. However, this is something that is difficult to confirm without drilling!

The evidence again comes from dowsing. It would appear that objects or structures, when placed in certain critical locations, attract small veins of underground water towards them over time - and may cause some of this water to rise vertically to form small blind springs. The frequency of this occurrence would depend on the geology and the fracturing of the bedrock, and on the presence of underground water nearby. Only where fractures exist beneath the object or structure, will water be attracted to it. Water of sufficient quantity needs to be flowing nearby. The size of the object would appear to have some bearing on the distance that water can be diverted away from the main stream. This suggests that the diversion of the underground stream may be due to the gravitational pull or some other unknown force exerted by the stone or object. The water, after passing underneath the object, can be traced using dowsing and seen to loop back into the main flow a little further downstream (see diagram below). The cause of this phenomenon could be a large stone, a pillar, a gatepost or anything similar.

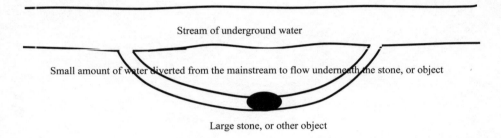

Stream of underground water

Small amount of water diverted from the mainstream to flow underneath the stone, or object

Large stone, or other object

It has also been observed that a structure such as a labyrinth will, shortly after construction, attract a blind spring to its centre, when there was none present at the time it was laid out. This would indicate that the presence of underground water at a location may be dependent on more than geology - and that it may be influenced by other factors, such as local topography and man-made structures. Whether or not these bring about subtle changes in the local gravitational field requires further investigation.'

Two examples of this type of attraction are included in *Megalithic Structures: Why?* The first is a quote from Sig Lonegren about the construction of a labyrinth at Benton Castle:

'Elizabeth Sulivan is a good water dowser. She has dowsed wells for her farm on the estate. She dowsed the location of every kerbstone that makes the walls of her labyrinth. When she began, she dowsed the sloping lawn that she intended to use.

At that time, there were no domes of water (blind springs) under that portion of her lawn. She just dowsed the best place to locate it.

Bill Cooper, a retired Major General in the British Army and at that time President of the British Society of Dowsers, told me that one day he had been at Benton Castle for lunch and he found that there was a dome of water under her dining room table. He had dowsed the castle on previous visits, and there had been no domes under the castle. They both found the new dome, and it appeared to be moving slowly towards the labyrinth!

When I arrived at Benton Castle, it was several weeks after Bill Cooper's visit. I found the dome to be directly under the goal of Elizabeth's labyrinth! This is not the first time this phenomenon has been observed.'

Another example of a labyrinth attracting water towards itself was observed by Billy and others, in a parkland area near to Moulton, Northamptonshire.

'A labyrinth had been constructed by the local council shortly before my first visit. Checking on that occasion showed that no blind spring was present in the area taken up by the labyrinth. However, there was one several metres to one side of it. I visited the park about six months later and found that this blind spring had moved close to the goal of the labyrinth. When I visited the site again several months later, the blind spring had not moved further but had remained in its new location. In addition, I found that the small underground flow that fed the blind spring had also moved towards the goal of the labyrinth.'

Billy may not be the only dowser to appreciate the relationship between detrimental energy and water lines, but he was certainly one of the first to investigate it in detail - and he carried out his research quite independently.

His understanding that it is the edges, or the centres, of the water lines (depending on the source), that have the adverse effect on the person standing above them, is a profound discovery. It is a principle that has yet to be taken on board by the wider world as a consistent, yet non-intrusive, way of improving or avoiding locations which may result in long-term harm to the affected subject.

Billy was one of the first to investigate the observation that substantial objects can attract veins of water - doing this independently of other dowsers.

This issue will be discussed in greater depth (if you'll pardon the pun) in the next chapter - concerning the purpose for the construction of Megalithic Structures.

At home with water

Before we leave the subject of water, however, it should be noted that when Billy was deciding where to build the house he and his wife now live in, he first located an appropriate and accessible source of water for themselves.

The water supply is pure and unfiltered and arrives at the tap via a pressure tank in the garage and a small pump in the well. Very nice it tastes, too.

'I am very aware that the water from my own well is different from mains water. There are two auras that come out of a glass of water - one representing the good energy in the water and the other that represents the bad energy in it.

When you look at a glass of mains water, the two auras come out to about the same distance from the glass. But when you look at the spring water here, the good energy aura will go all the way out into the yard! The bad energy is quite tight to the glass, and probably only represents the contamination of the contact with the glass itself. If you measured it on a scale of 1 to 100, you would get a reading of about 90 good to 10 bad with the spring water, whereas with the mains water it's about 50/50.

I've dowsed that many times - although the scientists would tell you that that <u>proves</u> nothing!'

Meaning in the Megaliths

Whilst Billy's work has spanned many decades and has covered a huge range of subject material, it is his work on megalithic structures, particularly in Ireland and the UK that forms the core of his research. These enigmatic creations have provided him with some astonishing insights into the mindset of their builders:

'The word 'megalith' simply means a large stone. When we talk about megalithic structures, we generally mean all the various types of large stone structures believed to have been erected in the mid to late Mesolithic and the Neolithic periods, which were roughly between 5000 and 1000 BC.

One of the greatest authorities on stone circles and other ancient structures is the Scottish archaeologist Aubrey Burl, who published *A Guide to the Stone Circles of Britain, Ireland and Brittany*. Megalithic structures come in many different shapes, designs and sizes. Of the many thousands that were constructed, there is a sufficient number remaining to suggest that no two of them were exactly alike. However in many cases what we now see are just the remnants of what was originally erected and that can make our understanding of them more difficult - as we are uncertain what they looked like at the time they were constructed. This may also be confusing when we try to comprehend their use and function.'

Stone circles

'First of all I want to make it clear what I mean when I use the term 'stone circle'. There are remains of many megalithic structures that are roughly circular throughout the landscape, but I would not classify all of them as stone circles in the true meaning of the term, as they do not meet the necessary criteria as far as I am concerned. Those that do not meet the necessary criteria I simply call circles of stone, remnants of a more elaborate structure that has over the years been removed from the scene. With many sites, there are numerous stones around the peri-meter, fairly close together. Additionally, the underground water present at these circles of stone does not conform to the pattern of water found at those that I classify to be 'true' stone circles. The Rollrights in Oxfordshire is one example of this type - and Stonehenge is another, in its current configuration. The characteristics I look for, that I believe define a stone circle, is that the stones are arranged - no matter the number - in an approximate circle, not touching, and usually irregularly spaced some distance apart. They are placed where several large flows of underground water cross, as well as several major energy lines.

The classification of these ancient circular structures into different categories should not come as a surprise. When archaeologists uncover the remains of slightly more modern structures, they differentiate between temples, places of commerce, dwellings, etc. However, with things megalithic, they tend to group them all together into 'ritual or ceremonial' - a term generally accepted as meaning 'I do not know, but that is as good a guess as any'. Dowsers are not immune to this blanket approach and many put all ancient structures under the umbrella of 'sacred space', another poorly defined term. There is also a tendency to feel that those who lived 5,000 to 6,000 years ago were primitive and superstitious in their beliefs - and that they had a lower level of intelligence compared to people today. Six thousand years is only about 300 generation spans. Mankind, mentally and physically, has not advanced significantly during that period of time. Therefore it is reasonable to assume that some of the structures that they built were utilitarian in purpose, whilst others may have been used for commerce or for worship.

However, I digress. Let us go back to stone circles as I have defined them.

Whilst they are called circles, only some are actually circular. Perhaps the most extensive research into their layout - and into the geometry found within their design - was carried out by Professor Alexander Thom. Thom included in his surveys many structures that would fall outside my definition of a stone circle. He was a retired engineer, who spent many years carefully surveying and meticulously measuring hundreds of ancient stone rings, as he preferred to call them, along with other stone arrangements, such as alignments and rectangles, in Britain and northern France.

He found that those that were not true circles could be divided into three basic forms, which he called Egg-shaped, Flattened and Elliptical, with various sub-divisions of each type. Thom believed that these shapes were arrived at deliberately, and incorporated a knowledge of advanced geometry.

He was of the opinion that in order to determine the position of the stones successfully, triangles, of certain dimensions and angles, had first of all to be marked out to find the position for a number of pegs. These would act as the point from which a series of arcs could be drawn to outline the perimeter, and create the desired shape and outline of the structure to be built.

Thom concluded that the builders of these ancient structures used a common unit of measurement, which he termed a 'Megalithic Yard' (M.Y.). He defined an M.Y. as being precisely 2.72 feet (32.64 inches). In his opinion, a second unit of measurement was also used, which he called a Megalithic Rod (M.R.), being two and a half M.Y.s (81.6 inches).

From observations made during the many surveys that he carried out, he suggested that diameters were measured in M.Y.s, and that the perimeters were measured in M.R.s. In cases where complete units were not used, half, quarter and, on rare occasions, eighths of M.R.s and M.Y.s were used.

In many cases, the perimeter of the structure did conform to a multiple of megalithic rods (2.5 M.Y.s), but sometimes it was not an exact number. Thom took the view that total precision was not achievable, given the crude construction methods available to the builders in those ancient times. He expressed the view that whilst they did not always succeed in perfect compliance, it was their intention that mattered more than the end result.

The existence, or otherwise, of the megalithic yard has led to a furious debate between, on the one hand, those who support Thom's view and, on the other, that of many leading archaeologists.

The latter contend that the rough shapes displayed in the design of stone circles simply reflect the lack of proper tools - and that the geometry contained in them is purely accidental. In support of this assertion, it has been shown that similar shapes can be achieved when people have been asked to mark out a similar circle simply by sight.

Thom's supporters, however, make the fair point that, even in those days, it would have been quite possible for a simple, but accurate, circle to be marked out using a central peg with a rope attached. This would have allowed structures to be built that would have been reasonably circular - certainly to a higher degree than the remaining examples incorporate.

There was also a great variation in the spacing between the stones. There was no consistency demonstrated - and again this could have been easily achieved, without advanced technology, to a reasonable degree of accuracy.

I would therefore suggest that there was probably a good reason why shapes, other than true circles, were built - and that it was actually necessary to have a differential spacing between the stones to achieve their intended purpose.'

Billy considers the implications of the work and approach of Professor Alexander Thom and provides a brief re-appraisal of his methods in Appendix C

The appreciation that the structures vary greatly, one from another - and that that variation may have been deliberately embedded in the design - causes the researcher to take a very different approach to other aspects of the construction and potential use of the megaliths.

The ground plan of these constructions is only one of many ways in which they differ:

'Firstly, their sizes vary enormously. On one hand, there are stone circles only a few yards across, with as few as four stones. These structures, known as 'four posters', are mainly found in Scotland. It is difficult to know whether a four-stone construction is really a circle or a rectangle, but they generally fall within the classification of circles.

At the other extreme is the great circle of Avebury, standing in the Kennet Valley in Wiltshire, England. It is one of the largest and best-known prehistoric

Four Poster at Lundin Farm near Aberfeldy, Scotland

sites in Europe, enclosing 28.5 acres (11.5 hectares). The structure consists of a circular bank of chalk 1,400 feet (425m) in diameter and 20 feet (6m) high, faced by chalk blocks quarried from an internal ditch 30 foot (9m) in depth. Inside the bank, a circle of more than 100 sandstone (sarsen) pillars, up to 50 tons in weight, surrounds two smaller adjoining stone circles, each consisting of about 30 uprights, each approximately 350 feet (105m) in diameter. There are also the

Avebury henge and circle

63

partial remnants of a third, smaller circle. Running from the eastern side of the main ring is the impressive West Kennet Avenue, flanked by dozens of huge sarsens. Originally, it extended all the way to a nearby site, now known as The Sanctuary. Another huge double stone row, The Beckhampton Avenue, is also thought to have existed, but only a few of its constituent stones now remain. This latter feature is reputed to have run from the great circle to the Beckhampton Mound, to the west of the Avebury complex.

Perhaps the world's best known example of the genre is Stonehenge. However, as I suggested earlier, Stonehenge in its later phases does not meet my definition of a stone circle. The first phase which included the henge and the first placement of the bluestones was more in keeping with my definition. One of the most significant findings to emerge from archaeological research at Stonehenge is that its design changed significantly, on several occasions, and over a long period of time. Stonehenge, as we see it today, is only a small part of the total story of the site. This discovery has raised questions as to why these changes took place. When we look at many other contemporary sites, it can be seen that changes also took place at those locations. Even in some of the simpler constructions, additions appear to have been made in later configurations. This would suggest that megalithic construction was a developing technology, and that circles were upgraded from time to time. The great difficulty with any construction in stone is that the stones themselves give no clue as to the date of erection or of any alteration in a later incarnation. It is only through dating artifacts, left by those who built and used the site, that any clue to its age can be gleaned.

A second major variance in design is that the size of the stones used in circles varies considerably from site to site - from a few hundred kilograms each at some remote circles, up to 50 or 60 metric tonnes in the larger examples found at Avebury.

The type of stone employed also varies greatly - and the fact that some of the stones were imported from a long distance away would suggest that type actually mattered. In some circles, the stones chosen had a high quartz and silicate content. This feature, too, has given rise to a fierce debate about whether the finding has any material significance.

There seems to be little consensus as to the probable purpose for building stone circles in the first place. Archaeologists generally suggest that they were places of gathering - for either ritual, ceremony or trade. Others, including dowsers, would suggest a more spiritual or religious use, regarding these places as being constructed on what might be termed 'sacred ground' - and contending that these were sacred sites, where gods were invoked and worshipped.

Both camps would largely agree that these events, whether they were religious or secular, generally took place at or around significant solar and lunar conjunctions - such as the summer and winter solstices. It is considered by some that this was the reason for cosmic alignments to be built into the designs; to mark significant solar and lunar solstices and equinoxes, and thus to ensure the correct timing of these ceremonials.

When we look at the myths and stories that surround many of the stone circles, and indeed ancient structures generally, there is an air of mysticism attached to them. They seem to have been looked upon as places where humans could make contact with spirits and also with what was generally known as the 'otherworld'. This included the periodic appearance of archetypal forms, such as great serpents, snakes, giants and beasts, which were to be seen there at certain significant dates in both the solar and the lunar calendars.

In Ireland especially, there was also the faery lore. The 'little people' controlled the land, and dear pity anyone who did anything to raise their wrath. In some ways, this helped to preserve many sites, as the foreboding of disaster and possible instant death to any who desecrated them, made country people think twice about removing them. There are many who could provide plenty of anecdotal evidence that awful things did indeed happen, either to those who desecrated the faery places - or to their domesticated livestock.

I was able to carry out a lot more of my own research into the location, operation and purposes of the stone circle, after I had built several myself - including the one in my own garden (see following chapter).'

Single standing stones

'Whilst little is known about the reason for constructing stone circles, even less is known about the purpose of erecting single standing stones. Archaeologists have only been able to split them into two categories - standing stones and outliers. Standing stones are those that stand alone, whilst outliers are those found close to a more substantial construction, such as a stone circle. There is no physical evidence to show whether outliers were put in place at the same time as the major construction, or if they were added at a later date. This creates the difficulty of not knowing whether to consider both circle and outlier(s) as one site - or whether there is no intentional connection between them. The suggestion made by some sceptics that all single standing stones were erected by farmers as rubbing posts for cattle has long been dismissed.

Again, standing stones come in all shapes, sizes and types. Some are only half a metre tall, while others stand up to seven metres in height. Most are rude stones, not worked in any way - whilst a few others have been carefully shaped. This might suggest one of two explanations. Either it did not really matter what size or shape the stone was - or the shape and size was all important and every situation were tailored to suit. I favour the latter explanation.

One or two have had holes cut in them, but again there is no uniformity in the size of the hole, or in its position.

Holland House
standing stone, Orkney

The most famous of these holed stones is the Men-an-Tol in Penwith, West Cornwall, which reputedly has healing properties. The healing was mainly associated with bone complaints such as rickets. Anyone who passed through the hole was thought likely to be cured. This belief is still well held, to the extent that when I visited the site in 1999, there were several parents who had sickly children with them that were carrying out the ritual of passing them through the hole. It has to be done in a certain direction, and repeated a certain number of times.

Close to where I live is a stone with a hole near to its top. Not surprise-ingly, it is called the Holestone. This hole is about four inches across and tapered on both sides. The story told is that it was a marriage stone, as it is just possible for a girl to pass her hand through the hole and clasp the hand of her lover. As with the Men-an-Tol, I believe this story is of quite recent origin - invented long after the real reason for either the stone or the hole was forgotten.

The suggestion that single standing stones may mark a place of burial is not well founded. Where excavations have been carried out in the vicinity of menhirs, signs of cremated bone or burial are rare. Another suggestion is that they marked land boundaries. Whilst it is true that some may be at a place where old town-lands meet, the formation of these land sections is again of relatively recent origin. The presence of the pre-existing pillar would have been an appropriate place to create the boundary, not the other way around.

Another idea is that they were phallic symbols and were therefore considered to be of some assistance to general fertility. This legend about ancient sites having the ability to improve fertility is widely known and deserves to be looked into more closely. There is a long held belief that energy coming from specific stones can assist with improved germination of seed and, perhaps, who knows, even fertility. Information that I have uncovered, and discussed elsewhere, would suggest that this belief is not unfounded.

However, the present trend of attributing a sexual meaning to ancient upright stones is only due to their phallic shape - and, I believe, does not reflect the true reason for their placement on the landscape!

As with stone circles, every stone that stands alone may not be an authentic standing stone. It may be an outlier or a remaining artifact of a more complex structure. It is necessary to be able to discern between one and the other. The determining features are the presence or otherwise of unique arrangements of underground water and energy lines at the location of the stone. An authentic stone would be situated at the crossing point of two, and sometimes three, underground flows that are sourced from downshafts. On page 53 I discussed the properties of such a flow, and I showed that detrimental energy, if present, rises from the centre line of such flows. The stone is therefore located directly over the intersection of the centre lines. The stone will send the disturbed energy back down into the earth, removing the detrimental effect of the downshaft from the landscape.

A stone that has not been located in this manner may still have some small flows of underground water beneath it, as these are likely to be attracted to the stone itself as described on page 55. There may also be energy lines radiating from the stone - but not a major crossing of earth energy lines.'

Stone rows

'There are a number of locations where whole series of stones have been erected in rows. Again, like the stone circles, there is no set pattern as to the length of row and the number or size of stones involved. Some are single rows, composed of relatively small stones, which stretch for some distance across the countryside. However, there are other instances of double, triple and even multiple rows.

The most striking example of multiple stone rows is to be found at Carnac in Brittany, northern France. Here, 1099 stones stand arranged in 11 rows that stretch to the horizon.

The next greatest concentration of stone rows, mainly single and double, is to be found in Devon and Cornwall in the south west of England. Another famous double row, mentioned previously, is the

West Kennet Avenue, which runs from the great circle at Avebury to the Sanctuary two kilometres away.

In a similar vein to stone circles, stone rows are rarely precise rows as such. They usually meander and are not in a perfectly straight line, nor are the stones in them spaced at even intervals. To construct them in alignment, and with regular spacing, would have been a relatively easy thing to achieve, even in Mesolithic times.

Again, one must conclude that it was either unnecessary for them to be sited in a perfect layout, or that the irregular pattern in which they were erected was intentional - and presumably for a specific purpose.

I believe it may be incorrect to lump all rows of stones into the same category, and to assume that they all had a common purpose. It is quite possible that some of them were erected with one purpose in mind, and some with another. The only opportunity that I have had to investigate this phenomenon to date, has been to look at a number of rows where a small number of stones have been placed randomly, a few metres apart.

Stone row with underground water as illustrated overleaf

This pattern indicates to me that these particular structures are something of a halfway house between a standing stone and a stone circle. <u>The stones were placed on the centre line of underground water fed from a downshaft</u>. As an underground flow is seldom dead straight, the centre line is usually sinuous. This explains the lack of alignment in most rows. Crossing this primary flow are several others fed from blind springs. Seldom do they cross at 90 degrees, but often at acute angles. The stones are placed over the centre line where it corresponds with where an edgeline of the crossing stream intersects. <u>The width and angle of intersection determines the spacing of the stones</u>. This combination successfully sends to earth any detrimental energy that may have risen from the underground water - and from any other source.'

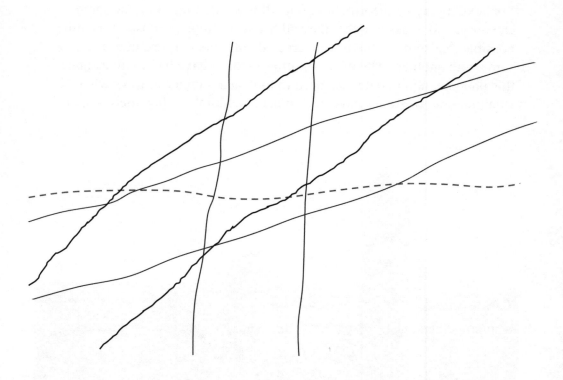

The solid lines are edgelines of underground streams from blind springs. The dashed line is the centre line of a stream from a downshaft

Dolmens

'Dolmens usually consist of a large capstone placed on top of three upright stones.

Photograph of a typical dolmen

It is generally considered that they were places of burial, and that originally they were covered by a mound of stones and earth. This notion is debatable, in that bones or cremations have been found in only a small percentage of cases where excavations have been undertaken.

There is no evidence of dolmens being found with the mound in place. The burial mounds that have been excavated exhibit a very different internal design structure to the chamber seen in dolmens.

Burial mounds vary, in that some are earth-covered and others are simply cairns constructed of smallish stones. Some have internal chambers, others not. Some have a passageway leading up to the internal chambers. As with stone circles, some of these passages are orientated towards the rising or setting of the sun at notable times, such as at the winter solstice.'

Chambered cairns and passage mounds

'The positioning of chambered cairns and passage mounds differs from other megaliths, in that generally they were constructed over just one major flow of underground water - whilst the others were constructed where several flows crossed. The width of this single flow is significant in that it is near to the overall width of the structure.

Usually two major energy lines cross near to the chamber. In some cases, as with smaller cairns and mounds, there is just one major line, with a minor line crossing it. As with the other structures, the presence of crossing points of major energy lines appears to have been a pre-requisite for the selection of the site.

Many cairns have three chambers, but others, such as the West Kennet Long Barrow, have as many as five. In some cases cairns were built in clusters.

Chambered cairns are considered by many archaeologists to be places of burial, and there is certainly some evidence to support this, as bones and cremated bone have been found in the chambers of most of these structures. However, very few complete skeletons have been found. In some cairns, bones from different skeletons had been bundled together, although it is not certain if this was intentional, or if it was simply to make room for further burials. In those cairns that were undisturbed when opened by archaeologists, the small number of skeletal remains is puzzling. Dating these bones showed that burials took place infrequently, and over a long period of time. Typical grave goods were pottery urns and bowls, beads and ornaments, flints and tools.

There is an abundance of such structures in the midlands of Ireland, and in particular around the Boyne Valley. Neolithic farming communities built these mounds about 5,000 years ago. Some structures here have clear astronomical alignments, such as the winter solstice sunrise at Newgrange and the equinox sunrise at Loughcrew. Alignments to either sunrise or sunset at significant events on the solar calendar is something that has been noted at many such locations throughout Britain and Ireland.

A similar, but smaller structure, classified as a court grave, is situated on the top of Browndodd Hill less than a mile from my house. It is now quite dilapidated, in that all the roofing slabs have been removed, but the passageway itself is still intact. Some years ago, I observed that the alignment of the passageway is similar to that at Newgrange.

Remains of chambered cairn on Browndodd Hill

It is no longer the perceived wisdom that the cairns and great mounds functioned primarily as burial sites. Contemporary scholarship regards the passage cairns more as sacred places associated with life, rebirth and regeneration.

In this context it is vitally important to consider the solar alignments of the passageways leading into the cairns. They suggest that perhaps, at ritually meaningful times of the year, such as the solstices and equinoxes, when the light of the sun shone directly along the passageways, the megalithic people would utilise the cairns as places of ceremony. Here they could co-participate with the earth spirits in the continuing regeneration of life. Perhaps those periodic times of potent celestial influence were also used for initiation ceremonies, and to awaken and amplify spiritual awareness.

However, there is a problem with this theory, in that there is conclusive evidence that many of these great passage mounds were closed off permanently. Some, like West Kennet Long Barrow, had the chambers infilled. Therefore they would have been inaccessible for ceremony and initiation after that event.

Newgrange and other chambered cairns are renowned for their stone carvings, and in particular the triple spiral. Energy lines often curve and form spirals. Spirals and vortices are amongst the most common and most significant characteristics that earth energies display. They nearly always terminate in a spiral, which, if looked at three-dimensionally, is a vortex. In studying many chambered cairns and passage graves, I have found that the chambers coincide with the presence of spirals of earth energy.

The standard crucifix formation of chambers, as found at Newgrange, was based on a triple spiral, with one of the spirals dowsable in each of the three chambers. West Kennet Long Barrow, with its five chambers, has eight lines terminating in spirals. The first two chambers to the left and right have two spirals each. The next two chambers have one spiral each, and the large end chamber has two spirals.

I began to look for these configurations in the open countryside, and I found various places where substantial energy lines terminated in spirals. In many cases, this was not confined to one single line, but several in parallel - which resulted in two, three, or more spirals at one location. One such place is in the garden of my house. Here, three lines terminate in a classical triple spiral. I marked out the orientation of the lines leading to the spirals and checked them with a compass. I was able to calculate that the sunrise alignment would be close to the November and February cross-quarter days, (November 5th to 10th being the Celtic Samhain and February 2nd to 7th Imbolc).

Subsequent observations confirmed that alignment. This is the same configuration as at Loughcrew, and at the Mound of the Hostages at Tara (the seat of the ancient Kings of Ireland) which has also been verified visually several times since then.'

Megaliths and human history

'If we look at the distribution of megalithic structures in the British Isles, we find that there appears to be a great difference in the density of sites, and in the types of construction, from one part of the country to the other. Many of them are found in what are now quite inhospitable locations, rather than in areas of high-density population. However, as many have been destroyed, and no traces of them now remain, it is difficult to be sure how many were originally built.

There appeared to be very little interest in the relics of these structures until John Aubrey, in the 17th Century, rediscovered Avebury and other sites in the area. Almost 100 years later Dr William Stukeley created another revival of interest. These early pioneers were not trained archaeologists but antiquarians. The development of scientific arch-aeology did not begin until the 19th Century. This was a big step from the antiquarianism and treasure collecting of the previous three centuries and it was due to three things: a geological revolution, an antiquarian revolution, and the propagation of the doctrine of evolution.

Geology was revolutionised in the early 19th Century, with the dis-covery and demonstration of the principles of uniformitarian strati-graphy, which determines the age of fossil remains by the stratum they occupy below the surface of the earth. This enabled archaeologists to more accurately date human activity and occupation, and the use of any particular site, by the strata in which artifacts were found. This ability to more accurately date artifacts brought about a realisation that meg-alithic structures were much older that first thought. Many of them had been incorrectly linked to the Druids but this new evidence demon-strated that they were built and used many hundreds, if not thousands, of years earlier.

The advent of carbon dating pushed the dates even further back. This soon led to a great upsurge of interest in the population generally, not confined to archaeologists.

There was a further awakening of interest by the observations of Alfred Watkins in the early 1900's who produced evidence to show that many ancient sites were in alignment. He used the term 'Ley' to describe such an alignment. His findings were published in *The Old Straight Track* in 1925. This fired the imagination of many people, and ley hunting became a common pastime. The Ley Hunters Club was formed and flourished for several years. Watkins and his immediate followers never claimed more than a visual alignment and certain rules applied.'

Dowsers enter stage left

'However during the 1940's and 50's some water dowsers began to take an interest in ancient sites and investigated them by the use of dowsing. The location of ancient megalithic sites appeared to be over substantial underground water. At many, blind springs or water domes were also present. Additionally, some dowsers began to state that they were finding straight lines of 'energy', which ran across the countryside from ancient sites - and in most cases coincided with the visual leys. The term 'energy ley' was coined to describe this phenomenon.

Guy Underwood was one of several who took the research a step further. In his book *The Pattern of the Past* he described that, as well as straight lines of energy, which give a dowsing reaction, there are many other types of dowsable energy line. These are not straight, but twist and turn, and form loops and spirals. With the benefit of hindsight, some of his conclusions appear premature, but it would be wrong to dismiss his groundbreaking work entirely.

This research brought to the fore a new breed of dowsers, who use the ancient skill to detect and investigate what we now call 'Earth Energy'. The term Earth Energy may not be totally accurate in describing what we observe, but it is possibly the most easily understood term.

All detectable energy on earth, including dowsable energy, is generally the combination of reaction within the earth itself and energy of cosmic origin. It is not possible to separate the two as the earth acts as both a receiver and transmitter. This is also true of all components that make up the earth. Each and every one of these elements creates its own interference pattern, which is unique to itself. It is these that we refer to as energy fields. An energy field is not a fog-like form around objects, but has structure and detail with many separate layers that function independently of each other, and are described in a subsequent chapter.'

Water at megalithic sites - the crux of the matter

'After dowsing for underground water at a very large number of ancient sites I have concluded that substantial underground water flows are present at all such locations.

However, my contribution to the study of the relationship of the sites with their associated water veins, was to mark out the edgelines of all the deep and wide underground streams that were present at each site. I believe I was the first to undertake this task in any detail.

These are water veins that would generally be deeper than a diviner would typically seek to provide a domestic supply if they were drilling to provide a borehole - as they would be too costly to access. Therefore, a person who specialised in dowsing for boreholes may well overlook this deeper water, unless their Dowsing Question was deliberately amended to take in water at a greater depth.

I found the results interesting, in that the diameter of the stone circles coincided with the width of these deep underground flows. Circles were always constructed at the intersection of several of these deep streams. In most cases, some of these deep streams were fed by blind springs, while others came from downshafts.

When I examined the locations of the megalithic stones I found that each of them had been precisely placed at a point where two edge lines of the streams fed by blind springs intersected - or at a point where an edge line and a centre line intersected where one stream was fed from a blind spring and the other from a downshaft. <u>That is, they were positioned directly over the place where detrimental energy (as identified by dowsing) generally rises to the surface</u>. The stones appear to have been accurately placed to counteract - to return to earth - rising detrimental energy and thus to take it out of the environment used by humans and animals.

The fact that at every ancient circle there are various different numbers and combinations of deep, wide water flows crossing underground, determines the number and spacing of the stones that would need to be employed to achieve this earthing effect.

The simplest combination would be where two streams cross, both fed from blind springs. Here, four stones would suffice - each earthing a crossing point that would otherwise give rise to detrimental energy on the surface. This is the configuration at four-poster 'circles' that I mentioned previously.'

Avebury revisited

'At the great circle of Avebury, in the chalk lands, there are many of these substantial underground flows, as wide as (and even wider than) the full width of the henge's ditch and bank. The largest of these is about 450 metres across. Within the enclosure, there are three very large blind springs, which feed major underground rivers flowing away in each direction. One of these flows coincides with the West Kennet Avenue. The stones to each side of the avenue mark the width of the flow and are at positions where lesser veins join with the larger stream. With just one exception, the smaller streams descend a downshaft into the deeper stream. At the exception, there is a blind spring. This large stream continues to the Sanctuary, where it descends down a downshaft into a deeper flow and onwards in a southerly direction. At the group of stones known as The Cove, there is another blind spring, which feeds an underground stream of equal proportions. This stream splits, with one part going to a downshaft at Windmill Hill and the other to the Beckhampton Mound.

Another blind spring rises in the front of The Red Lion pub, built almost in the middle of the henge. The water from this flows under the main street of the village, joins with the one from the cove and flows on to Beckhampton Mound. Three stones remain standing on the edges of this flow, and it is believed they are all that remains of another avenue that linked the main circle at Avebury to the mound at Beckhampton.'

Ancient and modern examples elsewhere

'I found a similar situation at the huge stone circle at Callenish on the Isle of Lewis, part of the Outer Hebrides off the coast of Scotland. There are several additional circles at the site (termed Callenish ii, Callenish iii etc.), which I found to be connected to one another by substantial underground flows of water. In every case, all of the stones marked crossing points or junctions of substantial underground flows.

The same applies to numerous circles that I investigated in Aberdeen-shire in Scotland - as well as many more in England, Wales and Ireland. By mapping the edge-lines of the large flows in relation to where the stones were placed in the different types of structure, distinctive patterns started to emerge. This finding was further reinforced by investigations I carried out at more recently erected stone structures.

There are now many modern circles and menhirs throughout the world, as people have been inspired to emulate their ancestors. Most of these have been erected either for their aesthetic or their spiritual value - and no attention was paid to the underground water present at the time of their construction. It is very significant that in most of them blind springs are now present, and the edgelines of the small flows running from them run under the perimeter stones.

This supports the important contention that small flows of underground water can be diverted and attracted to the larger stones of a structure.

Significantly, however, I have not found any <u>large</u> flows coinciding with the locations of the stones of the modern structures. At the few recently built sites where larger flows are present, the placing of the stones do not coincide with the position of these large flows.

At authentically dated ancient sites, the pattern I found was consistent. Where two large underground flows crossed, and the water in them came from blind springs (that is from an ascending source), there was a stone directly over the intersection of those edgelines. Where a stream fed by a blind spring crossed one fed from a downshaft, the stone was at the intersection point of the edgeline of the stream, which flowed from the blind spring, and the centre line of the other flow from the down-shaft. In cases where only underground streams fed by downshafts crossed, there was a stone at the intersection of the centre lines. This is also the scenario found at most single standing stones that are not classified as outliers.'

This important portfolio of research would suggest that the stones in any ancient stone circle are placed entirely according to the intersection points of edge lines or centre lines of pre-existing, large underground streams. They follow a 'blueprint', set in the earth by the presence of a network of deep underground flows of water.

It further suggests that the erection of the stones in a stone circle was probably totally dependent on the geology and hydrology of the underlying strata. It was, therefore, only necessary for those constructing them to be able to detect where these underlying watercourses were and to place the stones accordingly. If this is indeed the case, then could this possibly result in the approximately circular shapes and intricate geometry described by Alexander Thom?

As we have seen, many who have studied stone circles in detail have put forward convincing evidence that most of them embody precise solar and lunar align-ments. They have used this evidence to suggest that these alignments were deliberate, and imply that the designers would have required significant knowledge of the movements of the sun and moon.

If the stones were placed according to an aquatic blueprint in the ground, and yet the planetary alignments are found in completed circles, then the pattern of underground water must in some way be influenced by the interaction of the sun, moon and planets with that underground water.

'To determine if the only criterion for the design of a stone circle is for it to follow the blueprint found in the earth indicated by underground flows of water, I marked out and measured a number of possible locations for stone circles at various places on the farm near my home. I marked out some with wooden posts and, as we will see in the next chapter, I actually built one of them.

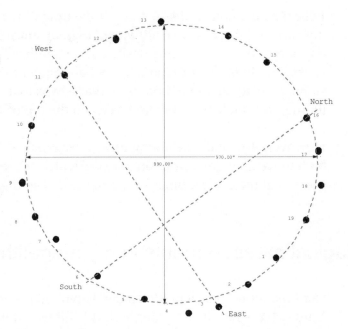

Design of circle in my garden at home which I later built

I measured the positions of the wooden posts, and I drew out the various shapes that were created. As you will see, these shapes are consistent with the shapes of many ancient circles. At several of them I looked for alignments across the stones for a correspondence with various solar events.

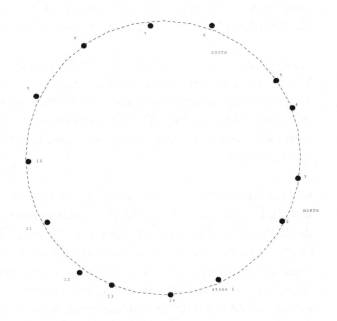

Another arrangement on my own farm

I checked the potential structures at the time of the autumn equinox. To my surprise, there was an alignment to both sunrise and sunset on that day across two of the stone positions. In another - the one that I subsequently built - I found a perfect alignment to the sunset at the summer solstice. Even more remarkable was that this alignment ran through the ancient chambered cairn on the top of Browndodd Hill.

However, it would take a long time to establish all the possibilities, due both to weather conditions and the difficulty of seeing clearly to the horizon at the critical times of the rising and setting of the sun and the moon.'

Magical measurements in my megaliths

'As I mentioned earlier, Alexander Thom identified the Megalithic Yard (M.Y.) and the Megalithic Rod (M.R.), and he found that the diameters and perimeters of ancient circles were very close to being multiples of those lengths. I measured and calculated the mean diameters and the perimeters of several of my potential circles - and I too found the M.Y. and the M.R. in each of them.

I also calculated how closely my circles complied with the 'Golden Mean', which is an embedded ratio that can be found in the architectural design of much ancient architecture, including most cathedrals and many old churches. The actual ratio is 1 to 1.618. Imagine a rectangle, where the short sides are 1 unit in length and the long sides are 1.618 units.

Golden Mean triangles are almost right-angled. The base is 1 unit in length, the vertical side 1.272 units (this is the square root of 1.618) and the hypotenuse (the longest side) is 1.618 units. To find this ratio in an elliptical or egg shaped form, we take the sum of the long and short axes and multiply by 1.618 to arrive at a calculated perimeter length. Alternatively, it can be calculated more easily by taking the mean lengths of all the radii and multiplying them by two.

In the stone circle I have constructed (see top diagram on page 81), the perimeter is less than 0.7 of one per cent away from conforming with the Golden Mean - and 0.07 of one per cent away from being an equal number of Megalithic Rods. It is inconceivable that such a close match could be sheer coincidence. It can also be seen how closely the stones conform to a regular arc, both at the top and at the bottom of the design.

I must stress again that all the positions for the stones were selected by dowsing, from the intersection points of the edge lines or centre lines of large underground flows crossing at the sites. No attempt was made to conform with any design - circular, elliptical or egg shaped. The final shape that I found, and the alignments that were created, were dictated by the blueprint of natural forces in the earth.'

Megalithic energy in three-dimensions

As we have already seen, Billy's ability to dowse with his eyes enables him to move one step (well, probably several steps) beyond the conventional dowser. When considering the size and shape of the stones in megalithic structures, this three-dimensional approach has led him to a further insight.

'At any intersection point of edge lines or centre lines of underground water, the detrimental energy - when it is present - will rise in the shape of a vortex. As we have seen, this is where the stones appear to have been deliberately placed.

The base of the vortex is at the level of the surface of the ground. The width of the base and the height of the vortex will vary depending on local conditions. Directly on top of the first vortex is an inverted vortex so that they meet point to point. On top of that is another base to base. This pattern is usually repeated several times and eventually terminates with a toroid at the top.

However, when studying a particular standing stone, I found that at certain times over the period of a month this vortex shape altered considerably - and on occasions changed to being cylindrical in form. The diameter of the cylindrical shape also changed from time to time. When I monitored this over several months <u>I found that the changes in shape and size corresponded with solar and lunar phases</u>.

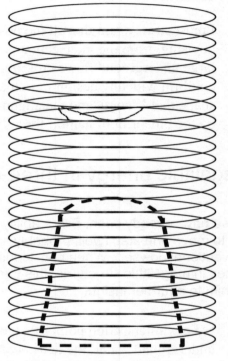

The vortex shape was maintained during the first and last quarters of the moon, but altered at the time of the full and new moon. These changes became greater with the onset of winter. The length of time over which these changes occurred became greater and the increase in diameter larger. Over the same period, I monitored the ability of the standing stone to successfully earth the detrimental energy. I found that when the changes that were taking place, in the form of the energy in the vortices, increased to a certain point then <u>the stone was no longer effective</u>.

Careful observation revealed that these periods of ineffectiveness were when the vortex changed into a cylinder and that the diameter of the cylinder became greater than the breadth of the stone. The stone then sat inside the ring of rising energy without making contact with it. See diagram above right.

At about 12 feet above the surface of the ground the line of energy forming the cylinder loops across the centre space before continuing on upward. To avoid these lapses of power and to ensure that the stone remains effective for the majority of the time, at this location a much larger stone would be required. This would then ensure that the ascending energy line, in whatever form it takes, would make contact with the stone and be earthed by it at all times. The diagram on page 85 shows a larger stone in place which would maintain the ability to earth detrimental energy. Because the stone is wider and taller it comes in contact with the detrimental energy cylinder, thus earthing it.

Therefore, it would appear that with megalithic structures, in many cases big is not only beautiful, but also necessary! Size does matter. The depth and volume of flow in the underground water at any given structure would appear to be the criterion that determines the maximum size of the energy cylinder there.'

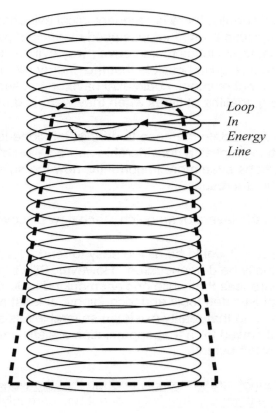

Loop In Energy Line

This is another profound appreciation, and again one that I have not found in the work of any other dowser or researcher.

It implies that the designers of the megalithic structures were aware of the width and impact of the rising detrimental energy. Furthermore, they designed both the location and the girth of the stones into the ground plan.

Whether those stones that do not fully cover the widest detrimental energy flow were incorrectly constructed, or whether it was just that there weren't large enough rocks in the logistical vicinity to cover the required necessary surface area, is a matter for further debate.

It is now apparent from research carried out by Billy, Hamish Miller and others - that earth energies react to the activities, and even the intent, of the observer. Given that many of the sacred sites were also used for ritual and spiritual purposes, especially at astronomically significant times, the interaction with the participants may well have had the effect of bulking up the earthing capacity of the stones at just the time that they needed it most - i.e. when the detrimental energy was leaking around the sides of the objects designed to block them.

Billy's observations of the behaviour of detrimental energy, when certain types of ceremony were taking place, confirm that it was pushed down into the earth for the duration of the activity, but that it returned soon after the activity ceased. The only procedure that appeared to embed a permanent improvement in the earthing quality of the site was the intoning of a Tibetan Chant.

Additionally, there is archaeological evidence of periodic burning at many megalithic sites. Fire was used by ancient people, and by quite a few more modern societies too, to drive away evil spirits (aka detrimental energies). It is therefore quite possible that the energy released by combustion, combined with the input of intent, could also have been used to increase the protective activity of the megaliths at times when they were in danger of losing their effectiveness.

To appreciate the need to do this, let alone to understand how to take remedial action, implies a considerable appreciation of how earth energy works - and, perhaps even more importantly, how the society can work with it to obtain the optimum results.

Like the layers of an onion, each new discovery raises a new raft of questions.

Clearly, it would be all too easy to read a lot more into these sites than can actually be demonstrated. However, Billy's work adds weight to an emerging awareness that while ancient mankind lacked what today we would consider sophisticated tools and technology, at least some groups did have an under-standing that reality exists on several levels at once. The physical interventions that flowed from that appreciation are still embedded in many of the structures they left behind.

I cannot stress strongly enough that the work undertaken by Billy Gawn appears to be unique in this field - and it has certainly been carried out quite independently of others. He acknowledges the influences and assistance he has had in developing his ideas, but the cutting-edge research has been his, and his alone.

As a further example of the work that Billy has carried out into the purpose and the positioning of stone circles, at Appendix B we include a description of a study he undertook into The Recumbent Stone Circles (RSCs) of Aberdeenshire, in north west Scotland. Here again, he shows that the precise location, size and shape of the component parts are all very relevant for the stone structures to achieve their primary objective. It is also reinforces the theme that the ancient circle builders were learning as they went along. They appear to have been adapting their con-structions to overcome shortcomings in dealing with earth energies inherent in the initial designs.

A Stone, a Circle and a Chambered Cairn

To take his research work to another level again, to put his theories to the test and to provide himself with a local laboratory to examine out his own suggestions, Billy took a quite remarkable series of decisions. He decided to erect, first a standing stone, then a full-blown circle of stones - and finally a modern cairn, complete with 'burial chambers' - in his garden!

The metamorphosis of coincidence into synchronicity in the current era may sometimes lead us to see parallel and related events and circumstances where none actually exist. However, in the case of Billy Gawn and his megaliths, the coming together of abilities, opportunities and locations does lead you to feel that these were structures that were meant to happen.

Now, there are several recently-built large structures that will hopefully last for millennia, and can be examined by existing, emerging and any future science for as long as they serve a purpose. If the project had been a failure, or it had just been inconclusive, that in itself would have been an interesting outcome - and Billy is the sort of man big enough to say 'OK that didn't work, let's try something else'. The fact that it worked in spades, after a certain amount of tweaking, and can be examined by anyone with a will to do so, was just the icing on the cake.

There are a growing number of modern megaliths in the western world. However, probably none of them, other than Billy's, have been erected deliberately using the principles discussed in the previous chapter.

So, just how did this massive undertaking come about?

'It was one of those things that started more or less by accident. About 15 years ago, when we were living at the old house (over the road), we were rearranging a bit of the garden at the bottom of the yard. My wife discovered a nice looking stone, about a metre or so long. It weighed about a couple of hundredweight, but we were able to dig it out by hand. We were able to lever and roll it to the part of the garden where we wanted to put it up, essentially just for decoration. We had no sense of putting it in a particular place - it wasn't dowsed into position - we just put it where it looked nice. Not surprisingly, putting it up there made no noticeable changes to the surrounding energies.

A couple of years later, we were further developing that stretch of the garden. My wife wanted me to put in a seat, with a paved area in front of it in the area where the stone was standing - which we did. I made it in the form of a pentagon shape, conforming to the golden mean as far as possible. That much was deliberate. Therefore, I had to move the stone to another location. By that time, I was starting to look into the placement and energy aspects of ancient standing stones. I had determined that they were positioned on the crossing points of two flows of underground water that were fed by downshafts. So, as an experiment, I found a place only about 10 yards from the stone's original location where two small streams crossed that were fed by downshafts - and I placed the stone at the centre of that crossing point.

The dashed lines indicate the centre line of two underground streams fed by downshafts.

What happened after that is fairly well described in *Megalithic Structures: Why?* I had been booked to talk to a dowsing group in Scotland. I was wanting to demonstrate muscle testing, but I didn't feel as comfortable about doing that in public then as I did later, so I got my daughter to help me with some preparatory work. We were working inside the house, which was 20 yards or more away from where the stone was placed. When I tried various locations where I knew her arm should test weak, I couldn't get any weak responses at all. It always tested strong. I tried and tried in various ways, but I couldn't get it to test weak. This worried me considerably, as it was only a few days before I was going over to Scotland to demonstrate it!

The next day, we were working out in that garden area, tidying it up - it was about 10 days or so after the stone had been moved. I took the opportunity of asking my wife to assist with the muscle testing experiment, but again I couldn't find any weak responses. No matter where I asked her to stand, I couldn't get her arm to go down easily.

I realised something had happened, and I wondered what I had done recently that brought about this change. I then realised that I had moved the stone to what must have been its 'proper' place.

I used my eyes to see how the energy was flowing - and I saw that all the detrimental energy that had been rising from certain locations was now being drawn towards the stone at ground level - and taken down into the ground. In looking around the immediate area, I did find one or two locations, but not many, maybe 20 or 30 yards from the stone, where a single shoot of detrimental energy was still rising. Without saying anything to her, I got my wife to stand on each of these locations - and to my great relief her arm went down easily. I then got my daughter to come out of the house, again without telling her anything about it, and asked her to stand near to these locations, where her arm was strong, and then to inch back on to them. When she stood directly over the lines of radiation, her arm went down.

A short time after that, my old friend and EEG stalwart, Dudley Wheeler, came over to visit me. We set out to see how far the effect of the earthing stone was reaching. We found that the detrimental energy was earthed for a distance of about 400 or 500 metres around it.

For me, that was a clear demonstration of two things. Firstly, that the muscle testing is not influenced by my thoughts or intentions, nor for that matter by the knowledge of the person being tested. The participants were aware that they could be standing on points of detrimental energy, so it wasn't suggestion that made it work. Secondly, it proved that putting the stone in its 'proper' location had a significant impact on the detrimental energies in the area around it.

So that's why I erected a second standing stone, a larger stone, which is now one of the stones in the circle in my garden near to the new house. It was a place where there seemed to be an abundance of underground water. I selected a stone, maybe a ton or more in weight, and I got a man with an excavator to bring it from where it was lying and to put it in place for me. By looking, I realised I had impacted on the energies around it for quite a distance. I got in the car and I drove in various directions - and I found that it had all but eradicated the rising detrimental earth energy for up to 6 or 7 miles around. It seemed that the area that was affected by the stone was the land surface above the underground water - and all the tributaries associated with it.

It seemed to deal with all the detrimental energy, not only from the underground water but from all other natural sources in that area as well. The only exception being one or two places where reversal points had been activated (which we will describe in a later chapter).

The area affected by the stone was smallest at the winter solstice - and increased as the days lengthened, to a maximum at the summer solstice.

After I discovered the effect that the standing stone had on the detrimental energy, I checked for its presence several times daily. I found that for a short while around the new and full moons, the detrimental energy rises out of the ground, increases in height and then gradually descends again. Many dowsers have observed that the lunar and solar phases have an influence on energy movement and its form. This temporary lapse in effectiveness is due to the vortex changing into a cylinder, as previously described, and the stone not being large enough to come into contact with the line of radiation. During the period that contact is lost, detrimental energy is no longer being earthed.'

Understandably flushed with enthusiasm, and on something of a roll, Billy went on to use the highly effective standing stone as the basis for a full-blown 'circle' of stones.

'A couple of years later, I went on to build the full circle, as I was hoping for much bigger and better things. However after it was completed, I found that there was only a small improvement in that respect. The impact varied from about a distance of seven to ten miles depending on the time of year - the greatest effect again being at the summer solstice.

The stone circle was constructed beside my house. It may seem strange that it is in two fields with a hedge across the middle of the circle, but that is what was dictated by the flows of underground water and crossing energy lines. Anywhere else and it would not be effective. The original standing stone (see arrow below) has now become one of the stones of that circle.'

After dealing with the detrimental energy, Billy turned his attention to what was left - the normal or beneficial energies. He sought to analyze them and to calibrate their effectiveness. He wanted to see if he could increase the range and the quality of the frequencies of beneficial energy with another tranche of megalithic property development.

'A few months after completing the construction of my stone circle, I decided that I would attempt to build a chambered cairn using, in part, the large number of stones that were left over from the circle building. I based the design on a triple spiral at the termination of three energy lines, which was about twenty metres away from the circle.

It took a lot of time and hard work to actually construct it, but when I checked to see what impact there had been on the energetic environment in the area around it, to my great disappointment I found there had been little change.

The cairn under construction showing the light box and blocked passageway.

Below is the wall with the quartz in line with the entrance to the cairn.

Having built the cairn out of natural local materials, I was a little concerned about the stability of the structure. With safety in mind and grandchildren visiting us frequently, I didn't want anyone to enter the passageway, so I placed a large blocking stone at its mouth.

This left a small slot near the roof of the passageway reminiscent of the light-box at the Newgrange cairn, through which light could still enter. I had read somewhere that when Newgrange was first uncovered a large piece of rose quartz was found blocking the light box. I subsequently built a stone wall in front of the cairn - and in it I placed three pieces of white quartz, in line with the opening into the passageway. This change blocked off the light completely from entering both the passageway and the chambers.

I checked to see if this addition to the structure had had any impact on the energies of the area. I found, to my amazement, that most detrimental energy rising from all sources had been earthed for a radius of about 30 miles around it, rather than the previous 7 to 10 miles.

It appears that the placing of the quartz in the mouth of the passageway - where the energy lines enter the mound - causes the cairn, my circle, and several of the ancient sites in the district to communicate with each other and work together as one single unit.

This is similar, but on a larger scale, to what I observed in experiments that I had carried out several years previously. Instead of placing a

The chambered cairn nearing completion, from the north side showing the wall at front of passageway

large single stone on an edgeline to earth the detrimental energy I built a small cairn with fist sized stones. I found that such a cairn composed of only one type of stone, in my case basalt, did not remove detrimental energy as effectively as a large single stone would have done.

It was only when I included some stones of a different kind in the fabric of the cairn that it carried out the intended function. By experiment-ation, I found that it required the addition of either quartz, limestone, or flint. This seemed to bind the stones in the cairn together, making them act as one single unit.

In the construction of many ancient cairns, there is a combination of different stone types - with limestone, flint, and quartz being among those most commonly found.'

Having established that the composition of the cairn had an unexpectedly strong impact on the working of the structure, Billy also wanted to investigate what effect other minerals and compounds commonly found in ancient cairns might have on the earth energy management.

'When we read reports of archaeological explorations at structures such as chambered graves the presence of several things appear to be common to most. The first is skeletal, or cremated bone. Others include wood ash, charcoal, quartz and what are termed grave goods. I could not get into the chambers, because I had sealed them off as mentioned above. However, I sprinkled various substances on the ground above the chambers to see if this would bring about any further change to the energies around the cairn. By experiment, I found that it was not the physical chambers themselves that seemed to be significant as such. It was the fact that each chamber coincided with one of the earth energy spirals or vortices, which in reality is a stack of seven vortices with a toroidal form at the top (see diagram page 83). These extend upward through the top of the cairn. If a substance is sprinkled, either in one of the chambers or directly above on the top of the cairn, it is the contact with the energy form of the spiral that really matters.

I sprinkled on bone meal, to simulate cremation. I also scattered on wood ash - as a lot of these places had evidence of fires. The third substance I tried successfully was very fine quartz crystal, like sand.

Each of these improved the quality of the beneficial energy to some extent. For calibration, I used a counting method. This enabled me to discover that the quality of the energy does fluctuate from time to time - again perhaps due to planetary influences.'

Quantification or qualification?

'At the end of the day, I am unable as yet to determine whether or not the raising of the quality of the energy levels has had any effect on the area or on the physical or psychological wellbeing of the people who live here. It would take a long time to work that out - and there are way too many variables! There is no immediate indication that the health of the population has improved, as so much also depends on their life-styles - what they eat and what they do.

What I <u>have</u> found is that the energies change to some extent every hour of the day. In this context, I am so supportive of Rory Macquisten's work *Dowsing Observations,* because he has taken the trouble to record fine details of the movements of earth energy lines over a fair period of time. Even he was confused, because the energy lines don't all do the same thing. When you are working in such a subjective field in the day -to-day world, as opposed to the tight paradigm you can establish in a laboratory, there are always going to be other factors that come into play, outside of your own experiment - and it's quite impossible to determine the impact of each factor in any detail. All you can deter-mine is that there is a trend in one direction or another. Therefore, I don't feel the fine measurement of the energies really adds too much to the value of the information you are getting. I think all you can do is to establish a trend.

Even the input of the dowser is important. The position where the dowser stands when carrying out the measurements can make a diff-erence. Even if you slightly adjust your angle, that can affect the reading you get. It's not an easy one to crack scientifically.

From my garden, I could see five or six miles across the landscape in several directions to the near horizon. With the stone circle in place, and the initial phase of the cairn completed, I could see that there wasn't much detrimental energy rising there - but I could also see hills beyond that, where detrimental energy was still rising quite clearly.

However, when I put the quartz into the chambered cairn, I could no longer see detrimental energy rising at all - it had disappeared over the horizon. I knew I had moved things on.

So, the next time I was driving to a job, about 100 miles away to the west, I just kept my eye on the landscape and asked the Dowsing Question 'where is the extreme edge of the influence of my structures?' For a long way it was in front of me, but eventually I realised I was coming to the edge of it. As I drove through that edge, I noted where I was and drew it on the map.

I had reason to visit that client several times, and I found the specific point where the influence ceased. It varied quite a bit, with the maximum influence at the summer solstice, and the minimum at the winter solstice. I checked to the north, south and west, but I couldn't drive to the east, as it runs out into the sea! However, I did map dowse that direction. The area of influence wasn't quite a regular circle - it was more of an egg-shape.'

Billy's work here must be some of the most exciting and incisive of modern times. The fact that he has been able to confirm in practice many of the concepts he unearthed at the remaining ancient sites raises the bar on the subject considerably.

In the emerging field of earth energy dowsing much effort is being concentrated, and understandably so, into minimising the adverse impact of detrimental energy and maximising the impact of beneficial energy. Billy has shown that this actually is quite possible. Improving the quality of earth energy - and, by extrapolation, the quality of the connected living environment is not an unfounded superstition, but a relatively straightforward, practical application - albeit engineering driven by enlightenment.

Billy's understanding of this subject, acquired through deviceless dowsing, has enabled him to reach more deeply into some of the motives and the intentions of pre-scientific man than almost anyone else alive today. It is just possible that he has reconnected with their chain of thought, and is actually pushing the process forward both academically and practically - effectively bypassing, or at least working in parallel with, three thousand years of scientific discovery.

Circle Building Elsewhere

While Billy's demonstration of putting the theory of stone placement into practice on his own land has been a revelation, it has not been his only sortie into this particular field. He has erected a number of single standing stones, with considerable effect, but he has also been instrumental in the building of other stone circles, using the principles described in the previous chapter.

A ring in Roscommon

'Before I built the stone circle in my garden in 2005 I had constructed two others in different locations in the Republic of Ireland. The first was in the hills near to the small village of Arigna, Co. Roscommon, an old coal mining area. To assist me in this project I enlisted the help of a small team, 12 in all, most of them members of the EEG. A report on the construction of this circle was published in the September 2000 issue of Earth Energy Matters. It was authored by Tony Hathway. It is accessible online through the BSD website.

The Arigna, Co. Roscommon circle

I marked the position of the stones to coincide with the intersections of 11 flows of underground water. Five were from blind springs and six from downshafts. This resulted in 17 stones being required to cover these intersections. The proposed circle had a diameter of about 60 feet. To assist with the construction the owner of the property supplied a JCB type track excavator with a skilled driver.

This, in itself, can give rise to a debate amongst modern circle builders in that some believe that the use of mechanical means violates the energies and the Spirit of Place. They feel that circles should be built manually as they were in ancient times. My response to this is that I believe that those who built megalithic structures several thousand years ago were working in what they looked upon as their modern times. They would have resorted to the most up to date technology that was available to them. If, perchance, the likes of a machinery hire shop had travelled back in time I am sure that the megalithic builders would have been some of the first to knock on their door and avail themselves of whatever tools they could get, to make the job easier and quicker to complete. If a JCB was one of those tools, I am sure that they would have used it - just as I did.

The use of the JCB and the willing team allowed us to complete the erection of the 17 stones in a record time of seven hours. In the time that remained we also used some spare stones nearby to construct a dolmen. The site chosen for it was over an ascending spiral of beneficial energy. The capstone had the effect of reflecting the energy back down into the chamber of the dolmen to form a sphere, which almost filled it.

Before the circle was constructed, I had examined the quality of the energies in the living environment for some distance around the site. In this area, there was the usual mix of beneficial and detrimental energies. After the circle was complete I found that most (if not all) detrimental energy had been earthed for about a three-mile radius around it.

Using a steel tape, Tony Hathway and Jim Lyons carried out a fairly accurate measurement of the position of the stones in the circle and they prepared a scale drawing of the site. It was not so much the position of the stones that they measured, but the position of the inter-section points, as dictated by the underground water, on top of which the stones were placed. On comparing the measurements to the Golden Mean, I found that the circle conformed to a high degree of accuracy. Unfortun-ately, at that time I was not checking for Megalithic Yards or Rods and as the site has now changed hands I am unable to carry out any further measurements.'

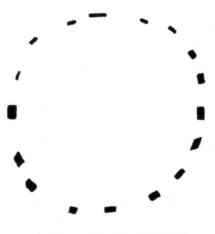

As measured by Tony and Jim

A circle near Askeaton

'I erected a second circle near to the village of Askeaton, Co Limerick. Again, I marked the location of the stones according to the intersections of large underground streams. It required 17 stones, which were sourced locally by the owner of the land. A JCB was employed, as at Roscommon, together with about six willing helpers. The circle was

The Askeaton, Co. Limerick circle

again completed in a single day. At the time that it was constructed I measured the position of the stones, and I calculated their conformity to the Golden Mean. Once more there was only a small degree of variance. In the spring of 2011, I had the opportunity to measure the circle again, to see if the measurements of the mean diameter and perimeter were multiples of whole Megalithic Yards and Rods. The result was in the affirmative with a very small discrepancy, well within the limits set by Thom. The actual measurements are to be found in Appendix C of this book.

On checking the quality of the energy after the circle was completed I found that almost all of the detrimental energy that had been present in the living environment prior to its construction had been earthed for about five miles around it.'

Continuing Professional Development

'My most recent involvement was in the construction of a stone circle, which took place in the spring of 2011 - in the hills not far from Ennis, Co. Clare in the south west of Ireland. I was contacted by John, the leader of a group of people who organise Earth Spirit camps, and are part of a group of traditional drummers. One of their members owned a piece of ground in a remote area, which they used for camps and drumming practices. They were interested in communicating with earth spirits through their activities, and they felt that a circle would be a good focal point.

I agreed to become involved in the project if I could be convinced that the circle would have more value than just its appearance. John emailed several Google maps of the property to me, along with some photographs. Through their own evaluation of the potential sites, they had selected a little plateau area in one of the fields as their preferred location - and they had actually deposited the stones to be used for the circle there. They had worked out a design based on the geometry of a flattened circle, as described by Professor Thom, incorporating the Megalithic Yard, and with a recumbent stone, similar to those found in some of the Scottish stone circles.

This was totally contrary to the approach that I would have taken, and consequently I was a little uncertain as to whether I should become involved - especially as my input had been limited up to that point. When I dowsed the Google maps, I could not see anywhere on the property where a number of large streams crossed to provide what I considered to be the necessary blueprint in the ground. However, it was interesting to find that the location they had proposed to site the circle was the only place on the property where any large streams did cross - but even then there was only one crossing point. They had actually marked out the design that they had created by hammering in fencing posts at the exact position where they believed that the stones should be erected. The photograph below clearly shows the posts in position. Again, I was amazed to find that three of the posts coincided with the edgelines of the wide stream - with two on one edgeline and one on the other.

Despite this remarkable accuracy, none of the group professed to be a dowser. <u>This suggests that dowsing and intuition are one and the same - and that many people use dowsing without knowing that they are doing so</u>.

John also mentioned the possibility of erecting an outlier, and he indicated a possible position which, in my opinion, would not have had any impact on the energies. However, I was able to find two possible sites where a stone outlier would complement the effectiveness of the circle - and without them it would have been lacking in performance. John agreed to go along with my suggestions, and I decided to fully participate in the project.

Consequently, I travelled down to Limerick where John picked me up and took me to the site. I spent five days there. It was an ambitious project, in that the stones were either large or very large - and they proposed to erect all of them purely by manual labour!

When I got to the site, I was pleased to find that what I had dowsed remotely was actually in the ground, exactly as I had envisaged. I was even more pleased to see that, in fact, four of the stones in the circle would cover the edgelines, not three as I had previously thought. I knew that that would increase its effectiveness. During the time I was there, they only managed to get three of the four critical stones in the circle erected - along with an outlier, placed about 20 metres away from it. However, I could see that even this minor amount of work had had a significant impact on the surrounding energies, and it had removed most of the detrimental energy I had originally observed.

One of the circle stones in the foreground with the outlier behind

A stone awaiting erection

When I had map dowsed the site at home, I had observed the position of
a large triple spiral on the ground, not far from a small ornamental lake
that they had constructed some time previously. I suggested to John
that we carry out an exercise there, which might also complement the

*One of the stones a few seconds after it became upright. The relief can be
seen on the faces of the workers*

other work being done. He was agreeable to this. I did not propose to build a chambered cairn as I had done at home, but rather to construct a solid cairn of small, easily managed stones - and then to place a large quartz crystal at the correct height, to intercept the three lines of radiation leading to the triple spiral. Four of us collected and wheeled sufficient stones to complete the task successfully - and to provide a platform at the correct height for the large piece of quartz.

On my way home across Ireland towards Dublin, I was able to look out of the train window and check on the state of the energies. I was able to identify the extent of influence that the stones that had been erected, together with the small cairn, were already having on the energies generally - and on the detrimental energy in particular. The cut off point of influence was slightly more than half way across that part of the island.

The group stayed on for another week, and they finally succeeded in erecting eight stones. One of those was the other outlier. That meant that all of the critical stones were in place and the circle was operating near to its full potential.

I intend to visit the circle again when it is completed, to make a final assessment of its effectiveness. However, even in its partially con-structed state, it has proven to be a particularly informative exercise. The chosen site was far from perfect and it required the combination of several structures to achieve an acceptable result. This may throw some light on the repeated use of outliers in ancient times. It suggests that they may have been later additions, intended to bolster an existing but ineffective structure, which may have been underperforming due to the selection of a less than perfect site - or the lack of availability of a better site.'

To repeat the formula in a number of cases - particularly where the design has had to be adapted to the extant landscape and the energy footprint - adds much credibility to Billy's hypotheses.

Given the hard evidence of these last two chapters, it would be difficult to argue that stone circles do not effectively manage detrimental energy. Additionally, these case studies imply that the erection of a modern megalithic structure, using either Bronze Age or Fossil Fuel Age technology, can have much the same dramatic effect under a range of different conditions.

Whilst I am sure it does not totally demystify the megaliths, it does go a long way towards demonstrating that they were tried and trusted technology, manufactured to manipulate subtle energies. As our society is only just starting to recognise the very existence of these subtle energies today, the stone circle remains as close to the cutting edge of science as it was four or five millennia ago.

These experiments clearly raise a series of uncomfortable questions, especially for those who feel that the embedded astronomical alignments in the megalithic monuments are proof of lost ancient knowledge. If the locations of the stones are based solely on the energy matrix of strong flows of underground water, yet the alignments were revealed after or during the event - then it suggests that lunar, solar and stellar alignments are encoded in natural earth energy emanations, independent of the stones themselves.

There is a growing awareness that ancient cultures were a lot more knowledge-able about the cosmos than archaeology would suggest at face value. Billy's findings, described above, would seem to imply that at least some of this archaic understanding was little more than the unfolding of natural processes - albeit with human intervention. Readers may be concerned that their intuitive feeling that the ancients were on to something big is being seriously challenged. However, please read on - for life is so much more complex than that.

Firstly, even if the cosmic alignments are a byproduct of the building of the megaliths, rather than their primary purpose, the recognition that they are there - and the appreciation of what that says about the workings of the universe - is itself a profound revelation.

Secondly, if the patterns and alignments are indeed totally natural, what does that indicate to us about the shapes and settings of other structures in the ancient - and indeed the not-so-ancient - world? What could it also lead us to infer about the other patterns that intrude into the physical world - labyrinths, symbols, even, dare I say it, crop circles?

Thirdly, it is apparent that many sites were employed, at least in the latter stages of their use, for astronomical and astrological purposes. Whether they were originally set up as earth healing sites, but were later modified to incorporate other functions is unknown (although you could, of course, dowse to find out!). It would be plausible to suggest that once the stones were in place - and the earth healing effected for as long as they were there - the original purpose would have been fulfilled, even forgotten. The more obvious parallel function, as an observatory, would then be accentuated. Add to that, the effect of the healed nature of the area on crops, livestock and inhabitants - and you have a one-stop-shop centre of community support and learning.

It also indicates that the designers and builders of the megaliths used a form of dowsing, initially to understand the need for their construction in the first place, and then to find the appropriate locations for the various components.

Let us not forget, that through both the ancient art of dowsing and also the most modern discoveries of science, there is a growing awareness that the interaction between the observer and the observed plays a significant part in the outcome of the process. Both people and the sites they construct are far more deeply integrated than we have previously imagined. It is a living demonstration of the Spirit of Place - a theme that we will return to later in this book.

Through a Portal in the Holestone

A mile or so from Billy's house stands the Holestone.   It is a fairly unremarkable standing stone, except, as its name suggests, it contains a perfectly formed, and probably man-made hole right through it.

It was here that he came across, quite literally, a touchstone on his journey - something that ignited his realisation that the world around him was far more complex than the thin veneer of the screen of the five senses. It was here that Billy's research into the wider world of dowsing really got underway.

A classic of the genre

'The Holestone is a genuine ancient standing stone that seems to have been set up to take account of the detrimental energy arising from the crossing water lines at that point. It also has various types of energy lines streaming through it.

When I visit an ancient site, I usually ask to be shown what the energies were prior to the construction of the megalith - and then again to find the current patterns. I think that's so important to the understanding of what the site has been used for - and you will usually get two completely different patterns of energy. You also need to ask about underground water - both how it flows now and also what the network looked like in the distant past. Again this is important because I believe, as do others, that erecting a stone can attract underground water to it.

At the Holestone, there are two substantial streams of underground water coming from downshafts, but one of those streams is also almost at the junction with a third stream coming in to it and joining at an angle. So, to all intents and purposes, the stone was once affecting three streams. There are also three major energy lines crossing at that point.

There's one that seems to run more or less in alignment with what you can see by looking through the hole in the stone in a westerly direction. If you look directly through the hole at the mid-winter sunset, you will get a very precise view of the sun setting into Donegore Hill, the site of an ancient Iron Age fort.

Looking across the top of the stone at 90 degrees to the hole, in a south-easterly direction, on that same morning, the winter solstice sunrise can be seen coming out of the top of a prominent hill several miles away.

I followed the energy line that is in line with the sight line through the hole, and I checked it at various places, right up to the top of Donegore Hill.

At one point it passes through the site of a hill fort, which is not visible now, but was excavated very extensively about 30 years ago, and was considered to be one of the main areas of habitation in times gone by in the district. The 'fort' was surrounded by two ditches, but they weren't continuous ditches - they were intermittent, with tree trunks placed in the sections of trench to create a palisade fence. The ditches were 20-odd feet long and about six feet deep, but backfilled to stabilise the tree trunks. They had been dug out of the solid basalt, at a time, 5,000 - 6,000 years ago, when there were no iron tools available. It must have taken a lot of work, moving thousands of tons of earth and rock. There was remaining evidence of the tree trunks, to the extent that the archae-ologists could establish their approximate size. They had been very substantial, so the effect would have been similar to building a stone circle - but using tree trunks instead of stones.

There were also a lot of shards of locally made pottery, possibly using the china clay available at Browndodd Hill nearby. The archaeologists were able to date the construction very accurately from the artifacts that were found.

The interesting thing for me was that the centre of the fort was directly in alignment with the line of sight from the Holestone at the midwinter sunset.

In a sense, that's what started me off with dowsing because, at the time, I didn't believe the mysteries and magical properties that were attributed to standing stones. That's why I put up an ordinary bit of basalt in my yard to test them out. The rest, as they say, is history.

My dowsing shows that there were already three major energy lines crossing at the site of the Holestone, prior to its being placed there. Whether the ancient people who erected it were dowsers in the modern sense of searching out a place to site it, or whether they just put it there through intuition, I don't know. If they were instinctive dowsers (like some of the experienced water diviners) maybe they just looked across the landscape and realised that that was the place where it needed to be erected to get the maximum effect - and they just plonked it there.

The erection of the stone would have caused a rippling effect on other energy lines across quite a wide area of the surrounding countryside. We will discuss this consequence in a later chapter.

My own experience and my dowsing has shown that the erection of a precisely placed stone like this has a marked and long-lasting effect on the suppression of the detrimental energies for a considerable distance around it. The area affected seems to be determined by the accuracy of the placement, the volume of the underground water flow and the mass of the stone – but, as I have discovered in the garden, even a small stone, well-sited on a small crossing point, will have a considerable effect. In my case, the first small stone that I put up affected an area of about 400 yards around it.

However, it's not just the impact on the detrimental energies. In recent years I have studied the impact on the remaining beneficial energies, and it is quite apparent that these can be enhanced greatly. It's possible that a megalith like the Holestone could well have been intended to address both of these issues.

In recent centuries, much of the rocky outcrop has been quarried away from around the stone and this has had some impact on its effectiveness. In fact, it has negated the original purpose of the stone. If you are putting up a stone over the centre lines of streams, the stone must not be large enough to reach out and cover the edge lines as well, or you will just eliminate the benefit it was erected to enable. It has to sit within the edgelines. So if you have two lines crossing, there is a square area on the ground inside which you must put the stone. (See diagram below)

Now, with the outcrop cut away from around the stone, the plinth that the stone is standing on, which is about 10ft higher than the surrounding field, is now acting as a standing stone in its own right – and that is well beyond the edgelines of the water flows. Consequently, this eliminates any original benefit from the standing stone on the top of it.'

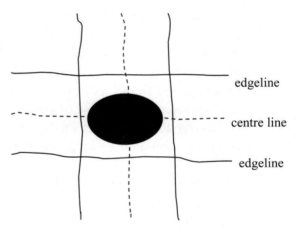

edgeline

centre line

edgeline

Standing by the Holestone with Billy, it seemed a rather pleasant spot energetically, despite the destruction of its energy earthing property. I wondered if that was because I was tuning into the energy lines, rather than the impact of the uncapped water energy:

'That may be true, but the work I have done at home, particularly by the building of the circle and the chambered cairn with its quartz lightbox, has cleared the detrimental energy from around this area - and that includes the Holestone. Consequently, the situation has been reversed once more.'

The megalithic environment

I was somewhat saddened to see that the area immediately around the stone was certainly not being revered. In fact, it was surrounded by fertilizer bags, discarded bottles and other rubbish. The public information sign had been felled and was lying face down in the mud. All in all, the site looked rather forlorn - and I asked Billy if he felt that this situation was having any adverse effect on the quality of the energy in the area. Billy's response was predictably unpredictable.

'Not a lot, really.'

We will re-examine this somewhat surprising comment in the chapter dealing with The Nature of Intent.

'What I have found is that providing the vegetation in the surrounding area is not up to the full height of the stone, it doesn't seem to make much difference. If there is gorse and whin close around it to the stage where it is overgrowing it, then it starts to reduce, and eventually eliminate the benefit that it previously had. Surprisingly, something as temporary and flimsy as a gorse bush, or even grass, seems to have an effect on the output quality of something solid like a standing stone. To be effective the stone needs to be the prominent feature rising above everything else on the immediate landscape.

Although we are looking at a holed stone here, you could get a similar effect by placing a tree trunk there instead. It might not last as long, but it would have a similar effect for the time it was there. You could use just about anything to get the same effect, even something made of concrete - or plastic.

I have occasionally visited people's houses to improve the energy, and I have used the first thing that comes to hand to demonstrate the effect of placing something at a specific location. As often as not it's a wheelie bin, empty or otherwise - but it seems to do the trick, just as well.

One question that often arises is that if you can eliminate detrimental energy just by erecting a stone, a wooden plank or a wheelie bin, why when you build a house over the line does that not eliminate it? I think it's something to do with the fact that the detrimental energy still rises up within the stone, but it seems to hit something towards the top of it. It is then directed back down into the ground, and is therefore removed from our living environment.

If, theoretically, you were inside the stone, you would still be able to see that there was detrimental energy present - and if you were in the wheelie bin, you could see that there would still be detrimental energy in it. But within the house, the detrimental energy rises through the structure and out through the roof. It doesn't just rise and bounce around in the house and return back down into the ground.

My research indicates that an object over the underground stream loses its ability to earth the detrimental radiation when it is a little wider than three times the width of the stream. Unless it is a very large stream, clearly most houses would be larger than that. If it is less than three times the width of the stream, it does seem to be able to earth the radiation.

I haven't totally resolved that issue yet, but I'm quite convinced that certain things do earth it, and also that if not earthed, detrimental energy goes through a house and off in to space - because I can see it. But there is some other factor at work there, which I have yet to discover, about <u>why</u> this happens.'

Implementing the wisdom of the megalith builders

While the discoveries that Billy has documented relate primarily to the structures he has erected in his own garden, or found in the surrounding countryside, he has nonetheless been quietly busy helping other people to rebalance the energies around their own homes.

'Although I have only mentioned one or two instances in my written work, I have actually put up numerous standing stones. In more formal gardens, where a rude stone would be inappropriate I have substituted and erected strategically placed birdbaths or sundials. It's the same idea - a monolithic structure in a very specific location. I have always felt most comfortable with that way of working.

From time to time, I <u>have</u> rebalanced energies purely by mental means, but I wasn't totally satisfied by doing it that way. Maybe that's why I haven't been as successful with my non-physical energy management as some people claim to be. To be good at anything it requires practice, practice, and more practice.

I think it's important that we all do what works for us - and we also have to consider our clients to see what they are most comfortable with. A lot of them like to see that something physical has been done. Just turning up, mumbling a few words and then asking for your fee can be a bit off-putting to some clients! Sometimes I think you do have to put a bit of theatre around the process - but not too much, otherwise the ritual can become more important than what you are actually doing. We have to be careful to avoid that.'

We will come back to look at Billy's views on the use of intent in his work later on. He certainly can and does apply a mental approach to a physical problem where he feels it's appropriate. However, as a practical and very down to earth man, he also prefers to provide some solid solutions.

Leying a Little Dust

There are few debates in dowsing that give rise to more heat and provide less light than the hoary old chestnut of ley lines.

For those of you new to the field, Alfred Watkins, a Herefordshire amateur archaeologist and local businessman, working in the early part of the twentieth century, discovered seemingly straight alignments of ancient sites, with widely varying dates of construction.

Alfred Watkins 1855 - 1935

He wrote up his findings in the seminal work *The Old Straight Track* in 1925. The book was seen as little more than a curiosity at the time, and went out of public awareness for many years. It reappeared in paperback, in a more auspicious era - and the 1976 Abacus edition rapidly became a cult classic.

Alfred Watkins was not a dowser, but he inadvertently set off the starting pistol on an entirely new area of research - Earth Energy Dowsing. To him, what he called Leys were no more than a series of locations on a map - and on the ground - that seemed to form a straight alignment. He deduced therefore that they somehow involved the input of humans, but right up to his death they remained a mystery to him. His best suggestion was that they might be trackways of great antiquity, which only remained in the landscape by virtue of structures of various ages that had been built along them. However, why tracks should cross mires or jump off cliffs was quite inexplicable, and the fact that many of these alignments included natural, as well as man-made features, only served to deepen the enigma.

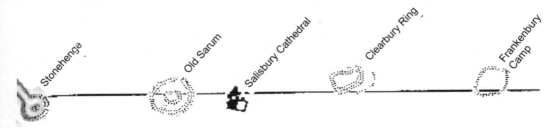

115

One example, shown at the bottom of the previous page, is the Old Sarum Ley, spanning the border between Wiltshire and Hampshire. It can be seen that the line of the ley does not run through the centre of many of the constituent sites.

Although to date it has been considered a basic tenet of a ley line that the alignment is straight, it is Billy's view that the Watkins leys are almost straight. This is a subtle, but significant, distinction, to which we will return shortly.

During my own introduction to dowsing, I was taught that leys were lines of consciousness - effectively entities that were thought into place through human thought. I was even shown how to set one up - a surprisingly simple process - and then how to take it away again afterwards. Yet some years later, I was to read that the US Dowser, Sig Lonegren, had found leys that did contain earth energy - although, at the same time, he felt them to be man-made. He termed these lines Energy Leys - and the plot thickened even further.

Since then we have had a period of (sometimes heated) debate, with various camps trying to explain the seemingly conflicting evidence of their own experience. Billy's view is characteristically straightforward and logical:

'When I, and others, compiled the little terminology booklet for the use of Earth Energies Group members, definitions of the terms 'Watkins Ley' and 'Energy Ley' were included:

WATKINS LEY - A significant alignment of sacred and secular sites across a landscape, generally inter-visible. The minimum number of aligned sites to qualify as a ley is five. The term was first used by Alfred Watkins in 1921. There is no associated energy line indicated by the term ley as Watkins described it, and therefore it is not to be confused with Energy Ley.

ENERGY LEYS - Lines of dowsable energy which generally run straight, are 6-8 feet wide at their central core, and often have further bands or edges to either side. Influenced both in width and strength by lunar and solar cycles. They are often found at what are called sacred sites. Whilst energy leys are considered to be natural energy phenomena it is also thought that they can be created by the formation of structures (and in some cases have been observed to appear after a structure is built) and are drawn to the site as the result of human activity of a spiritual nature.

Therefore it can be seen that we need to be careful as to the term we use to describe what we observe. <u>The word Ley is not a dowsing term and should not be used as such</u> as it often leads to unnecessary confusion. As stated above, it has been considered a basic tenet of a Watkins Ley that the alignment of structures is straight. But here it is important to ask what is meant by straight in this context. Most of the structures that Watkins considered to be valid components of a ley are large and their centres are poorly defined. Also, we need to understand how much variance from dead straight is allowable before a line ceases to be a ley in the eyes of the ley hunter. Apparently, the criterion judged necessary to qualify an alignment as a ley is that it only required any part of a site or structure to fall within the visual alignment.

In my opinion, the term Energy Ley should be used only to describe energy lines that are straight and run through several ancient sites or other structures. However, I am aware that some dowsers claim that energy leys are not always present where a Watkins Ley is to be found. It is also commonly found that an energy ley does not cross an ancient site at the geometrical centre.

I appreciate that the previous few paragraphs do not fully remove the confusion from the ley debate - and in some places may even add to it! So, let me add a little more detail to try to clarify the situation.

A few years ago, I carried out experiments with three or more small, easily-moved objects - placing them a distance apart and in approximate alignment. This gave me great insight into the origin of what are called the Energy Leys that we find linking many ancient sites.

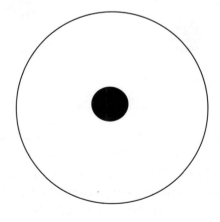

Any object be it a small stone or an ancient site, a stone circle, cairn, building or any other structure - when it is viewed in isolation, and not in alignment with any others in its range of influence, has an approximately circular aura around it. (See diagram at bottom of previous page.) Confusion can arise in that this aura is often referred to as the energy field. I am as guilty as anyone else of doing this. The energy field is a much more complex manifestation with the aura being only one of many different - and independent layers. A series of radial lines is another of these layers. Radials do run in straight lines until they terminate in a spiral, but do not at any time form part of an energy ley.

At first glance, the aura appears to resemble a circular halo around the object, which is not the case. Careful examination will show that it is more like a geoglyph, formed from a single convoluted line. In certain circumstances, this can be made to unwind into a straight line extending for some distance.

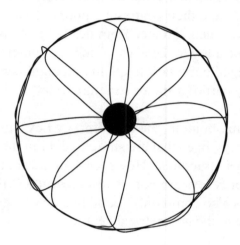

When three objects are out of alignment by more than four degrees, the energy fields around them remain unaffected by one another.

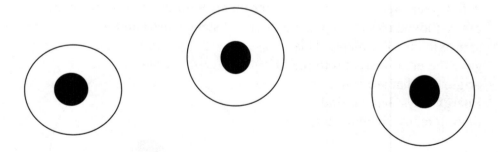

However, when any mixture of three or more objects, structures, or sites are in near alignment, and they are not over a certain distance apart - the lines forming each of their auras unwind. They combine to form a straight line flowing through all of them, and extending further beyond the objects in both directions. See diagram overleaf.

This is the reason why straight lines of natural earth energy form what dowsers call Energy Leys.

In fact, when any three objects - be they stones in the garden, ancient sites, or planets in the cosmos - approach three degrees off alignment, and are sufficiently close in relation to their mass, they begin to interact with each other. The lines that comprise the auras around them start to unwind. At first the lines will become sinuous and head towards the other objects. Then they progressively straighten as the objects come, or are brought, closer into alignment. <u>They will be perfectly straight only when they are a fraction of a degree out of precise alignment</u>. As the objects are brought even closer to alignment, the lines start to fragment and the 'eclipse effect' takes over. When perfect alignment is achieved, the lines of radiation are drawn back into the objects and appear to disappear. As we can dowse during a planetary eclipse, as soon as the objects are taken out of alignment again, the lines reappear. When they are several degrees off dead straight they return to the normal energy fields. This may be one explanation why some dowsers fail to find energy leys at places where there is an obvious alignment of structures - for if the alignment is perfect, then no energy leys will form.

At a full moon, when the earth, sun, and moon are close to alignment, but not eclipsed, an energy line can be 'seen' linking the moon to the earth, which would run on to link to the hidden sun on the other side of the earth. Approaching an eclipse, which is total alignment, this line again starts to break up and roll back into the source object and disappear altogether along with most energy lines on the face of the earth.

Where Energy Leys are found, the sites related to them are, of necessity, ever so slightly out of alignment - although this is not easily detected given the nature of the natural or man-made markers, and the distances involved. Energy Leys formed in this manner are just straight lines of earth energy. Some occur naturally, the result of the inter-location of hilltops and other significant topographical features. Others have been assisted, or perhaps encouraged into existence, by the judicious or casual placement of stones, mounds and other features by man. It is difficult to know whether those who put the structures in place were aware that they were causing a dowsable line of subtle energy to be put in place as well. In my opinion, these dowsable lines are not man-made, however in some cases they may be 'man caused' which is an entirely different thing. The energy in the lines is natural. However, man can emphasise the energy flow, by adding stones, earth mounds and other features, which extend the line and enhance its presence.

Nigel refers earlier to lines of consciousness, and suggests that some dowsers are of the opinion that the energy in them is different from what we refer to as earth energy. However, I am a firm believer in not over-complicating any issue and tend to go for the simplest credible explanation. I believe that as far as all subtle energy is concerned, there is only one type and source of it no matter where we sense it or how we deal with it. As I have mentioned already the term 'earth energy' is not a proper descriptive term. However, it is the one that we appear to be stuck with for the time being and it is appropriate enough, provided dowsers are aware of the possible confusion that it can cause.

Similar lines of energy can be found linking any structures that have been put in place in modern times, provided they meet the conditions of mass, alignment and distance apart. The distance apart within which this interaction takes place is dictated by the mass of the objects concerned. I feel the reason that dowsers have not remarked on the presence of these lines connecting modern structures is simply because they have not gone looking for them - or, if they have found the lines, they have not investigated their source.

I have found out more about the energies dowsable at ancient sites when working well away from them - usually whilst looking at more mundane things. Those who want to become familiar with Earth Energies should spend a considerable time dowsing the open landscape well away from ancient sites. This will help them to establish what is the norm as far as energies are concerned, and then when they do visit an ancient site it is easier to evaluate the difference that the structure has made to the underlying energy patterns.

My view is that man has never actually made anything, and never will - either in the physical world, or in the realm of subtle energy. Man assembles things that are already there - or at most rearranges a few molecules. The same applies to earth energy lines. It is a bit like throwing a pebble into a pond. It creates ripples. The ripples would not form if the water was not already there. We do not create energy lines. We can throw thoughts into the sea of energy that surrounds us and create ripples that take the form of a line, or whatever. We are only rearranging that which is already there.

So how does this relate to what we generally call thought forms - lines of consciousness? Everything is an individual entity - a planet, a person, even a stone or a tree - and a thought also has an existence of its own, as soon as it is created. A thought form is a real phenomenon, an entity in its own right, and is therefore different from imagination (although it could also be argued that imagination is itself an entity, and therefore exists, but we digress!).

Once created, thought forms can remain in the ether, possibly for all time. A thought form could therefore remain as a straight line on the landscape - dowsable, but simply being a rearrangement of existing earth energy. Accessing consciousness through dowsing may allow us to go beyond the range of the electro-magnetic spectrum, and this is where I believe what we call earth energies exist.'

Billy has never been one to court controversy. Indeed, throughout his published works, he has gone out of his way to avoid offending or unnecessarily contra-dicting the opinions of his fellow researchers. In this short chapter, however, new ideas are raised that are significantly at odds with the views that many of us have held over the years in the great Ley Line debate. Some degree of controversy is unavoidable in the pursuit of a new enlightenment.

The Statement that the concept of the Ley Line is not primarily confined to dowsing is a useful clarification. Watkins merely discovered that there were straight alignments of sites in the landscape - nothing more. A ley, therefore, has nothing intrinsically to do with earth energy, even through it drew many of us into the field in the first place.

The endorsement of the term Energy Ley, to describe the Watkins alignments that also have straight flows of earth energy running between them, is also quite clear. Personally, I would also like to have a term for those that do not to appear to contain energy, but that's just my own preference.

The appreciation that leys are formed by slightly off-straight alignments is a real breakthrough. It throws much light on to the debate about the precision of the leys - and it ties in closely with Billy's work, explained elsewhere in this book, on the Eclipse Effect.

The understanding that Energy Leys are formed from the unravelling of auric energy is more contentious on a number of counts. Auras are conventionally considered to be composed of several layers or types of force - and many will assert that these do not contain earth energy at all. There is a general assumption that the aura of an inanimate object is in some way comparable to that of a human. How a human aura would or could be affected by the Energy Ley formulation process is unclear. It is also difficult to understand how some objects, such as sacred sites, could form an Energy Ley line in this manner over a long distance, while there are any number of other natural and man-made features in between the sites - both on and off the alignment - that do not form part of it.

However, Billy never claims to know all the answers and, like any scientist worth his salt, he only purports to open doors for others to investigate. What I have come to appreciate during the time that I have known Billy is that no matter how unexpected the concepts and the phenomena are that he investigates, at the end of the day his descriptions tend to be pretty close to the mark. So, while auras that deform and join to make a unicursal line may sound a bit far-fetched today, I have a funny feeling that we may be nodding wisely in years to come, to indicate that we found it all rather obvious really!

Everyday Energies and Gigantic Grids

The way that earth energy lines display themselves has given rise to years of debate amongst dowsers. Some have found straight lines, while others have found lines that are anything but straight. Most modern dowsers find both types - and that just adds to the general confusion.

Precisely when people first observed lines and fields of radiation - the kind of patterns we now call earth energy - is difficult to determine. Certainly, a picture discovered in temple ruins indicates that ancient Mesopotamians dowsed, and that they embedded the lines they sensed into their buildings

However, before the arcane art of dowsing was banned in Britain for four centuries, the earth energies we dowse today were acknowledged by some of the most influential people in the Kingdom.

Milestones of earth energy dowsing

'One of the earliest references to invisible lines being found in the ground comes from a colourful character, who lived in the 16th Century. His name was Dr. John Dee, and he became Astrologer Royal to Queen Elizabeth I. He was born in 1527 and was educated at Cambridge, entering the halls of St. John's College at the remarkable age of 15 - and graduating as a Bachelor of Arts.

Dee straddled the worlds of science and magic in a way that would seem inconceivable today. One of the most learned men of his age, he was invited to lecture on advanced algebra at the University of Paris, while still in his early twenties. Dee was an ardent promoter of mathematics and a respected astronomer. He was also a leading expert in navigation, having trained many of those who would later undertake some of England's landmark voyages of discovery.

By the early 1580s, Dee was growing dissatisfied with his progress in learning the secrets of nature. He began to turn towards, what we would now term, the supernatural as a means of acquiring additional knowledge.

Dee was also a prolific writer. In one of his books, he wrote:

"The true mathematical science is that which measureth the invisible lines and immortal beams which can pass through cold and turf, hill and dale. It was for this reason, it was accounted by all ancient priests the chiefest science; for it gave them power both in their words and works."

It is clear that Dee did not claim to be the first to become aware of these lines - and it is reasonable to suggest that the knowledge of their existence was something that had been handed down through time immemorial.

In the late 19th and early 20th centuries, the eminent French dowser Henri Mager took up research into the subject, and wrote a number of books on dowsing-related topics (dowsing not having been banned in France, as it had been in England).

However, the search for displays of subtle energy greatly increased after Alfred Watkins published his seminal work *The Old Straight Track* in 1925 - and coined the term Ley. Watkins was not a dowser and the Leys he described were purely visual straight alignments of ancient and more modern significant sites. Although his book is considered by many to mark the beginning of earth energy dowsing, at no time did Watkins himself suggest that Leys marked or contained subtle energy.

In the 1930's, two British dowsers, Captain F. L. M. Boothby and Reginald A. Smith (Keeper of the British and Roman Antiquities of the British Museum) linked prehistoric sites, such as earthworks, barrows and temples, with underground streams and, what they termed, 'magnetic currents'. These they observed through the use of dowsing. Clearly, these two gentlemen were well-educated and well-respected citizens of their day - not the type of person subject to flights of fantasy. Their work triggered the search for what became known as 'Energy Leys'. These were dowsable lines of radiation that were claimed to join ancient sites, in much the same way as Watkins' Leys. Energy Leys were assumed to be inherently straight - as a line of sight is necessarily straight.

The concept that lines of natural subtle radiation are always straight was later challenged by the eminent dowser, Guy Underwood, working in the 1950's. Underwood had an impeccable record as a water diviner and turned to energy dowsing as an interesting sideline. His research was partly inspired by the claim that ancient sites were placed over underground water; something that Underwood and other qualified dowsers of that era were able to confirm. He concentrated his work on the energy lines he found at sites, rather than on those that connected sites.

His work is well-documented in *The Pattern of the Past*. However, his work was so controversial at the time that the book was only published in 1969, five years after his death.

What Underwood found was that whilst some lines were reasonably straight, most were far from it. They weaved about, all over the place.

However, his suggestion that the outlines of some of the fallen stones at Stonehenge and elsewhere indicate that they were deliberately in those positions, on pre-existing energy lines, we now realise is not correct - and unfortunately this has detracted somewhat from a broader appreciation of the importance of his work. (See Appendix C).

Another person who made a significant contribution to the understanding of earth energies was Colin Bloy. Although he is probably best known for founding the Fountain Group in Brighton in 1981, I believe the extensive research he carried out into the nature and form of earth energies, and into the way those energies respond to changing circumstances, was even more significant.

Colin Bloy

It was Colin who drew attention to the existence of spiral shapes, as well as other geometrical, geoglyphic, even archetypal, energy forms. He was one of the first to realise that these energy displays are not confined to ancient sites, but are present throughout the landscape. He highlighted the influence on earth energies of changes in local circumstances, and also the impact of the human mind - through properly directed thought, meditation and prayer - to effect change.

Colin became aware that changes in the form and nature of the energy display could have an impact on the way that the human mind operates, which in turn affects our behaviour.

This appreciation inspired him, together with a few colleagues, to form the Fountain Group, which gathered to 'send' healing energy into the global energy network, using a well-known and easily visualised landmark, the fountain in Brighton, as a focus.'

No book covering the work of Billy Gawn would be complete without a description of his work on energy grids.

Whilst, as Billy explains, research into the nature of energy grids has rumbled on for decades, there are many dowsers, let alone scientists, who remain unconvinced of their very existence.

When attending one of Billy's courses on the subject, you are left in little doubt of their empirical existence - but then, when your tutor can 'see' what you are finding with your rods . . .

Grids galore

'Perhaps the most discussed configurations of energy lines are those that take the form of grids. Of these, the two best-known were first identified in 1951.

One was reported by the German physician and radiesthesist Dr. Ernst Hartmann. (1914-1992). He described a grid of radiation composed of rectangular cells surrounding the earth, which had a north-south by east-west orientation. He called it the 'Global-Net Grid'. Today it is simply referred to as the Hartmann grid.

In the same year a second similar grid was discovered by Dr. Manfred Curry (Founder of the Bioclimatic Institute in Bavaria) and his colleague, Dr. Wittmann. This grid runs at a 45 degree angle to the north-south alignment of Hartmann. It is now called the Curry Grid.

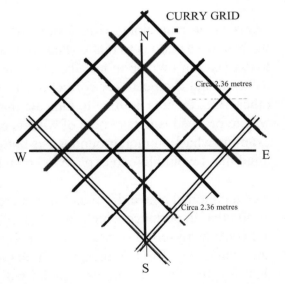

These physicians felt that it was detrimental to health to sleep directly over where the lines of the grid intersected with each other - especially when this intersection coincided with an underground aquifer.'

Meanwhile in Northern Ireland . . .

'All this took place, either before or at the same time that I became involved in the earth energy scene. Due to my isolation from it, I was totally unaware of what others had found until my own research was well underway. Like Colin Bloy I had dowsed lines and associated patterns that appeared to emanate from stones. I had also found a multitude of lines and geometrical forms, as well as more complex patterns, within the energy field of every stone I studied. The main difference between what I was investigating and what others were doing was that I had used 'common-or-garden' stones - stones with no apparent religious or spiritual associations.

In later experiments, I also examined stones at places that many dowsers regard as 'sacred sites'. However, my view is that there is no significant difference in the energy displays of most stones, or any other objects that contain mass, no matter what they are - or no matter where they are found.

I must stress that, along with all other dowsers examining earth energy, the best we can do is to relate what we have found as individuals - and to express our own opinions. To date, there is no proof that what any of us has found is objectively correct other than by dowsing, but on the other hand, there is nothing to indicate that it is incorrect. The only fair way to proceed is to take note of what is being said by all parties and to examine what common ground exists between us. It is with this in mind that I would like to explain my own experience of the subject.

As I mentioned above, from an earth energy perspective, I found it was of no great importance which stone I used, or where it came from. I did not confine myself to stones, but used objects of all descriptions, natural and man made. I found displays of radiation coming from nearly all of them - with a few exceptions, which I will refer to later. These displays, of which I have identified about 11 different and distinct layers, go to make up what is generally referred to as 'the energy field'. When dowsing the energy field, only one layer will present itself at a time. There can be confusion in that we tend to refer to a particular layer as the energy field. The layer that is most commonly referred to is the multi-ringed aura.

In nearly all cases, there was a great similarity in the displays that I observed. None of them was absolutely identical in detail, but that was understandable, as it is not often that we find any two things in nature that are exactly the same. We humans are a good example of this. We all have the same bodily features, but every one of us is unique. No matter how small the object I used, I found a similar display. The only real difference between the objects was that the smaller the object, the smaller the area covered by the display.'

Grids around objects

'Grid forms are one of the layers of the energy field that I refer to above. If you take any everyday object, there are generally five different orientations of energy grids associated with it, forming a dense surrounding energy matrix.

The grid with the greatest number of squares has 14 x 14, and is generally in a North-South, East-West orientation. Whilst we refer to them as grids, they are actually three-dimensional manifestations - and are cubic in form. If the object producing the grid is on the surface of the ground, half of the cubic form is submerged under the surface of the earth.

14 squares x 14 squares

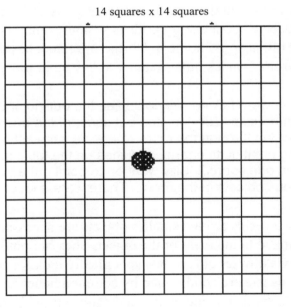

Basic grid form in energy fields around most objects

A second grid has 10 x 10 squares. The spacing of the lines is wider and, although it has fewer squares it covers a greater area.

Next is a grid with 8 x 8 squares with a wider line spacing and an even greater total area.

A fourth grid has 6 x 6 squares with a much wider line spacing, but a smaller total area than the previous grid.

The fifth grid has 4 x 4 squares, again with greater line spacing and a total area less than the fourth grid.

Whilst I have noted that the 14 x 14 grid is orientated approximately North-South by East-West, I checked this with a compass and find that it reads a few degrees west of magnetic North. I want also to clarify that these findings are what I find here in Northern Ireland, and I do not know if the orientation of the grids changes with location or other factors. However, I would be interested to know what dowsers find in this respect in other parts of the globe.

I think that the prolific nature of grids and their sources is why the debate about energy grids is so confusing. For example, Browndodd Hill, near my home in Northern Ireland, has this series of grids coming from it, in a similar manner to any other topographical feature.'

While we were talking, we could see the outline of Browndodd Hill on the north-western horizon. Billy pointed out some of the energy grid lines emanating from it, and passing through the room where we were sitting. He also identified a crossing point of its energy grid lines on the table in front of us - and all that was just from one source! Billy went on to point out a number of other grids generated by various objects in the room. There were a lot of them!

'The grids around smaller objects are necessarily small, as the size is linked to the mass of the object. They are not so likely to be picked up by a dowser unless they specifically look for them. I believe that dowsers are conditioned by common belief and that our dowsing mechanism is inclined to a default setting, based on that belief. The fact that the Hartmann and Curry grids were the first to be recognised and that the spacing of those grids is reputed to be about 5 to 6 metres apart, would encourage dowsers to find grids that have spacings in that order of magnitude. Those with much finer grid spacings would generally be ignored by our dowsing consciousness. Until we acknowledge the possibility of the existence of grids below the spacing range of Hartmann and Curry, the smaller grids will remain unexplored. However, the bigger ones, especially those from topological features, can - and will - be picked up by most dowsers, because their dowsing radar is open to receive them. Because of their size, I feel they could be confused with the width of the Hartmann and Curry grids. I think that that's one reason why there's a lot of debate about the spacing of the lines in the various grids.

I think the Hartmann and Curry grids are formed by the earth as a whole, or at least by significant components of it. I find there are also other grids formed by the earth as a whole, but that their component lines are a little further apart than the Hartmann and Curry grids.'

Billy pointed some of these out to me as we sat chatting in his conservatory. They were composed of a rectilinear mesh - with lines about ten paces apart.

'I think people who feel there are no earth grids are just not tuning into them. If you doubt strongly that a thing exists, you are unlikely to find it through dowsing.'

This is another of the themes that is engrained in Billy's approach to dowsing - and for that matter to the whole of the human approach to discovery. You have to believe in at least the possibility of something existing, or that an event can happen, before you can realise it for yourself. He feels it is probably the biggest barrier to the widespread uptake of the skill - and many of us feel that the dam of public and scientific incredulity will burst soon, as the evidence from books such as this one gain more common currency. I dearly hope that Billy is still around to see the flood, as his work will doubtless play a considerable part in forging the breach.

Types of energy display

So far, we have touched on subjects that, if not yet mainstream, are moving towards mainstream scientific acceptance. Beyond this point, Billy moves out into little-charted territory, but his conviction - based on his personal, practical research and his visual dowsing ability - is unshakeable. When talking to those who doubt that energy lines exist, Billy will merely encourage the more open-minded critic to try locating one for themselves. However, he also likes to offer a word of caution to those new to Earth Energy dowsing, and who have found an energy line to play with in their back garden.

> 'Quite often they will ask another dowser to confirm that they have indeed found an energy line. A difficulty of confirmation arises in that there is such an abundance of energy lines, radiating from millions of sources, that in any small area, even a back garden, the dowser is completely spoiled for choice. It is virtually impossible for another dowser to confirm or refute a colleague's findings, unless both dowsers are aware of both the source and the exact nature of line that has been found. This is where the dowsing question requires continuous rewording to get to a compatible answer to the intended request.'

In its modern form, dowsing is still a very young and immature discipline. Consequently, much basic work on the nature of the beast, in this case the energy line, has yet to reach a complete consensus amongst dowsing practitioners, let alone be accepted by the wider scientific community.

Most people are pleased to have assured themselves that they are dealing with a real phenomenon, and maybe to have discovered that energy lines differ, one from another. As we have seen, Billy moved beyond this stage many decades ago, and he is now engaged on the finer points of the subject - such as answering the questions 'what are the different forms that earth energy lines take? - and what are their component parts?'

> 'Lines of radiation coming from an object take many different forms, but they can be grouped into four categories:
>
> 1. Straight   2. Sinuous   3. Spiralling   4. Convoluted

Whilst earth energies mostly display themselves as three-dimensional manifestations, they are usually observed two-dimensionally - and it is to those that I will refer first.

1:     Straight lines in energy fields can take the form of grids, radials, rectangles, and triangles.

Grids found on the surface of the earth can have many sources, some of which we have already considered:

- The earth as a whole - of which the Hartmann and Curry grids are two examples.

- Topographical features on the face of the earth such as mountains, hills and valleys.

The amount of deviation from the plane, whether it be incline or decline, that causes the formation of undulating ground and hills and valleys, does not need to be that great. Experiments that I have carried out show that when the deviation exceeds a little more than 3 degrees and less than 4 degrees, the area affected by this change in profile acts as an energy generating unit in its own right. This helps to explain why there is a considerable variation in the display of grids, energy lines and other forms across a rolling landscape.

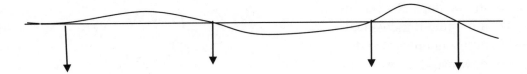

- Trees, all rocks (large and small), buildings, and man made structures, including posts, pillars, and most artifacts that rise above ground level, project their individual, but similar, energy imprint on the face of the earth locally to them.

- Planetary sources - the five planets closest to the earth, plus the moon, have grid forms that project out far enough to reach the surface of the earth.

As I described on pages 129/130, within each energy display around an object there are usually five different grids - with a different number of lines, spacing, and orientation in each.

Each of these grids is formed by a continuous energy line with a series of 90-degree bends, which continues until the complete grid is formed and the line returned to the source. As stated earlier, most energy forms are three-dimensional, so what we are really observing is an energy lattice in a cuboid form. Naturally occurring cubic lattice structures are well known in nature.

Radial lines radiate out from a central point within the source object. They can vary in number depending on the interaction with other energetic objects. Radial lines terminate in a spiral, which sometimes curls clockwise, sometimes anticlockwise. The spiral can have a varying number of rings, again due to external interaction. Radial lines are three-dimensional, pointing upward and downward, as well as outward.

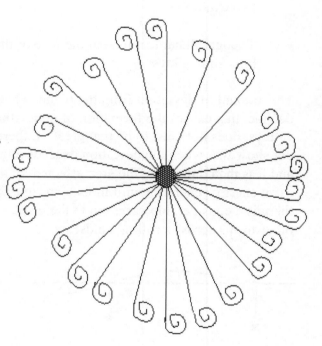

The most prominent example of the portrayal of two-dimensional radial lines in the world is on the Bolivian plains in South America. These were marked out by the indigenous people living near Nevado Sajama, and cover much of the Altiplano, or High Plain.

Rectangles, triangles, and other geometric shapes with straight sides are usually formed by several straight lines intersecting.

2:     <u>Sinuous lines</u> are generally observed as a sine wave with a regular frequency, although they can also appear serpentine with no regular frequency.

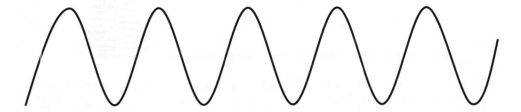

What we see as a two-dimensional sine wave in plan form would be observed as a horizontal spiral in three dimensions.

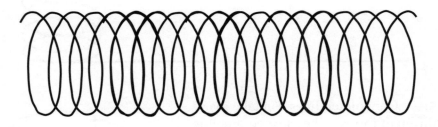

3:     <u>Vertical spirals</u> are commonly found where a line terminates. They are never in isolation. This is a vertical spiral in plan form as would be marked out on the ground.

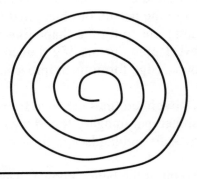

Spirals in three dimensions appear as cone-shaped vortices.

If the curvature of the spiral is such that it meets up, two-dimensionally it will appear circular. Seen three-dimensionally it resembles a coiled spring.

4:     Convoluted lines can take many different forms. The most common is the aura - an energy manifestation found around the human body as well as all other objects. On first exam-ination, the aura can appear to be a circle of radiation of varying projection from the source. In fact, it is a continuous line of radiation, emanating from the person or object that twists and turns to form a shape like the overlapping petals of a flower, with the outer edge forming an imperfect circle.

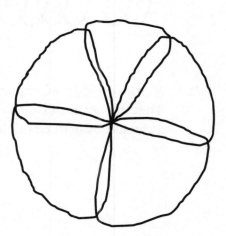

Convoluted lines can also form shapes that are reminiscent of the archetypal imagery found throughout the world - such as that seen in rock art and landscape figures.

Some of the better-known examples include:

Multiple spirals as seen at such places of antiquity
as Newgrange in Ireland and Gavrinis in Brittany.

The prehistoric chalk hill figures of Britain

The Cerne Abbas Giant

Long Man of Wilmington

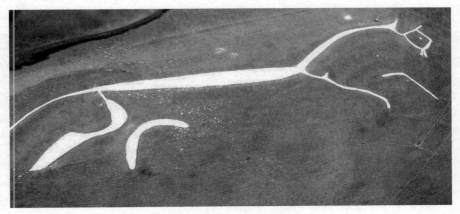

The Uffington White Horse

The effigy mounds built throughout North America by the indigenous Indian tribes - of which the Ohio Serpent is probably the best known.

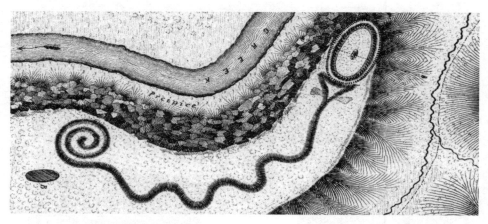

The Nazca lines and geoglyphs of the Nazca desert in southern Peru.

The convoluted lines of radiation that form shapes similar to the geoglyphic and archetypal imagery described above are to be found as offshoots of straight lines radiating from the source object. These lines are not to be confused with the other, much shorter, radial lines that simply end in spirals.

The size of the images found reflects the size of the source object. Some can be as small as a few inches across, whilst others of a similar profile can be several hundred metres across.

When these images formed by the convoluted lines emanating from objects are observed regularly throughout a year, it can be seen that like all energy lines, some are static, but many are not static – and that they move according to the seasons. When observed in groups, rather than as isolated individual figures, they appear to play out scenes that are reminiscent of some of the stories from ancient mythology that have been handed down through the centuries.'

Images in the ether

Billy's work on the archetypal images is both fascinating and disturbing. As he acknowledges, it echoes both the work of Colin Bloy and Hamish Miller, but it takes the dowsing definition much further. While Bloy and Miller could only find elementary shapes, albeit some with quite complex forms, Billy sees well-defined outlines - and connects them to natural energy lines emanating from nearby ranges of hills and mountains. This clearly implies that the archetypal forms are natural projections or interference patterns, but how can a man with a club or an intricately-feathered humming bird be produced by geological means?

I have no reason, and certainly no means, to question what Billy is visualising, but even as a reasonably experienced dowser, I find it difficult to grasp the reality of such a cutting-edge piece of work.

However, in attempting to come to terms with this aspect of his research, I can tender two possible lines of reasoning. The first possibility is that the earth itself is communicating these archetypes. I am quite used to having a virtual discourse with what some would term Gaia - the planet as a coherent entity. The 'spirit of the planet' certainly responds to the investigation of various earth energy phenomena - and it is just about conceivable that such a dialogue could stretch to a non-verbal exchange of icons or pictograms.

Beyond the Far Horizon

The other possibility is that the observer is becoming part of the process - and it is the observer who is striving to make some order out of the chaos of convoluted lines. In the case of the chalk figures of horses or giants, the images could have been interpreted in times gone by as forms that were familiar at the time - and then somehow set in aspic in the ether. This would only be one stage on from setting down visual ley lines, the more ancient of which are now so firmly etched into the ether that we can no longer change them.

Neither of these possibilities gets anywhere near to explaining why a farmer from Antrim would find the same archetypes in his fields. I can only let Billy put some flesh on the bones of this remarkable aspect of his portfolio.

'I stumbled on this phenomenon. When I intersect any line of radiation I always turn and follow it for some distance to see if it is straight or convoluted. To be able to get any feel for what lines of radiation are like it is important that all earth energy dowsers develop the skill to enable them to follow a line at walking speed. If a line is simply intersected at intervals it is impossible to be sure as to whether it runs in a straight line between the points or is curved or convoluted.

It was when tracing out some lines that I observed that they appeared to resemble figures of one kind and another. I found one - and that led on to another and another. In all, I found, maybe, a dozen different shapes that had some resemblance to human, animal or bird-type images. It was at that stage that I began to see a resemblance to the landscape figures of southern England and also to those in the Americas. I think the serpent (similar to that in Ohio) was one of the first images I found. The more complex shapes remind me of the ones in the Nazca lines in South America.

Although I have never had the resources to go there, my colleague Jim Lyons was kind enough to lend me a video of the Nazca images. Using the eyes as the dowsing tool it is possible to dowse from a video, or in fact any TV image, just the same as if one was present at the time that the video was shot. From that, I was able to see that the shapes had a source in the hills and mountains behind them. They are much the same configurations that I find attached to the energy lines coming out of any stone or object. However, when they are coming from a range of mountains, which are relatively linear, it gives rise to a wide range of straight and convoluted lines, which tend to form patterns - very similar to what has been marked out in the earth on the Nazca Plains.

I have also visited the Cerne Abbas Giant (in Dorset) and I have looked at the way the energies form patterns around it. What I saw there didn't quite align with what is there today, although I accept that energy lines can move over time. If you were cutting it today, and using the earth energy pattern in the ground as something to trace over, it would be taller and longer - and the feet in particular would be further down the slope. However, the way it's drawn out now, it's visible on the hillside from head to toe. If it was drawn in line with what I could see, the head and the feet would come onto more level ground, but they would not be so visible all in one go. So, I think that alterations have been made to it down the years, on subsequent cuttings, to make it more observable.

The pattern of the giant is an offshoot of lines that originates in hills several miles away. Although I have never visited those hills to see the exact location of their origin, I was able with my eyes to follow the line back to the range of hills in the distance.

The Ohio Serpent Mound certainly conforms very closely to the lines and patterns that I found there. There were one or two minor deviations, but nothing more than a foot or so. I was able to trace the line of origin back for 7 to 10 miles to a range of hills. It was just one of a series of lines that emanated from that range of hills.

The images can be very complex, but they are again composed of a single convoluted line. I believe the correct term for such a line is a unicursal line. It's just one line that comes out of the source object, weaves about in a convoluted way, forming various patterns as it goes, and then ends up back in the source object.'

Billy is not the only experienced practitioner to associate convoluted energy lines with the shape and form of landscape figures. Alanna Moore, the well-known Australian dowser and author, came across a similar phenomenon when dowsing at the site of a Stone Serpent (which appears to be a depiction of the Aboriginal deity Mindye) in the countryside of Victoria State. It is laid out in rocks. The figure was clearly of considerable age but its outline was still traceable as being etched out in the ground by earth energy lines. Writing in the online magazine Geomantica, September 2011 she describes how:

"Dowsing the line of stones I soon detected a telluric energy flow (earth energy line) *that followed the path exactly. This energy flow suggested where missing stones had once been placed. Technically speaking, one might describe its form as a toroidal vortex flowing horizontally across the ground . . . Close by the last boulder I soon discovered, by dowsing, the presence of a very powerful geo-spiral some 10 metres or so across."*

Billy takes this correlation of energy lines and landscape figures one stage further, by suggesting that features in the ether, described by the late Hamish Miller, may also be greatly scaled-down versions of the similar process in action.

'I believe the Pictograms described by Hamish Miller and Colin Bloy are formed in exactly the same way. I am of the firm opinion that the geometrical relationships found within the molecular structure of the object and the interaction of those molecules are the reason why a line of radiation coming from an object is either straight, curved, or convoluted.

This opinion is based on some simple experiments that I carried out in the garden of a house at St Laurent, not far from Carnac, France in May 2001, where I was staying with fellow dowsers Paul Barnett, Jim Lyons and Dudley Wheeler. It was during an interlude between visits to the megalithic sites of that area that we were inspired to carry out a series of experiments.

1. Three wood blocks were placed on the ground approximately 72 inches apart to form an equilateral triangle with base angles of 60 degrees. This caused disturbance to the energy in that area and certain nodal points were formed as a result. As Colin Bloy and Hamish Miller had observed elsewhere, it is at these nodal points that pictogram images and other deformities in the energy field can be observed. I dowsed the energy form at these nodes and found them to be similar to the stylised shapes of flowers with either four or five petals.

2. As the wood block at the apex of the triangle was moved a little further away from the base line, the geometry of the triangle changed. This brought about changes in the flower patterns in that the petals were larger, incomplete semi-circular and/or overlapping.

3. When the apex wood block was moved further away still, until the base angles were approximately 68 degrees the manifestations at the nodal points had changed further to adopt the shape of seven circuit labyrinths.

We continued the experiments through a total of 16 stages, with the apex angle decreasing and the base angles getting progressively larger. Every stage showed changes in the energy display. These included wiggly shapes like arms with triple spirals, and S shapes, a Maltese cross, Ohio Serpent shapes, spider and bird patterns and shapes reminiscent of the Nazca patterns, the Long Man of Wilmington and the Cerne Abbas giant. When a slight adjustment was made beyond this stage the images found at the nodal points ceased to be present - and another phase of manifestations appeared.

Many of my experiments, including the one described above, using small objects demonstrate that critical geometrical relationships exist between objects of whatever size that cause lines of radiation to bend and turn in particular ways. It is reasonable to suggest that this kind of critical relationship would - and does - occur at all levels including the atomic and the molecular level.

If we move a few objects, even such mundane objects as flowerpots, around in the garden - or even if we stand in different places ourselves - we can change the patterns formed by the energy lines quite considerably and very easily. Another person can dowse and record the changes. That much is pretty straightforward.

I feel that the shape formed is derived from the geometry that exists within the molecular structure of the objects themselves, creating these critical relationships, which react by distorting and deforming energy lines, dependent on the angle between the atoms and molecules. This is reminiscent of the holographic principle and the science that governs it. The production of a holographic image is dependent on the exact angle of the laser beam projected across the material under scrutiny. In other words, a critical relationship or angle must exist, or the holographic image would not appear.

The next question is, 'What criteria are necessary to bring about a critical relationship?'

Some clues are available from my experiment with the three bricks. In that case, the critical relationship that was necessary was a triangle that conformed to the Golden Mean (1.000 - 1.272 - 1.618). This ratio is one of several, so called, irrational numbers that cannot be expressed by an ordinary finite fraction. No matter how many digits there are after the decimal point it will never resolve to zero.

At the other end of the numerical scale are many numbers that are divisible with the answer being a whole number. These are termed rational numbers.

I am of the opinion that it is the geometrical configurations that are constructed incorporating irrational numbers which are most likely to cause critical relationships to occur. When mountains, objects, atoms, or no matter what, are placed at these critical angle points they communicate with each other and they seem to act as one unit.

Other experiments have shown that when three objects are positioned to form a triangle, and that their relationship can be expressed in whole numbers, there is no communication between the objects and their individual energy fields collapse within them. This is similar to the eclipse syndrome.

If we examine this finding more closely and apply logic, the possibilities that come to mind are really quite interesting. An irrational number, not being precise, is always changing. It is moving about between two parameters, depending on the number of decimals used. The parameters can get ever closer, but they never meet. It could be said that the irrational number is oscillating and vibrating - the very forces that are necessary to maintain life and our very existence. Everything that vibrates gives off energy, so anything constructed incorporating an irrational number could be said to be 'alive' - and because it can never be resolved to zero it will never "die", or stop emitting energy. It is not a precisely perfect or definite shape. It can only be constructed to the degree of accuracy that the irrational number allows. As there is no limit, or end, to the number, it is possible that any construct using this geometry will have no limit placed upon its range of communication with other similar entities. Indeed, its influence may go on to infinity.

On the other hand a rational number has a single and precise value. It does not oscillate, and anything carefully constructed to those measurements will be perfect every time. It will not give off energy and could be termed as energetically "dead".

Between these two extremes there are other ratios that resolve themselves after a few decimal points. Entities incorporating these ratios will emit energy for a short period and distance from their source and then fizzle out, a bit like a spark shooting out of a fire and quickly disappearing. Anything based on these ratios would have the ability to communicate briefly over short distances.

Large mountain ranges tend to be relatively static and unchanging from a brief human perspective, and therefore the natural shapes they form may be more durable than the pictures you can form using flower pots on the patio.'

The previous day we had moved a stone in his field that affected the pattern of energy around an ordinary fencing post about twenty yards away. It was a simple experiment, but one with profound implications.

Billy has never tried to establish over what distance the effect of such simple, everyday changes to the relationships of objects would remain active. However, he does think there will be a limit, or at least a point at which the changes will no longer be discernable by humans. Of course, on the other hand, they may go all the way to the end of the universe - but I doubt if we could measure them there! What this implies is that everything we do - even something as simple as getting up out of a chair and walking across the room - may be felt at some infinitesimal level throughout the cosmos.

Billy's suggestion that even quite intricate patterns and pictures can be natural emanations of complex atomic structures provides enough feedstock to keep an army of PhD students going for generations.

It also gives an unintentional shot in the arm to all those who have been trying to explain that archetypes and archetypal stories are just natural phenomena translated into the language and iconography of their time.

As ever with Billy's major breakthroughs, he manages to mention them as asides to a much deeper discussion. This indication of the function and purpose of energy lines, fields and patterns could provide succour to both the scientific and the spiritual lobbies of the dowsing community. It is so profound and potentially so wide reaching that it deserves a book - no, a library or a database - in its own right.

The feng shui interface

Yet another interesting facet of Billy's work is the way it crosses over into the realms of other disciplines. This tends to give his findings added credibility, in that he is discovering by one route what others have concluded from entirely different channels of investigation.

One such piece of unintentional dovetailing concerns the finding that the straightening and simplification of earth energy patterns can be beneficial in encouraging the improved flow of beneficial energy - and subsequently the reduced negativity of stagnation.

This will ring some very loud bells with anyone who has experience of the eastern discipline of feng shui.

'The removal of objects from an area would certainly improve the energy flow - it would simplify the patterns. It would certainly reduce the number of convoluted lines, which in turn would reduce the number of restrictions and increase the speed of energy passing through an area. So, I would tend to agree that it could have a benefit. There are a lot of feng shui principles that I would agree with totally.

However, I have a concern that some people go on a weekend course and come back an expert - or read a book and feel they have all the answers - just as with earth energy dowsing. Sometimes the precise placement of an object is critical to achieving a particular result in one house, but would not be of benefit in another because circumstances are different.

I would encourage people to study feng shui, but also to stay in touch with their intuition. I believe it is important that the practitioner is able to dowse to ensure that they have had the desired effect - and that they have not just moved the detrimental energy from one room to another!'

The composition of energy lines

Ever since Guy Underwood made the breakthrough back in the 1960s that earth energies are not just single strands of something - and made a first stab at trying to disentangle the woven threads - dowsers have been working on understanding the constituent parts of an energy line.

Billy has carried out more work in the field than most, and has put forward this analysis, using his visual dowsing technique:

'An energy line is, as I see it, a composite structure with nine strands in total. It is made up of four lines of different types of energy on either side of a central neutral line. The four lines on either side of the neutral line are mirror images of each other. Each of the nine strands is made up of small sections of line interlocking together to form a longer line.

The overall width of this combination of lines can be as little as a few inches, with each strand very close to each other but not quite touching, up to a veritable motorway of energy many metres across with each strand some distance apart.

The terms I use to describe the four types of energy in any given line are: Negative and Positive - Minus and Plus. These are used by me simply to indicate opposite types of energy and are not intended to describe electrical charge. Again, I believe that this form of radiation, which is only detectable through dowsing, is outside of the electromagnetic spectrum.

1. The most commonly found arrangement of strands in an earth energy line is:

POSITIVE	— — — — — — — — — — — — — — — — —
MINUS	··
PLUS	– – – – – – – – – – – – – – – – – – – ·
NEGATIVE	— · · — · · — · · — · · — · · — · · — · · —
NEUTRAL	———————————————————————
NEGATIVE	— · · — · · — · · — · · — · · — · · — · · —
PLUS	– – – – – – – – – – – – – – – – – – – ·
MINUS	··
POSITIVE	— — — — — — — — — — — — — — — — —

2. The next most commonly found arrangement is:

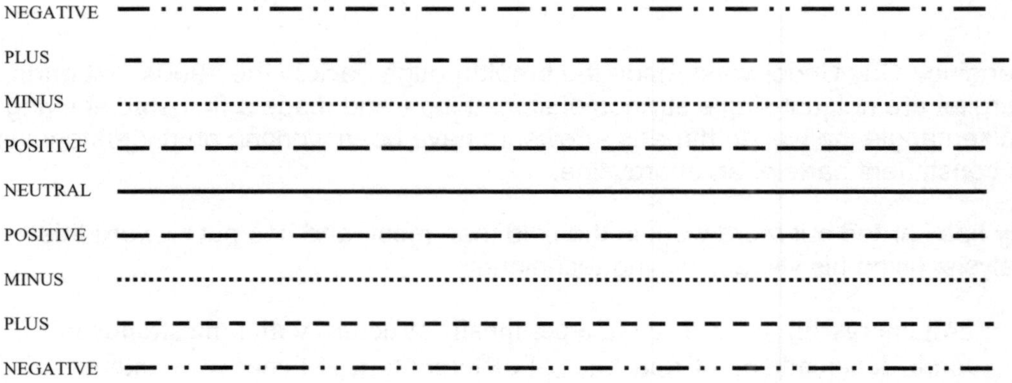

NEGATIVE

PLUS

MINUS

POSITIVE

NEUTRAL

POSITIVE

MINUS

PLUS

NEGATIVE

3. Then less common:

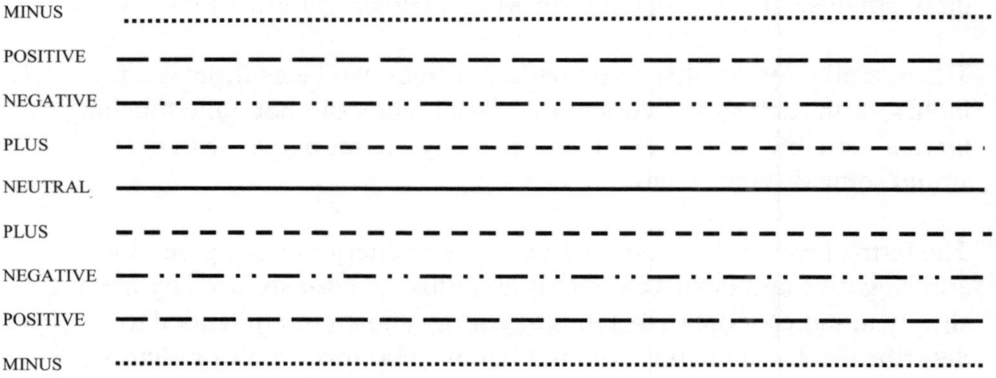

MINUS

POSITIVE

NEGATIVE

PLUS

NEUTRAL

PLUS

NEGATIVE

POSITIVE

MINUS

4. The least common arrangement:

PLUS

NEGATIVE

POSITIVE

MINUS

NEUTRAL

MINUS

POSITIVE

NEGATIVE

PLUS

The first arrangement is generally found in an undisturbed landscape, and this gives rise to only beneficial and harmonious radiations being emitted into our living environment.

The second arrangement is caused by the coinciding of landscape features such as hills and mountains with Reversal Points - all of which are naturally occurring features that have an impact on the quality of energy. This arrangement can cause detrimental and unharmonious radiations to enter our living environment - unless other topographical features act as earthing tools. Commencing on page 178 we will discuss Reversal Points in detail and study their effect on naturally earthed detrimental energy.

The third and fourth arrangements - where the Plus and Minus lines are to the outside of the energy band - are caused where an energy line composed of one of the more common types of arrangement crosses over a large vein of underground water at the same location where a specific energetic form exists on another crossing energy line. Hence, they are comparatively rare. This causes the lines to loop upward and, as they descend again, they switch order.

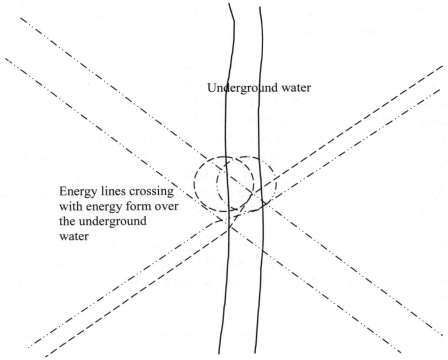

Underground water

Energy lines crossing
with energy form over
the underground
water

The permanence of any energy state depends on natural energetic and geological change, on ongoing human activity - and on the way that these forces alter the face of the landscape over time. Whether these changes occur through intent, or whether they occur casually, does not appear to make any significant difference to the outcome. Even with a sound knowledge of the situation, it is therefore difficult to stabilise energy states at any given locality over a long period of time without periodic intervention.'

Teasing apart the strands

'Whilst the natural state and composition of an energy line is to be in balance, as described above, in some situations that balance has been disturbed. In such cases, individual energy strands can become separated from the others in the line. This can happen when an energy line comes into contact with specific conditions, which exist at certain locations. To describe these locations, I use the term 'Energy Separator'.

An energy separator is essentially a specific energy form, which is the result of the line becoming convoluted in a particular and unique way due to certain local circumstances.

One example of such a circumstance is where underground water forms a shape similar to a siphon - that is where it descends down a shaft and rises again almost to the same height a short distance further on. This is quite similar to the arrangement of a U bend beneath a household sink. This particular type of energy separator will cause the negative and positive elements to be drawn down into the earth, while the plus and minus elements continue to flow across the earth. The plus element will flow above the surface of the earth, and the minus element beneath the surface of the earth. (See diagram at top of next page)

In a different type of separator, the plus and minus elements are drawn into the earth and the negative and positive elements flow onward. In some cases only one type of element survives, with all the others being earthed.

All this change, movement and modifying behaviour causes variations

in the energies to occur on a local basis - with no two locations disp-
laying exactly the same energetic characteristics.

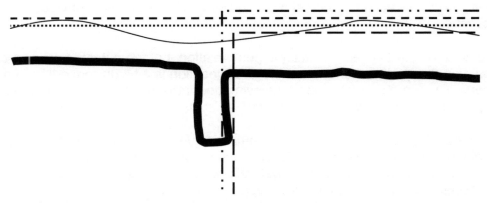

*An energy separator caused by underground water descending and rising
again within a short distance. This causes some of the lines of radiation to be
pulled down into the earth*

If you find some of the concepts described above to be a little challenging, join the
club! Billy has two big advantages over the rest of us. Firstly, he has worked with
the constituent parts of energy lines for several decades - and secondly, his
method of dowsing allows him to 'see' what is happening to them as circumstances change.

However, his work gives us a remarkable insight into the mechanics of earth
energy 'physics', and it enables us to get a feel for the scale of change that is
going on behind, or beneath, the scenes. Without the visual input, getting to grips
with the nuances of energy lines is difficult, to say the least. After all, it would take
even the most gifted engineer some while to figure out how a car engine works if
they couldn't see inside the bonnet!

Billy's work also gives us a vital insight into why earth energy lines seem to
behave differently under different circumstances. To date, they have generally
been regarded as essentially static energy forms - hence the association with
standing stones and other megaliths, which don't tend to move about too much.

However, Billy is not alone in realising that some earth energy lines are moving all
the time, especially away from the better-known sacred sites. The work of Rory
Macquisten, concerning the trademark signatures of different types of energy line,
describes how they move in cyclical patterns in real time - and it is part of this
unfolding area of study.

Energy line movement can be caused by natural geological activity, of which volcanoes and earthquakes are the most extreme examples. It can also be caused by movement on a planetary scale - and the seasonal and periodic gravitational interaction of the celestial bodies would be the most obvious instances.

That human activity is also a factor is no revelation, but the extent to which it can impact on the quality of energy at any given location is a bit disconcerting - unless, of course, you are a practitioner in relieving geopathic stress, who could see this chapter as something of a blank cheque!

The underlying message here is that earth energies do change over time, albeit not always on a dramatic scale. To maintain a good quality of energy in any given area, we have to be aware of both natural and human interventions (either intentional or unintentional) that are happening all the time.

Undertaking this work without being able to 'see' the cause of the change would be no mean task.

Segmented energy lines

The aspects of earth energy that Billy has investigated through visual dowsing just keep on coming.

Most of us naturally assume that an energy line is a single continuous strand that goes from one place to another, for whatever reason. Period. No such luck - not only has Billy found that they are multi-stranded, but he has also observed that each strand of each line is itself a composite feature, consisting of a large number of individual segments.

Prior to discussing this concept with Billy, I had heard of people trying to re-balance - to heal - an energy line by intent, using a section-by-section approach to the task, but I hadn't taken the idea too seriously. However, experience has told me that with dowsing it never pays to dismiss anything too lightly.

'Earth energy lines are composite structures made up of two basic components which can be arranged in several different ways. They are fractal, in that lines are composed of smaller and smaller identical parts, all having the same characteristics and form.

These basic components are:

1:

This form is not constant. It can change from being a straight line to a single point, or any other transitional stage depending on circumstance. It can be either positively or negatively charged.

2:

The line forming the helix is also fractal and helical with each layer being progressively smaller and smaller. I believe it to have no charge. However, it does contain quanta of information.

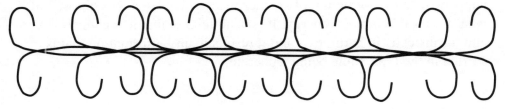

Type 1 segments are attracted together to form a longer line as shown above.

Generally they are found attached to a similar, but reversed, image back to back. If the amount of curvature to the short sections on both lines is equal the line will be straight. If one side has more curvature than the other this will result in the line bending in the direction of the greatest curvature. If this difference is regular then a circle or a spiral will be formed. When it is irregular the line will become convoluted. This type of line provides the structure to energy lines.

The curved lines attract sections of the helical line (type 2) to form a double helix, as shown below. This type 2 line contains and conveys information which travels in both directions.

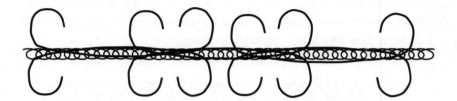

Where two positively charged type 1 lines intersect, a ball of positive energy is created at the point of intersection.

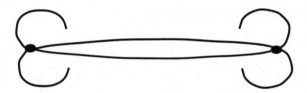

When three or more intersections occur in near alignment, the balls of energy unwind and form a line. As we saw earlier, this is similar to what happens with the formation of an energy ley. This line is composed of what we term beneficial energy. It is beneficial in that it is concordant and intrinsically in harmony - and it results in any information that is carried in the type 2 line being coherent.

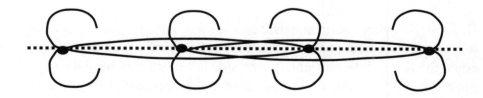

Where negatively charged type 1 lines intersect, as above, a line of negative energy is created between the intersection points. This line is inharmonious and discordant, and it causes any information carried by the type 2 line to be incoherent and thus detrimental in nature to the living environment.

If basic type 1 segments become disconnected, they can form shapes not dissimilar to the scrolls you find in wrought-iron work. These scroll shapes are macro versions of one of the basic component parts of energy lines - some forming clockwise and anti-clockwise spirals at the ends, giving a C-shaped spiral. Sometimes you can find the scrolls with both being clockwise or anticlockwise in rotation, giving an S-shaped display. These can be found in isolation, whilst on other occasions, they form clusters or groups that can go to make up geoglyphic forms.

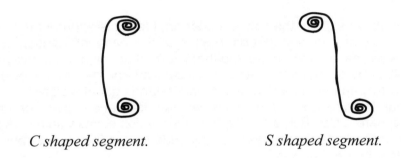

C shaped segment.   *S shaped segment.*

Fractured energy line.

There seem to be circumstances where an energy line fractures completely. As with anything flexible that is under tension, when it breaks up, it will curl back on itself and form spirals. A prime example of this in the natural world is the stem of dandelion, which if de-headed will curl back on itself to form a curled stem. That's very similar to what a damaged energy line does.

Lines, or at least sections of energy line, vary in length, some of which are only a few inches long, while others can be several hundred yards in length.'

As so often in one of his talks, or in a piece of his text, Billy manages to introduce a fundamentally important concept as something of an aside to the actual topic in hand. Such is the integrated nature of his work that it is clearly difficult not to do so - the whole worldview is a unified process, without a definitive start or finish.

However, although we explain the concept later on, I feel it is appropriate here to draw attention to the observation that earth energy lines carry information as well as 'energy'. People have often suggested that information might be conveyed from place to place by energy lines - and specifically by Energy Leys. However, this view has partly been superseded by the understanding that we are surrounded by an information field, on which we can draw at any place or time, given the appropriate tools. Billy's finding that information exists within energy lines - and that those lines form a mesh of tiny grids across the planet - brings the two scenarios together rather neatly.

The function and purpose of energy lines

'Having discovered these enigmatic lines of energy, I was faced with two fundamental questions. <u>Why</u> are these lines of radiation present, and <u>why</u> do they present themselves in the various forms that they do? A few simple experiments gave me sufficient clues to suggest a satisfactory answer to both of these questions.

There are a few objects that do not emit lines of radiation when placed well away from other objects. Pure crystal, and stone where the atoms are magnetically aligned, are good examples. In both of these cases there is inherent order within the structure of the substance. When an object with this property is placed in isolation - where it does not have lines of radiation coming from it - and then a non-crystalline object is introduced close by so that its energy field is covering the crystalline object - it will then be found that lines of radiation can be observed coming from the crystal. <u>This suggests that lines of radiation are the result of disorder or chaos in the structure</u> - and that the inherent order in the crystal is disturbed by the presence of the nearby object.

In another experiment, I marked out a section of a straight energy line that crossed a level area of ground. I placed an ordinary object, in this case a watering can, about 12 inches away from the line. Checking it again, I found a significant bend where it passed the watering can.

The rope marks the energy line   *Bend caused by watering can*

I then placed a second object - a plastic flower pot with a broken brick inside it - close to the other side of the line - and a little downstream of the watering can. Checking once more, I discovered another bend, opposite the second object. On moving both objects closer to the line, more curves appeared - like a decreasing rippling effect, just down-stream of where both objects were placed. The placing of more objects in various relationships to the line caused more bends to occur.

With flowerpot added   *With three objects there are more bends*

Whilst carrying out experiments such as this, I became very aware of the influence that the dowser has on the energy line under scrutiny. In this instance the influence I refer to is from their body mass, not their mind. If, when following an energy line, the dowser walks directly on top of it, the line will not move sideways as I discovered to be the case with the watering can and the flower pot which were placed several inches to one side of the line. However, there is a ripple of energy which precedes the dowser as they progress. This makes it difficult to establish the precise form of any line at any given moment in time.

Experiments with two and three objects placed in a critical relationship with each other are described in the experiment with three bricks - which also sheds light on the cause and form of lines of radiation (see Appendix E).

This simple, low-tech research points to an explanation of <u>why</u> radiating energy lines are produced from most objects - be they watering cans, standing stones or planets. It also suggests how they come to adopt certain forms. <u>The specific form of the line and the nature of its display appears to be dependent on the make up or structure of the object</u>.

It is the relationship that exists between the basic particles of matter, and the geometry thereby created, that dictates whether a line of radiation is straight, sinuous, spiralling, or convoluted.

Where the atoms and molecules are arranged symmetrically, as in crystals, the lines are still present, but they remain locked firmly within the object. My dowsing suggests that there is a spin which causes a centripetal force within crystals and similar substances, which continuously draws the energy towards the centre of the object - and that keeps the lines of radiation firmly within the mass of the object itself.

In the case of most other objects, the atoms and molecules are arranged more randomly, with less regular patterns. This reflects their conglomerate nature - and also the degree of impurity in the composition of the object.

In those that display more chaos in the arrangement of atoms and molecules, the spin is in the opposite direction - and these exhibit a centrifugal force. This causes the lines of radiation within the object to be projected out into the space around them and it results in the displays that can be found emanating from nearly everything - from small objects to larger objects, (including humans), to the earth as a whole, and even to the most massive celestial bodies.'

The ability to use internal vision to identify shapes and forms, that are only perceptible in the crudest manner by the rest of us, clearly gives Billy a departure point that is way ahead of the rod-based two-dimensional dowser. While he is not alone in 'going deviceless', he was certainly one of the first earth energy dowsers to do so - and he was probably the first to use this ability to address questions about the nature and function of energy lines and radiations.

To date, most of the research conducted in this field has been directed at proving the existence of the lines, and to a lesser extent, to describing their shapes and types. From his enhanced viewpoint, Billy can take all that as given - and he has moved on to consider the role played by these radiations in the cosmic context.

Quite apart from Billy's ability to 'see' these emanations changing in real time, his reasoning has a beautiful internal logic that could be academically deduced, even if it could not be 'seen' or dowsed.

The fact that much of this research has been undertaken quite successfully using garden tools and everyday artifacts has brought cutting edge science to the masses in a manner undreamt of in modern times. Who needs multi-billion pound installations surrounded by barbed wire and armed guards, when a few bricks and a smidgeon of intuition can produce similar results?

Even as I am writing this book, the full extent to which Billy has prized open the doors of knowledge - at least to those with an open mind and a lack of fear - is only just sinking in.

Energy lines that move

Until quite recently, it had been generally assumed that although energy lines have been shown to move a little over time, they are essentially fairly static phenomena. Billy's work shows something rather different. Certainly with regard to the smaller energy lines, they seem to be moving all the time, in reaction to modest changes in their physical environment and to the movement of the planets.

'I think there is a good analogy here to trees. You can see the branches waving about all over the place, but the main trunk isn't moving very much.

If you take the main energy lines, they may not deviate very much over the time we are likely to be looking at them - over a few decades, or even a few thousand years. Again, this is similar to a tree. Even thousands of years would be quite a short period of time in relation to an energy line, taking into account the millions of years since the earth was formed. The smaller energy lines are more like the twigs of the tree that wave about in the wind, in that they can more easily be moved about - and some get broken off!

Major energy lines appear, to all intents and purposes, static – especially those anchored at sacred sites. At the other end of the scale, however, there are some that are very volatile. I feel there's a comparison to the science of physics here. Classical Newtonian physics describes a very stable universe, made up of large objects where there is little movement, and unchanging laws and rules - whereas quantum physics investigates the frantic and unpredictable world of the very small.'

Billy, like most people who actually have something significant to say, merely mentions that there are a number of doors that he has stumbled across, some of which he has opened out of personal curiosity. It will be up to the generations that follow him to decide which they wish to walk through.

When I came to compile and consider the vast canvas of Billy's work and ideas at the start of this book, I knew I had a few big issues to address. The first was clearly the sheer novelty and the inherent complexity of the subject material. The second was where to stop! The very nature of the subject sets off multiple, inter-woven trails of reasoning that lead . . . well, you tell me.

So far, we have tried to stay on fairly solid ground. We have looked at Billy's archaeological work, which can be reproduced and re-examined by anyone with the motivation and means. We have considered his in-depth examination of the form and nature of earth energies. Again, this can be trawled over and dissected by dowsers - and by mainstream scientists, once the understandable inherent prejudice against frightening new ideas has been overcome.

From here on, we venture out into the wildwood. But before you get the idea that Billy's New Frontiers are more Alice in Wonderland than the familiar zoo full of creatures you could poke with a stick, always remember - everything in this book is based on visual dowsing and the logical trails that lead from it.

NEW FRONTIERS

Detrimental and Beneficial Energies

Much of the modern work of earth energy dowsers has concentrated on the identification and treatment of detrimental energy. There are certainly very well documented issues resulting from its adverse impact of on humans - dating back at least to Baron Gustav Freiherr von Pohl's study of the houses that seemed to suffer excessive health problems in Vilsbiburg in Southern Germany in 1929. However, it would be all too easy to get the problem of 'bad vibes' out of perspective. Billy has a characteristically down-to-earth view of the subject:

Baron Gustav von Pohl with his unusual dowsing rod

'It is generally accepted by all earth energies dowsers that the subtle radiations that are present everywhere within our living environment can be broadly divided into two specific categories. The terms commonly used to describe these are 'detrimental' and 'beneficial'. The suggestion being, based on much anecdotal evidence, that they in some way affect our wellbeing, either adversely or for our benefit.

Because of the possible harmful impact on our health, detrimental energy - and how to eliminate it - is the main interest of many of those who study and practise in this field. However, little research has been done to establish why it is present in the first place.

In the U.K. streams of underground water are considered to be one of the main sources of detrimental energy. However, detrimental energy can also be abundantly present in desert countries where underground water is scarce. Quarries and large natural outcrops of rock on hillsides often also send out wide bands of disturbed radiation, which answer positively to 'detrimental' when dowsing. There are other lines of detrimental radiation where the cause or source is less easily determined.

A little known, and poorly recognised source, from which lines of detrimental energy can rise into our living environment, is from most ordinary objects - large and small. I observed that where detrimental energy had not been earthed from an area - and it was rising freely from the edge lines of underground water - even mundane objects such as fist sized stones, bricks, small logs of wood, (and even a seemingly ludicrous example, a tin of beans) will have lines of detrimental energy radiating from them, which rise for two metres or more into the air. If they are placed in such a way that one of the lines of detrimental energy coming from the object passes through a person's head, their arm offers little or no resistance when pressure is put upon it just above the wrist. See diagrams below. (A full description of this muscle testing technique is given in Appendix A).

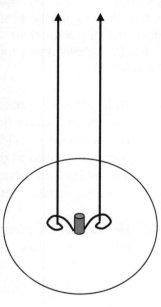

The circle is the extent of the basic aura. The left and right 'ram's horns' are the location of two rising lines of detrimental energy. It is when one of these is directed through the head that the muscle of the arm becomes weak.

However, if detrimental energy from underground water is properly earthed, the detrimental energy that radiates from all the objects with which it comes into contact will also be earthed.

In the section "The Composition of Energy Lines" (page 147 and 148) I list the most common arrangements of line types. I describe there that where the negative strands of the lines are to the outside (as shown in item 2 on page 148) that is the greatest contributing cause for unexplained lines of detrimental radiation.

Negative energy lines, on their own, do not necessarily emit detrimental energy. However, when two negative lines intersect, at that position, a small point or dot of detrimental energy is brought into existence. If two or more intersections occur less than a certain distance apart, the dots join up and a line of detrimental radiation is born. The dot is actually the tightly wound up ball of a single line of radiation. The unwinding of this line is similar to what happens on a grander scale when an energy ley comes into being. (See page 119)

It is important to determine what is meant by detrimental energy. Is 'detrimental' detrimental to all living things? To a large extent, I believe it is. It seems to have an adverse affect on almost all life forms although there are some that seem to be able to tolerate it. Those able to tolerate it are generally life forms with a relatively short life span.

I feel that the reason for this may be that they have developed from further back in the evolutionary chain than we have. Because of that, they have been around much longer than humans and also they tend to have a shorter life span - so they have had many, many more opportunities to evolve and adapt to their surroundings than we have had. For example the 'Smart Bugs', that are so notoriously difficult to deal with in hospitals, have developed very quickly an ability to put a protective shield around themselves.

I have observed the same type of reaction beginning to develop in one or two individuals.

When I started dowsing for detrimental energy lines that rose vertically into our living environment, I was muscle testing everyone that came forward - and everyone's arm went down. But one day, during a lecture that I was giving, a person came forward and their arm muscle showed no sign of weakening at all. I tried the same experiment, in the same place with someone else and it did work, so I knew the first subject was standing on the right spot. Later, I took this person out into the car park to see what was happening. To my surprise, I found that he had a protective energy shield around him, which pushed the detrimental energy away from him. I am not sure if he had put it in place intentionally or whether it was just there. This made me recall another experience.

Some time previous to that, but not at a lecture session, I met Major John Ferguson-Cunningham, a charismatic member of the BSD who is immune to muscle testing. I found a big egg-shaped shield around him - it was about 20 feet across. This protected him from any detrimental energy that he came close to. As he walked over a place where a line of detrimental energy was rising, the shield pushed it aside - and he did not come into contact with it.

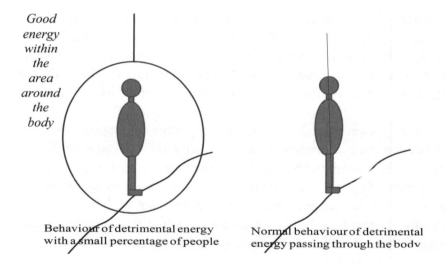

Good energy within the area around the body

Behaviour of detrimental energy with a small percentage of people

Normal behaviour of detrimental energy passing through the body

Of the hundreds of people on which I have carried out muscle testing, there is maybe about 1% that have this ability. However, I believe that in time the human race will evolve in such a way that everyone will be able to cope with the effects of detrimental energy.

Some people seem to be coming through the evolutionary chain in a different time line from others. Perhaps they are coming from a different place, their ancestry goes further back in the chain, so that their evolutionary cycle is more advanced and consequently detrimental energy does not seem to affect them so much.'

How old is detrimental energy?

Has detrimental energy, as we know it today, been around since the earth was created - or is it of more recent origin?

'The presence of detrimental energy is a local rather than a universal feature. It has the potential to radiate from certain underground sources and other objects, but this is not always the case.

Those within the animal kingdom, especially humans, perform actions - casually or intentionally - that give rise to detrimental energy. Where nature has been allowed to proceed without interference very little, if any, detrimental energy is present in the living environment in that area - and almost all of it is kept well beneath the surface of the earth.

If then we go back more than 10,000 years, to a period before the advent of farming, it is likely that very little detrimental energy existed in the biosphere. The subsequent clearance of land to make it free from rocks and trees - and to render it suitable for the growing of crops - would have removed some, if not all, of the objects that were critically located to keep detrimental energy in check. As a result, in many areas detrimental energy would have been released into the living environment. The spread of farming methods to most areas of the globe took several thousand years to complete. It would only have reached the British Isles less than 1,000 years before the commencement of the construction of megalithic structures - around 4,000 - 3,000 BCE. Could this building programme have been prompted, in part, by the need to deal with the amount of detrimental energy being released by the activity of farming practices - which possibly resulted, in turn, in lower fertility and the poorer general health of livestock and people. It would soon have been realised that not everything needed to be relocated - only specific objects in specific locations.

As we have seen, the precise manner in which megalithic structures were sited and constructed would have had a positive impact on our environment, by earthing this detrimental energy, regardless of other probable subsequent uses.'

The use of structures, megalithic or modern, for geopathic stress relief is as relevant today as it was in pre-historic times. Our language and construction methods may have changed out of all recognition, but the basic need to improve and maintain the health of the community and its food sources is as relevant today as it was 5,000 years ago.

Billy's suggestion that circles and menhirs rebalance 'bad' energy has a strangely modern resonance. Always remember, Billy only stumbled upon this line of reasoning as a result of easily repeatable experiments that he undertook on his own land. He has demonstrated that detrimental energy is bad for us - in that it seems to interfere with the communication system within the body. He has also shown that localised, dowsable detrimental energy can be rendered harmless by the judicious placing of a large stone or two. If it works - and it certainly seems to work - then we shouldn't knock it.

We are very aware in the 21st Century that the actions of man can have intentionally adverse impacts (as in warfare) or unintentionally negative effects (as in climate change). It is reasonable to assume that Neolithic man probably had much the same mindset as ourselves.

However, being that much closer to nature, they may also have come to realise that there was a way out of the dilemma. They could continue to clear the land, but they had to deal with the detrimental energy arising as they went - and they could do that by using geological acupuncture.

Detrimental energy in the network

Over the years, Billy has had the good fortune to be part of many of the more important pieces of earth energy research - which have often provided quite unexpected, yet rather interesting, results.

'I would like to say at the beginning of this discussion about detrimental energy that it is something that we should not be paranoid about. Whilst detrimental energy exists, it is only a very small proportion of the whole energetic environment. However, it is considered wise that we avoid it when we can, as exposure for lengthy periods may have an adverse impact on our wellbeing.

Some years ago, I took part in an experiment which was set up to attempt to determine the parts of the brain that are affected by detrimental energy passing through it. People had parts of their scalp connected to a computer by wires, and were asked to stand where I felt there was detrimental energy - or not - that I had previously found by muscle testing.

This computer had software installed that was able to measure brainwave activity.

On the edge of a water line, where there was detrimental energy, the muscle testing of a subject connected to the computer showed weak, as one might expect. However, when the person was moved to the centre of the water line - where you would normally expect the reaction to be strong, it was weak there too. This was puzzling.

It was only when I got the person holding the computer to stand on the centre of the water line next to the experimental subject, so that none of the cables or wires connecting the computer to the subject were in contact with the detrimental energy rising from the edgeline, that the expected strong reaction returned. It was a revelation to me that the rising detrimental energy coming up from the edge of the water line seemed to be carried by the electrical cables attached to the computer that was connected to the person's head.

The data gained from the computer programme indicated that something was happening to the brain waves of the person under test, when they were subjected to detrimental energy. Up to that point the results were inconclusive, and many more tests would have been required to establish definitive findings. However, the information that detrimental energy could be carried by the cables leading from the computer to the person's brain was far more important to me.

At a later date, I took this experiment one stage further. These tests were carried out indoors where there was a level floor. I exposed a few inches of wire at one end of a piece of ordinary electrical flex, about 12 feet long. I taped it to the ground at a point where I knew detrimental energy was rising. I got a person to assist with muscle testing and stand away from this point as far as the electric flex would allow. This was necessary because if the subject was standing beside where the detrimental energy was rising, the point on the floor would move away from where the wire was taped to the floor. It would then no longer convey the detrimental energy. This is yet another example of the physical presence of the experimenter affecting the outcome of the experiment.

I put the other end of the flex against different parts of the head of the subject. This radiated only a small section of the brain at a time. By so doing, I was able to determine which parts of the brain were affected by detrimental energy, and thereby caused the arm to be easily pushed down. The parts affected were those involved in communication and the co-ordination of muscle movement, as well as those that influence the chemical and hormonal balance of the body. There is likely to be a negative impact on our health and fertility if these functions are adversely affected. As I noted in an earlier chapter, it appears that detrimental radiation causes the information being sent from the brain to become somewhat incoherent. The messages sent become scrambled and are not understood by the body part concerned.'

This implies that an electrical grid, or possibly any other wire or cable, captures some of the rising detrimental energy that it crosses, and then circulates it around the built environment. The implications of this finding for those of us who work in office blocks, or even at home, are legion. Yet more detailed research will be required here, I feel!

Reduced detriment

One of the great joys of having had the privilege of being part of the compilation of this book has been the number of times that optimistic themes seem to have emerged - often from the most unlikely of places, such as through the TV!

'I am very aware, particularly when I go over to England, that the amount of detrimental energy in the landscape has reduced over the last twenty years - although I wouldn't for one minute claim that it was anything to do with what I have done here or elsewhere! However, when I have gone to a village hall or an hotel to give one of my talks, quite often I've had to overcome the lack of detrimental energy, by placing something on a reversal point to cause it to rise into the space within the hall - otherwise I would have had nothing to work with!

My method of using my eyes as the dowsing tool allows me to look at ordinary television programmes with scenes of the landscape in them and determine the amount of detrimental energy that is rising into the living environment where they were filmed. <u>My dowsing clearly shows me that there has been a great reduction over the last 10 years in many areas of countryside.</u>

Whether this reduction is the sum of whatever earth energy dowsers corporately have done in their own areas is difficult to say. What we do locally radiates out - perhaps indefinitely. However, it is likely also that a significant amount is due to changes in natural forces of which we are unaware.'

Beneficial energy

'Professor Philip Callahan was a radio operator for the American forces stationed in Northern Ireland during World War II, where he became familiar with the Irish round towers. After the war he became one of the leading entomologists in the world. Phil Callahan has done more than anyone else in building a worldwide appreciation of low-level energies in agriculture. His work on insect communication systems, low-level earth

Antrim round tower.

energies, and the paramagnetic force in rock and soil is changing our ecological approach to agriculture.

He maintained his interest in round towers and carried out some investigations into how they affected plant growth. He carried out experiments, whereby he planted quick-growing seeds, such as mustard, in a large flowerpot. He put a little standing stone as a simulation of a round tower in the middle of the crop - and as a result of the energy coming from that stone, he found that plant growth was much stronger in some areas than others. There were distinct patterns resembling a trefoil cloverleaf where there was weak growth compared to the area around it.

He compared this with control plantings where there was no stone. In these control plantings the growth was fairly uniform. He demonstrated convincingly that energy is emitted from mundane objects such as stones and can have an effect, one way or another on plant growth around it.

Professor Callahan went on to identify several different and distinct energy wavelengths coming from stones, and by inference, from round towers. He believes that they are powerful amplifiers in the alpha brain wave region, 2 to 4 Hz., which would be at levels achieved through meditation. This is of particular interest as round towers were attached to monasteries where meditation would be regularly practised.'

Activated cairns

'A few years before I constructed the cairn in my garden, discussed in pages 92 and 93, I carried out an experiment using the remains of the ruined cairn on Browndodd Hill.

I placed a chicken leg bone in one of the chambers in the passageway of the cairn. Although I was trying to mimic the effect of a burial, I did not bury the leg bone in the soil, but just placed it on the earth. On checking, through dowsing, I found that when the bone was placed in line with the chamber, and in one particular orientation, that is the light

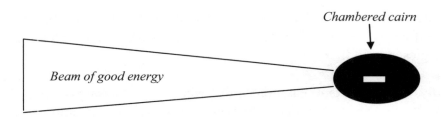

A bone marked in light grey in one chamber within the cairn

end of the bone pointing inward and the heavy end pointing outward, there was a change in the earth energies for part of the way around the cairn. This produced a torch-like beam of beneficial energy, projecting out of the entrance and towards where I live - about three quarters of a mile away. It widened out by a few degrees as it crossed the fields. See diagram at the top of this page.

I left the bone in that position and followed the path of the energy until its extremities, which I marked. This was less than 100 metres from my house. I kept checking it every day to see if any change occurred.

About one week later I could no longer detect the beam of beneficial energy. I went back to the top of Browndodd Hill to discover that the bone had disappeared. There was no sign of it anywhere, and I concluded that it had been eaten by either a dog or, more likely, by a fox.

I expanded the experiment by replacing one bone, as before, and a similar beam of good energy reappeared. I then placed a second bone in another chamber and found that the angle of the beam had increased to close on 120 degrees. When I placed a bone in each of the other chambers, the beneficial energy then formed a complete circle so that it was like an aura around the cairn.

To thwart foxes or dogs, I placed a smallish stone on top of each bone. Again I kept checking for the presence of the aura every day. After about three weeks it also disappeared. Another excursion to the top of the hill revealed that the small stones had been overturned and all the bones disappeared. I did not repeat the experiment.

From this I learned two valuable lessons. Firstly, that bone, when placed in a specific way within a chambered cairn, has a beneficial impact on the energies around it.

Secondly, I got important reassurance that what I was dowsing really existed. It came about by placing the bones correctly in the chambers, and not as the result of my imagination or intent. If it had been either of these, I would not have noted the disappearance of the beneficial energy when the bones were removed by agents unknown to me.'

How beneficial are sacred sites?

'Something that I want to emphasise in this book is that we look on sacred sites as being 'good' places, yet they are all sited over underground water. If underground water runs beneath someone's house, we would usually regard that as a 'bad' place, because of the bad vibes that can come from it.

However, as we have seen, my research implies that by placing a structure of a certain type in a certain way on the   so-called sacred spot, it is possible to suppress the detrimental energies that would normally come from it.   When you do suppress them, being over underground water has an enhancing effect, as water tends to carry the quality of the energy it flows over.   Generally, I would regard being above underground water as beneficial to humans and most other life forms, providing you can get rid of the detrimental energy that can arise from it.   However, I emphasise 'can' as this is not always the case.

I am concerned that sometimes people go out to dowse houses at the request of worried residents, when they are not totally up to speed. They can dowse underground water running beneath a house and proclaim that it's a terrible situation - without checking to see if there are detrimental energies rising from the edge lines of those water flows. I think that's absolutely essential - to determine if there is actually detrimental energy in the living environment of the people who live in the house before you take any action.

If the energy is in the ground, and is going further down into the ground, then it's of no concern to the people living in the house - and therefore you don't need to do anything about it.

I think there can sometimes be unnecessary interventions taking place, which may be making a pound or two for the unscrupulous - or those with insufficient experience. I consider this to be a serious moral issue.'

What on Earth is a Reversal Point?

We have already come across the term Reversal Point a few times. However, I hesitated to describe it in too much detail before explaining some of the more basic building blocks of the mechanics of earth energy.

While the idea of a Reversal Point is conceptually quite simple, surely only someone with the insight of a visual dowser could ever have come across this idea in the first place.

Billy's work has taken him to some unusual places - places that not even he would have thought existed. As far as I am aware, <u>the discovery of the Reversal Point is yet another aspect of earth energy dowsing that is quite unique to his research</u>.

If you are a lay reader, with no prior knowledge of the subject, please don't be put off. There are plenty of us, who have dowsed for decades, who still struggle with concepts like this.

Whenever I left the room after a talk by Billy that included the reversal point idea, I felt I had grasped it at last - but I'm still glad I have his original 2007 script to work from in seeking to explain it!

So, just what is a Reversal Point and why is it so important that it has a section all to itself?

> 'In a nutshell, a Reversal Point is the opposite of an Earthing Point. A reversal point is a location on the earth's surface where if something is placed on it, it will push detrimental energy up to rise into our living environment. An earthing point will push the detrimental energy down into the earth.
>
> Before I move on to describe the importance of reversal points, I feel it is necessary to fully understand how earthing points are created. As discussed earlier, an earthing point is usually a location where either the centre lines, or the edge lines, of underground streams intersect. However, it is not the underground water itself that causes the detrimental energy to be put to earth but an object, such as a large stone, being placed on top of it.

Under an authentic standing stone, there will be at least two sizeable energy lines crossing at the intersection of the water lines. At a stone circle there are, in most cases, many more. When the energy lines meet the water lines they twist and turn and form a knot of energy. It is the combination of this deformity of the energy line and the mass of the stone that attracts the detrimental energy and pushes it down into the earth.

It is possible to find crossing energy lines away from underground water that are similarly affected. In these situations, it is caused by some obstruction such as a tree or a mound coinciding with the crossing point. However, whilst these features will earth detrimental energy, the absence of the underground water will restrict the area affected.

Most dowsers who involve themselves in Geopathic Stress Relief will know that it is possible to earth and suppress detrimental energy through a type of earth acupuncture. This can either be by hammering stakes into the ground, or by the placement of an object such as a stone, or even a garden ornament, at certain critical locations. In the case of physical intervention, it is also well known that great accuracy is required in identifying the exact position where these objects are to be placed to make this process work effectively.

However, the importance of reversal points is not confined to those who get rid of detrimental radiations through physical means. It is equally important to those who use spiritual and mental processes to change the behaviour of energy that would otherwise contribute to geopathic stress in humans and other life forms.

Many dowsers who work in the field of Geopathic Stress Relief, find that in some cases detrimental energies return in due course - and sometimes with a vengeance. The reason for this is not always clear.

Even before any human intervention takes place, it can be observed that there is a great variation in the quality of the energies being radiated from the earth. In some areas there is very little detrimental radiation, even though underground streams and other features that usually emit detrimental radiation are present. However, a few miles away there may be similar geological features, which can coexist with an abundance of detrimental energy.

Therefore, it is apparent that something is happening locally that is contributing to the situation. These local circumstances may be the result of natural evolution, or of human intervention - either casual or with intent.

The impact of casual human actions is not always fully recognised. Indeed, some people may consider that action without intent does not have any energetic impact at all. My experience leads me to believe that this is not the case. In my view, intent can focus the impact of the action on to a specific problem or area - whilst without intent it will tend to have a more random effect.

There are precise locations on the earth's surface, which could be described as earth acupuncture points. When such places are activated, local detrimental radiation will be removed from our living environment - and driven back into earth. These are earthing points.

However, I have also observed that there are other critical locations, which will upset the harmonious nature of earth energies if they are disturbed by placing any object of mass in that position. Any earthing action of detrimental radiations, that may have taken place through natural or human intervention, will be reversed. It is this type of location that I have termed a Reversal Point.

In some cases, the influence of these reversal points can be significant, while at others it can be very slight. The area over which they reverse the earthing of detrimental radiations can also vary considerably. At a minor reversal point, the influence may almost go unnoticed, possibly only allowing one small line of detrimental radiation to rise. At a major reversal point, an area several miles in radius could be affected - greatly reducing the quality of the energetic environment in that area. So, what gives rise to these points, and what activates them?

Most subtle detrimental energy in our living environment rises vertically from the earth. It emanates from well-understood geological features, such as fissures filled with underground water and other mineral resources. For us to influence them, or be influenced by them, we need to be directly above the geological feature. However, some detrimental energy does flow horizontally over the face of the earth, and it can come from such places as quarry faces or craggy hillsides. Detrimental energy can also come from the energy field associated with most objects, small and large.

Reversal points are not located directly above any underground geological feature, or underground water. They are found as part of some horizontally-radiated lines coming from either the earth itself or from major topographical features like hills and mountains. These lines, which form reversal points, are an integral part of the energy web within all energy fields. Therefore, there is the potential for millions of these points to exist! Fortunately, most only have an effect for a short distance around where they are found. It is only very large objects or notable topographical features that produce lines that are significant enough to cause concern.

A reversal point is found where a type 3 line has fractured. (That is, where the strands are in the order of Minus - Positive - Negative - Plus : Neutral : Plus - Negative - Positive - Minus.) The ends curl back as in the diagram below. The area inside the oval marked by the dotted line is the position of the reversal point.

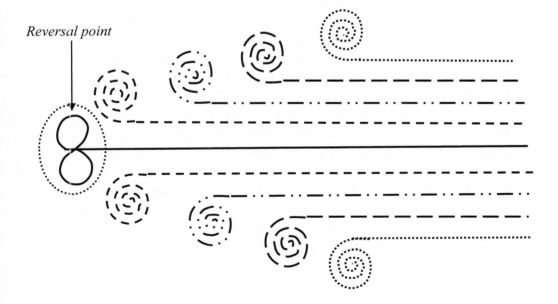

Reversal point

Reversal points can also occur as a result of local conditions affecting the line, which cause it to twist by a half turn, before continuing to its termination point. The neutral line at the centre forms a series of figures of eights. The reversal point is inside the oval shaped dotted line.

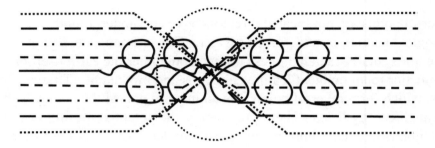

The conditions that cause lines to form these patterns, and thus the reversal points, are as yet unclear.

What activates them is better understood. When the patterns that form reversal points are located on ground that is reasonably level, they are not usually active. However, they can become active if the contour of the earth's surface is either concave or convex at an angle slightly greater than three degrees (see diagram page 133).

Alternatively, activation can occur, even if the ground is flat, if something has been placed directly over the energy pattern - like a stone, a planted tree, or a stake driven into the ground. This is where your personal actions can come into play. Even when something has been casually placed there for a short period, like the parking of a car, the reversal point will be activated - and it will remain active until the object is removed. Even inoffensive artifacts, such as flowerpots, can be moved on to one of these spots, with dire consequences for the quality of the energy within any houses nearby.

If we are to ensure that detrimental energies remain suppressed, we need to be aware of the presence of reversal points. We need to identify them, and to inform the owner or custodian of the property of their locations - so that they can be kept clear of anything that will make them operational.

Problems can occur when a critical reversal point is located outside the boundary of a property, and thus beyond the control of the custodian. Nevertheless, if dowsers become aware of the locations of reversal points, and inform the residents accordingly, then it is more likely that at least some of the energetic damage could be avoided.

This brings us to the crucial question - how can dowsers identify them? The answer is simple; go and look for them. In dowsing, it is first necessary to be aware of the possibility that certain things exist. Then, by careful study, establish the precise nature of the Dowsing Question. Finally go forth and do something about it!

When tackling a new concept it is necessary to travel slowly, and try to get verification. Verification can be gained through the use of the muscle testing technique, described in Appendix A of this book.

To take positive action:

- Find a location over the edgeline of underground water, where the muscle tests weak.

- Place a marker close to the spot (but never directly over it, as the marker may affect the detrimental energy rising from the spot).

- Take action to suppress the detrimental energy, by whatever method you may wish to use, at a location away from where the person was tested.

- Check if muscle strength has returned. You will then know if the action to suppress the detrimental energy has been successful.

- If you have been successful, seek out a reversal spot by dowsing, and place an object on it.

- A further muscle test will demonstrate whether or not the detrimental radiation has returned.

- If it has, then you were successful in finding a reversal spot, if not try again until you do find one that does work.

- Having established the site to your satisfaction, remember to take the object off the reversal point again, and to keep the location clear.

    Rome was not built in a day, nor should a successful dowser be put off by one failed attempt!'

This procedure is much easier to demonstrate than to describe but, in a nutshell, Billy encourages us to find our local reversal points, by dowsing, and to ensure they are kept clear of objects - even quite inconsequential decorative ones. If we can do it for our friends, neighbours and clients too - so much the better.

It may seem a somewhat esoteric idea on first reading, but you come to appreciate that the idea of the reversal point is probably one of the fundamental building blocks of an understanding of how earth energy works - and of how it interfaces with the physical world. If you can grasp the essence of this, you are well on the way to appreciating why earth energies matter.

As ever, Billy presents this practical and pragmatic approach to a potentially serious problem. But, as he is quick to explain, most of us live with a range of sources of detrimental energy all the time. Most of these are caused by human activity, yet only a few of us come badly unstuck.

However, the benefit of removing a weight from a critical reversal point can be significant - and you'll only find out how significant it is once you've cleared it. Coming back to the description of the composition of energy lines that we encountered in the chapter describing Everyday Energies, on page 147 Billy is able to tie together the two threads of thought that show how reversal points occur.

'I mentioned on page 181 that a reversal point is found at the termination point of a type 3 line. As these lines can change position over time due to earth and planetary movement, many reversal points are only temporary features - but they are cyclical and seasonal.

Each activating phase lasts for five to six weeks, with about a six to seven week interval. As the position where the reversal point is located also changes over time, it will possibly only be in a critical location for a part of this period. This can lead to significant variations in the quality of natural earth radiations in any given area at any given time.

I have named this location, at the termination of a type 3 line, a reversal point because if an object of any kind is placed there whilst it is active, it will cause a reversal of the natural earthing of detrimental radiation to occur - and it will allow detrimental energy to rise into our living environment.'

Breaking news!

Prior to commencing work on this 'biography', Billy seemed to have reached something of a plateau - he had found out more in one lifetime than most, but he had not undertaken much new research for some time. However, a few unexpected questions from yours truly seem to have brought him back into action with a vengeance - and now it's the narrator that is struggling to keep up!

'I have been carrying out more work on this subject in recent months, and I have been able to determine what the circumstances are that cause a reversal point to exist. In other words, <u>why</u> they exist at all.

A reversal point is created as the result of two energy lines crossing each other, and on one of them is a convoluted energy form of a particular type. This convoluted form is on the neutral line and is in the shape of four double helices at right angles to each other, forming a type

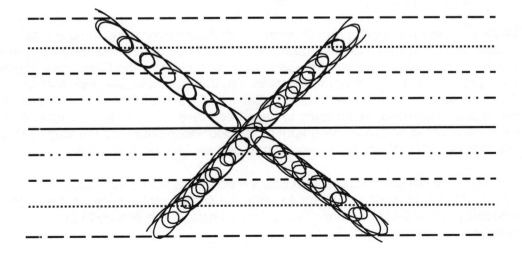

of cross. When this double helix cruciform figure is in contact with a standard nine-strand energy line, it causes the strands in the line to flip into the format of a type 3 line. If this line fractures further upstream, the ends curl back to form spirals, as shown in the diagram on page 181. The existence of a reversal point can be transient, as seasonal fluctuations may cause both energy lines to lengthen - and the double helix cruciform may no longer trespass on the other energy line.

A reversal point will only be harmful if:

1.   An object is placed over it

     or

2.   The reversal point moves to be beneath an object

In either of these circumstances, detrimental radiation will rise into the immediate environment. The area affected appears to be determined by the importance of the energy line and the size of the object. In many cases only a few square metres are affected, and there is little cause for concern unless this includes a domestic living or growing space. However, in a few cases - where a major energy line is involved - the area affected can be significantly larger, and for the benefit of everything in the living environment, action should be taken to minimise the damage being caused.'

And I thought algebra was complicated!

While discussing the discovery of reversal points, it's interesting to note that, in recent years, the whole idea of earth acupuncture has performed something of a U-turn. There was a time that it was standard practice for the Geopathic Stress (GS) practitioner to hammer metal stakes into the ground of the client's garden. This may well have had the effect of radiating GS away from their client's home - and it could be shown by dowsing to have been cleared. However, who knows what it did to the energy environment of the poor neighbours, as the fragmented beam of detrimental energy was scattered across their living spaces.

Today, many GS practitioners take Billy's much more subtle approach. Either the careful placing of an object where it earths the detrimental energy, or the targeted removal of an object from a reversal point, will restore the energy to being beneficial.

Billy's approach is so much closer to the spirit of acupuncture. Here, the precise positioning of a stone is being used to strengthen the earth's natural defences. This, in turn, can boost the well-being of all life, including that of humans, in the vicinity.

Dark Matter and the

Missing 2/3rds of the Universe

Don't say it too loud, but most of the universe has gone walkabout. If you work out the mass of the cosmos and then look around to see what it's composed of, you will find an uncomfortable equation that implies that the majority of it is . . . well, it isn't.

Clearly, this is not the case, and while the greatest minds in the academic community are searching the depths of space to find the rest of creation, the absent balance has been dubbed 'dark matter'.

However, it's only 'dark' in the sense that we can't see it in any part of the spectrum that we can detect. We know it's out there somewhere, but maybe we're just looking in the wrong place.

Billy's dowsing offers an intriguing, but very rational, explanation as to why we can't sense it. He feels it's because it's composed of fragments of energy that are below the radar of our current science. While the lads and lasses at CERN are beavering away at detecting the next most minute sub-atomic particle (as I write, the Higgs boson is the current holy grail), Billy's dowsing indicates that there may be five or six layers of particlette below that, before we eventually get to the fundamental building blocks of existence.

He was inspired to dowse this chain of thought by his own work on the fracturing and reassembling of the component parts of energy lines.

'Basically, I don't feel there is any difference between dark matter and ordinary matter, other than dark matter is matter broken down into its very basic components and it is stationary. I would liken it to all the spare parts of a motor car sitting on a shelf, waiting to be assembled. It doesn't become a motor car until you connect them all together, but they all exist in the garage.

I believe the relatively small amount of matter that has come together to form the universe, as we know it, is a consequence of the various components of this basic matter, this dark matter, coming into a critical relationship with each other. If I am correct in saying that the relationships require geometry associated with irrational numbers - as discussed on pages 144 and 145 - then the opportunities for this coming together to occur are few and far between. This may help to explain why there is a comparatively small amount of matter that has come into existence, compared to the large amount of dark matter.

When a critical relationship happens, these basic components firstly communicate with each other and are then attracted towards each other in a local area. Subsequently, they aggregate to become larger and more complex units. When a unit passes a certain stage of assembly, it ceases to be what we would call dark matter and simply becomes 'matter', which is measurable, detectable - maybe even visible. Only at that stage, does it begin to emit electrical and magnetic radiation.

My dowsing leads me to believe that dark matter is composed of electrical and magnetic components - possibly single monopole components with a negative or positive electric charge firmly locked within them. Whilst these elements are static and do not come into a critical relationship with one another, they will not become assembled, or emit radiation. It is only when something stirs them up, agitates them, and starts to move them around in a chaotic fashion that they may come into these critical relationships and be attracted to each other.

At the very beginning of this phase of existence, be it the Big Bang or some other catastrophic event (a debate that is far from over!) everything was broken down into its constituent components, which today we call dark matter and dark energy. But, because it was moving about in a chaotic state at that time, it hadn't settled. Some of these basic elements would find themselves in critical relationships, which would start them off on the pathway to reassembly back into conventional matter. Eventually, the basic elements started to come together to form larger particles, which in turn became the sub-atomic particles (quarks, leptons, bosons, etc.) that we are now beginning to discover. My dowsing indicates that this is about the fifth or sixth stage of assembly.

Modern science knows what follows on from there - the building up into atoms, molecules and beyond. Because the catastrophic event, which caused the chaos, has run its course, vast amounts of dark matter are still hanging there in space, not moving and therefore not getting into critical relationships. Only when something else happens, such as a supernova explosion, does more of the dark matter become agitated and start out on the road towards more complex atomic structures. I see this as an ongoing process, with the decay of matter over time and the formation of new stars - essentially from the invisible pool of unass-embled dark matter.

I have come to this line of thought entirely from my own dowsing questions and answers. It all stemmed from looking at the breakdown of energy lines into their basic components - and their reassembly, when they are put into a critical relationship with other unattached elements. I believe that what we observe as earth energies today is the holographic imagery of matter as a whole, which would have been present from the commencement of time as we understand it. Therefore, the under-standing of the behaviour of energy lines in the present day will give us an important insight into how the creation of the universe came about.

I feel the current scientific paradigm - even string theory - misses out one very important component, and that is tiny quantum packets of information. I believe these are important components of basic particles - and that they are also part of dark matter.

In essence, that shouldn't be too hard to comprehend; after all we are now quite aware of DNA and RNA, and of the impact that they have on the formation of life and matter. Essentially they provide the blueprint that makes us what we are. You could even envisage the tiny quantum packets of information as minute sub-elements of DNA, separated out into their component parts, mini genes or nucleotides.

It is currently assumed DNA and RNA did not appear until some time after the commencement of life. I would argue that they have existed in a fragmented form since the beginning of time - but only became DNA and RNA, as we know them today, when suitable circumstances prevailed that allowed them to cluster in their individual way. That may mean that the blueprint for the different species that exist has been around for all time and it only required favourable local conditions to prevail for them to come into being.'

There is a helpful comparison here with the development of language - letters, forming words, forming language that conveys information. Similarly, the elemental parts of the information that underpins matter, are inert until they come together to form packages that contain more complex information - and that allows matter to develop in very specific ways. Indeed, in this analogy, the letter would be the very first building block in the process of creation. One could even stretch the analogy a little further by referring to the biblical quotation - 'In the beginning was the Word . . . (John 1:1)'. Perhaps that was just another way of explaining, in another time and culture, that the essence of matter, life and consciousness is built up from elementary entities, which today we might term 'information'. On the other hand, perhaps I ought to leave the theological references to my more experienced colleague!

I mentioned earlier that Billy's work is more of a process than a story, in that it has no specific start and end point. He may have come to it through dowsing (which I have always felt was a virtual bridge between the planes of the physical and meta-physical), but once in the loop it has taken his intuitive research to the ends of time and space.

It may seem a long journey from rearranging watering cans on the patio to investigating the template for the origin of life - but having engaged with the process, every aspect of reality can become equally self-evident. Those practitioners who use the strapline 'Dowsing is only limited by your imagination' have captured the essence of this worldview.

Hubs of Attraction

As we saw earlier in this book, one of the insights that started Billy off on his epic journey of discovery was that most objects have lines of attraction that link them with all other objects.

It was a fundamental breakthrough, both in understanding how dowsing works and, perhaps even more importantly, in starting to unravel the very nature of energy and matter.

In recent years, Billy has taken that line of research further. He has observed that all objects also have a single point, a central core, from which this attraction stems. It takes him, and us, deeper into the emerging realm of theoretical physics.

'I find that in all matter, regardless of size, there is the potential for a hub or central point that acts as a force of attraction. Usually from these hubs, three or four lines of attraction extend outward for some distance. The distance is relative to the mass of the source object. The indications are that this force is not gravity as such, but it is something akin to it, in that it can attract certain things such as underground water and energy lines towards it.

I believe that it is possibly a "magnetic" force, but it is unique in that it is a monopole magnetic force - rather than dipole (as found in a bar magnet). Monopole magnetic forces have never been identified in science, although they are believed to exist theoretically. Physicists have predicted that monopole magnetic forces must exist, but they have yet to be detected in the laboratory. Currently (early 2012), this phenomenon is being studied using the CERN accelerator.

Hubs of attraction are composed of a clump of these magnetic forces. They are like little spinning wheels of energy that attract other things to them. It is not the magnetic force itself that causes the attraction, but the spinning vortex of the associated field that activates it. Spin is not to be confused with movement as it occurs around its own axis. The basic particle can be stationary in one location and still spin. I believe that this is the force that causes subtle energies, and even underground water, to be diverted towards objects of some mass, such as standing stones.

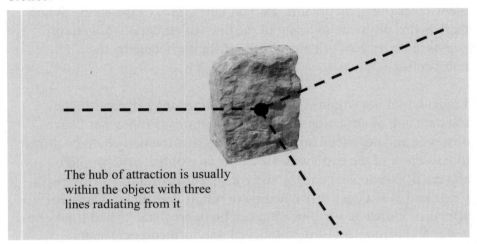

The hub of attraction is usually within the object with three lines radiating from it

When you are earthing detrimental energy, with a standing stone or whatever, and you follow the path that the detrimental energy takes into the ground, it is attracted to one of these hubs of attraction and it is forced down into the ground. Again, looking at the earth in a wider context, I see that there are major hubs of attraction deep in hills and mountains. I believe it is topographical features such as these, along with the geology of the earth, that dictate the pathways that underground water takes.

When underground water is beneath the stone the hub of attraction is drawn into the earth below

When work is undertaken in an area to remove detrimental energy, and to improve the quality of that which remains, the hubs of attraction present in stones, and even in hills, are drawn down to a greater depth. They reach a point where they are no longer present in the components themselves (hills, mountains, etc.) on the surface of the earth. When there is this physical lowering of the hubs of attraction to greater depths, a larger area of land at the surface is affected by the intervention.

Logical thinking would suggest that, with regard to the earth, the ultimate hub of attraction must be at its centre. From what I have observed and described above, if all hubs of attraction could be drawn to the centre of the earth then all the surface of the earth would be cleared of detrimental energy and enhanced accordingly. However, whether this is a desirable outcome or not, is debatable. The side effects of global geo-engineering can be unpredictable, and it may be better at this moment of time to leave it in its theoretical state.

This is a phenomenon that I have only come to appreciate over the last few years. It is something I can 'see' through my dowsing technique. I am very aware that this is only a projection of my own mind. Dowsing is something that happens in the mind and nowhere else.

One of the best places to observe hubs of attraction in relation to the landscape, and how they appear to influence the pathway of underground water and energy lines, is up in an aircraft on a clear day when the ground is visible.

I see some similarity between the operation of hubs of attraction and the way that crystals behave. A perfect crystal does not radiate subtle energy in the way that other matter does. That is why crystal can be such a healing thing - it can draw the detrimental energies into it and sequestrate them away. It is how the crystal healing process works - and it is why you have to wash it out of them occasionally.

The difference between a crystal and a stone is that generally the stone needs to be placed directly over the line of detrimental radiation in order to earth it. A crystal can be placed away from the line of detrimental radiation and will still attract the line to it and then earth it.

It is interesting to note that if an ordinary stone has certain symbols (such as a triple spiral) carved into it, then it also will act in the same way as a crystal - and it need not be placed directly over a line of detrimental radiation to earth it. A good friend of mine, Patrick Pugh, who carves symbols onto stones, kindly lent me one of

his pieces for use in my experimental work - and that allowed me to find this out. This finding may have some relevance in helping to explain the original purpose of some of the Rock Art that is a common feature of many ancient sites, both in Ireland and throughout the British Isles.'

Billy's description of Hubs of Attraction as 'little spinning wheels of energy that attract other energy and matter to them' will have an immediate resonance for those involved in healing through the manipulation of the chakras of the body. Barbara Brennan is another visual dowser, whose seminal work on the subject 'Hands of Light' contains diagrams of the human chakras, which show a similar process in operation. Her visualisation of the process includes cone-shaped hubs, rather than circular ones, but the inference is much the same.

By this point in the story of Billy's research, I am starting to run out of ways of indicating that a discovery is profound! The concept of the Hub of Attraction is so simple, yet it explains so much about <u>why earth energy dowsing works</u>.

Interconnection - A Vision of Information

Since Billy last committed his ideas to paper, the areas of investigation that have flowed from his earlier breakthroughs have continued to multiply. He may have tired somewhat of talking and travelling, but his mind is still working away at whole areas of study that would have passed the rest of us by.

Having expanded the theory that the energy-matter spectrum should really be thought of as an information-energy-matter continuum, he was then primed to make a further leap into the unknown by coming to appreciate that the interconnectedness of all things isn't just a philosophical concept.

The energy vanishes!

'In 2010, whilst I was undertaking some preparatory work for another experiment, I discovered a type of manifestation that I had previously been unaware of. I believe this may well play a big part in the inter-communication of all things, animate or otherwise. For me, it was the first time that I had observed that intangible connection is an objective reality. It is an obvious, but important, point that inter-connection between all things can only arise through information being communicated and a response being generated.

When I was examining the energy emanations of an object in my house, I observed that as I moved the object from one location to another, there were changes in its energy output. This was not unexpected as any change in relationship with other objects will bring about gradual changes in the energy output in most situations. However, at one location, I was very surpised to find that all its outward energy emanations ceased. The lines of radiation that had been extending away from it were suddenly drawn inside the mass of the object at that point. This is again similar to what occurs in an eclipse scenario, but on this occasion there was no third object in the vicinity as is necessary for that to happen.

In this experiment the conditions were different as I was only working with one object and it was not in a relationship that would cause this outcome. I looked more closely to see what was happening and, by asking an open-ended Dowsing Question, I found that where the object was placed there was an unusual energy manifestation. It was something that I had never come across before, although I had observed similar, but smaller forms, two in number, within the energy field of all objects, including humans. I feel that the identification of these forms is a very significant development in the understanding of the relationship between information, energy and matter.'

The football of enlightenment?

'The energy manifestation that I had discovered within my workroom was about the size of a football, and toroidal in shape. There was a clockwise rotating field at the centre of the toroid and an anti-clockwise field around the outside. It was just above the surface of the table on which I had placed the object, although subsequently I found that it is not stationary but moves in a thirteen day elliptical orbit. The football-sized manifestation did not appear to have any lines of radiation coming out of it, nor any going into it.

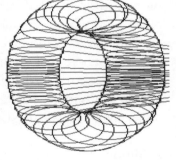

I moved the object that I was checking away to where normal lines of radiation extending from it could be observed. I then moved it back closer to the manifestation in easy stages, and I found that at a certain point the aura and other lines of the object were being attracted into it - until eventually they were all absorbed.

Not surprisingly, I was astonished by this feature in my workroom. I looked outside to see if I could observe any more of these manifestations in the open countryside. Again, to my surprise, I found several of them. They were a little larger than the one in the house, around 200 to 300 paces apart and at various heights above the surface of the ground.

I couldn't find any dowsable energy lines, as such, connecting them with the other objects around them. However, I observed that there appeared to be some communication between them - and also communication with all objects of matter within their specific area of influence. I detected, what could only be described as an exchange of small pulses, or packages, of energy or information - moving from the one to the other in rapid succession. These packages are in various shapes, but mainly in C and S segments as seen on page 155 along with short helical sections as described on page 153.

It is just possible that this could be supporting evidence, acquired though deviceless dowsing, of the process postulated by the theoretical physicist, Max Planck. Planck described the theoretical transfer of light and other energy between one object and another. It could be highly significant here that the transfer process occurred as distributed quanta (individual 'packets'), rather than as a steady stream.

Max Planck

Additionally, it would appear that these manifestations are 'wirelessly' connected with other manifestations at an even greater height above the ground. This latter scenario is further confused by the fact that, regardless of the time of day, the connection appears to remain stationary and directly overhead. One would expect that with the rotation of the earth, this would change over time.

The only tenable explanation I can put forward that would allow this to occur is that the whole of our reality, our universe, is contained within some gigantic manifestation that lies beyond the horizons of our universe.

This could be seen to align visual dowsing with the evolving reasoning of modern physics, in that it suggests that our cosmos is moving between two Branes (a Brane is a different type of spatial dimension, of which there could be many!)'

Billy's work here seems to be dovetailing with that of the eminent Cambridge academic Neil Turok who, working at very much the other end of the spectrum of theoretical physics, wrote in The Cyclic Universe (Edge Magazine 2007):

. . . we find that if the universe collapses to make a singularity, it can bounce, and the universe can come back out of the bounce. As it passes through the singularity, the universe becomes full of radiation - very much like what happens in the colliding brane model . . .

Interconnection in action

'My original objective, prior to stumbling across the information processing footballs, was to carry out an experiment to look for evidence of the interconnectedness and influence of one object on another over distance.

I used some everyday objects, mainly small stones that were lying on the ground near to a hedge in a field, distributed naturally over a distance of about 100 yards. All my measurements were undertaken by dowsing.

Before starting the experiment, I checked these objects for two aspects of their energy fields. One was the aura, and the other was the number of radial lines emanating from the object.

I was careful to note the exact position of where I was standing when I made these initial observations, so that I did not change the result by the unintentional intrusion of my own energy field. I was careful to do this, as I had noted on previous occasions that the aura of the object could alter in size considerably. This was especially the case if I dowsed for it by starting away from the object and walking towards it, as opposed to starting with my back towards the object and walking away from it. I had found that the number of radial lines emanating from the object also changed in some cases.

When this preparation work was done, I lifted one of the small stones and moved it a little over one foot away from where it had been lying. On checking the other stones, changes were observable in both the extent of the aura and the number of radials from each of them. I repeated the experiment several times, moving one stone at a time - and on each occasion additional changes to the aura and the radials were noted.

I did not carry out this experiment over a distance greater than 100 yards, so I do not know if there is any limit to the effect of this interaction.

It is important that we bear in mind that many elements in the landscape are on the move all the time, and any of these could influence the outcome of this experiment, as well as my moving the stone.

One of the core problems when dowsing for earth energies is that it is very difficult to replicate results precisely - especially between different dowsers. However, it may be that this, in itself, is a clear demonstration of inter-connectedness in action.

As well as people and objects on the move, we have the movement of the earth and the other planets to contend with. All this would make it impossible to precisely get exactly the same results, as described above, over time or in a different location. I feel the most that we can hope for is a degree of similarity in our findings.

Further complications arise from the necessity to form a clear picture in our mind of exactly what it is we are trying to find. The clarity of that picture is determined by the observer's personal baggage and beliefs.'

The idea of the interconnection of all things, ourselves included, is clearly not new. However, up to now it has either been regarded as spiritually or philosophically self-evident (but therefore not provable) or restricted to a limited physical reality (we all breathe the same air or are physically recycled over time - ashes to ashes). What Billy is putting forward here is that we, and everything around us, are connected - both at an energetic level and also at an informational level.

Once you get to this point, then the universal consciousness emerges as a practical demonstrable reality - and I can almost feel Carl Jung chortling 'I told you so!' somewhere out in the far reaches of the network. <u>Dowsing itself would then be a predictable side-effect of that deeply embedded universal knowledge</u>.

Clearly, Billy's experiments raise a number of issues across a whole range of practical and academic approaches to the subject - and much more research would be required before even tentative conclusions could be drawn.

However, the evidence it provides for quantum physicists to work on is quite ground breaking - and it will be interesting to see if anyone from the scientific community picks up and runs with Billy's research (and indeed if they give him the credit he deserves).

Cosmic Strings and Other Things

In a similar vein . . . for a man with no formal training in theoretical physics, the experience that Billy has gained through dowsing has led him to consider some profound areas of thought. One of these is the ongoing research into the existence of anti-matter.

The existence of anti-matter was initially postulated by Hicks and Pearson toward the end of the 19th Century. However, it was the work of the renowned physicist Paul Dirac in the 1920's that brought the theoretical concept into sharper focus - although he did not use the term anti-matter, as such.

Resulting from this work, Carl Anderson later discovered anti-particles, and the whole field moved into one approach to the realm of reality.

The hypothesis is simple enough - that for every piece of matter, as we experience it, there is a corresponding piece, which exists in an opposing energetic state. Getting your head around quite what that means in our everyday lives, and why we don't just disappear in a personal explosion, is another matter entirely.

Paul Dirac

Billy's work on subtle energies has led him to form his own hypotheses. He takes the existing understanding of anti-matter one stage further, by embracing his understanding of the world of subtle energies as revealed to him through dowsing.

'The position held by present day physicists is that every elementary particle in the Universe appears to have a partner particle called its antiparticle. This particle shares many of the same characteristics, but many other characteristics are the opposite of those in the original particle. For example, the electron has as its antiparticle the anti-electron. The electron and the antielectron have exactly the same masses, but they have exactly opposite electrical charges. It is considered possible that these antiparticles can come together to form antimatter, and that there exists an antimatter universe similar to our own, as yet undiscovered.

One of the problems that confronts physicists is the assumption that for every particle there is an antiparticle, and that when a particle and an antiparticle collide they annihilate each other. The common under-standing of the term annihilation in this context is that the two particles destroy themselves completely, and nothing is left. However, some scientists claim that there is no such thing as 'nothing'. They argue that if at the time of the Big Bang, an equal number of particles and antiparticles were formed, and annihilation took place as described above, it is likely that there would be no particles left to form the universe of which our earth is a part. Clearly, that was not the case, but currently there is no reasonable explanation as to why an imbalance in favour of particles came about.

Perhaps a better understanding of the term 'annihilate' is contained in the first law of Thermodynamics which states that: "energy can be transformed, i.e. changed from one form to another, but cannot be created nor destroyed". To fully accept this law in this form the logic would imply that there is indeed no such thing as 'nothing'. Instead, there is something which takes another form that, as yet, we are unable to observe.

The scale of the imbalance is reflected in the amount of matter that has been calculated to exist, derived from all the other known elements that make up the observable universe. These are: Dark Energy 72%, Dark Matter 23%, Atoms 4.6% - which leaves a small proportion unexp-lained. However, it is far from certain that we have already found every component that makes up the universe. Some physicists believe that there are other elements, as yet undiscovered. This belief comes from two sources. On the one hand, evidence from cosmic microwave background fluctuations in deep space have been observed by the Wilkinson Microwave Anisotropy Probe (WMAP). On the other hand, additional particles have been predicted through work aimed at formulating a Grand Unified Theory. This line of research has proposed that at extremely high temperatures (such as in the early universe) the electromagnetic force, and the strong and weak nuclear forces are not actually fundamental forces. Instead, they occur as a result of the breaking down of spontaneous symmetry. This is known as the Single Gauge Theory, which predicts the existence of a number of heavy, stable particles that have not yet been observed in nature.

Of these, the most notable is the magnetic monopole, which is a kind of stable, heavy "knot" in the magnetic field. <u>The Grand Unified Theory predicts that monopoles will have been produced copiously at extremely high temperatures - and that they should have persisted to the present day in such quantity that they would have become the one of the primary constituents of the universe we know today</u>.

If additional new particle forms are eventually observed, then the percentage of atoms in relation to other elements would decrease accordingly. Therefore, the scale of the imbalance between matter and antimatter could be quite small, and much smaller than presently calculated.

Whilst we feel that balance in our lives is desirable, to achieve equilibrium and attain complete balance would appear to bring our existence to a halt! Equilibrium occurs if we have two opposing forces with equal amounts of energy, resisting each other, and bringing about a stationary state by cancelling each other out. As the maintenance of life, and the continuing process of evolution, are dependent on an ever changing environment within the universe, and in our case on the earth, some inherent imbalance appears to be necessary for this process to continue.

However, a total imbalance would also seem to be disastrous. Therefore, to create the correct conditions where a living universe could come into existence, and could continue to exist, a specific level of this imbalance is necessary within its structures - and also a regulating force that keeps the imbalance within certain parameters. As I mentioned earlier, my view is that matter, or indeed antimatter, will only form when the basic elements of which it is composed occur in specific geometrical relationships.

Just because something that we are observing ceases to be observable, it may be logically incorrect to assume that it no longer exists. It is likely that it still does exist, but in another form that is beyond our present ability to observe it. I have discussed this in the section on Dark Matter (see page 188). There is sufficient evidence to support the existence of Dark Matter, and also to support the assertion that there is much more of it than observable matter. If my proposition that Dark Matter is actually observable matter that exists beyond the electromagnetic threshold is correct, the theory that matter has been annihilated by antimatter can be refuted. It would also support the proposition that Dark Matter has been transformed back into its basic elements.

It has been observed at CERN that when particles and their antiparticles collide in a particular way, energy is released in the form of gamma rays. It is possible that the collision between a particle and an anti-particle causes a fracturing of the bonds within the magnetic fields of both, resulting in north and south pole magnetic monopoles being formed. Such a fracturing would allow some of the electric charge to be released in the form of gamma rays, as observed. I therefore believe that monopole magnetic forces are the major constituent of Dark Matter and Dark Energy. Dark Matter still retains some electric charge firmly bound within it, whilst Dark Energy is devoid of all electric charge.

The problem of non-observability is one that dowsers also experience. On occasions, something that we are observing seems to disappear. This may be due to the narrow focus of the dowsing question in our mind at that time. The dowsing question focuses our mind in one specific direction. If we are unable to widen the scope of our search with a new dowsing question, then much information could be missed, or possibly incorrect conclusions could be drawn. On page 148, I described the composition of energy lines as I understand them. I have described them as Positive - Negative, and Plus - Minus with a mirror image pairing. What I now need to add to that narrative is that when the dowsing question was widened to include the possibility of radiation from antimatter, I found an identical series of lines in close proximity to those described above. However they are kept at a safe distance apart, and do not often come into contact. On the rare occasions that they do interact, they both disintegrate into their basic elements (as described on page 155), and continue to exist side by side in that dormant state.

If what happens to subtle energies is replicated by particles of matter and antimatter, then the process of annihilation would not eliminate them. Instead it would reduce them to their basic elements, which I believe are Dark Matter, Dark Energy, and their antimatter equivalents. In this state they could survive side by side without any further interaction, because any energy that they contain is firmly locked within them. In the field of science, the existence of dark antimatter is still a matter of conjecture and open for debate. If, immediately after the singularity (or the Big Bang), that led to the creation of the present universe, there was an equal amount of matter and antimatter, then equal amounts of Dark Matter and Dark Antimatter would still exist. They would continue in that state until conditions changed to those which could cause them to reassemble.

However, it is more likely that when the catastrophic event occurred at the beginning of our universe, the outcome was not an exact balance between the dark and the observable elements. As I have discussed elsewhere, it would appear that the forces of nature operate between certain narrow parameters, but these are never precise.

A recent analysis of findings from The Planck Surveyor space probe, launched by the European Space Agency in 2009, shows that there are minor, but distinct, variations in the cosmic microwave background radiation. Additionally, data provided by WMAP implies that the cosmic microwave background suffers from such anomalies. Some observers have also pointed out that the uneven temperature distribution in the WMAP data did not appear to be consistent with the Big Bang picture. As the cosmic microwave background closely reflects the situation shortly after the big bang, it is evidence that a small imbalance may have existed from the very start of this cycle, and that that imbalance was in favour of matter.'

New names for old energies

'How then does all this square up with what we can find when we are dowsing the subtle lines of radiation emanating from matter?

It is easy to assume that when energy lines are found radiating from an object that the source of the lines is the matter itself. I held that belief for many years myself. It is only recently that I have come to realise that <u>the source of ordinary energy lines is not the matter itself, but something else contained within the mass of the matter. That something, I believe, is a small clump of the basic elements that go to make up Dark Matter. A short distance away from any object, but still within its mass, I find, through dowsing, another similar clump. However, this clump consists of Dark Antimatter</u>. It is from this source that anti-energy lines are radiated.

I find that lines radiating from both Dark Matter and, what I believe to be, Dark Antimatter have exactly the same composition although they respond differently. It is this difference in response that leads to local imbalances.

The following description is applicable to all the forms of energy lines that I have observed.

Plus and minus energy takes the same form as ordinary earth energy - and shadows it most, if not all, of the time. Plus and minus energy strands are components within most energy lines.

These components are sometimes separated from earth energy lines at a siphon - an unusual underground water arrangement (described in pages 51 and 151), or at a unique energy configuration. On these occasions, the positive and negative elements within an energy line are separated out and drawn down into the earth. The plus and minus elements are thrown back out to form a band of plus and minus energy, which is beamed across the surface of the ground - with the plus energy being slightly above it and the minus energy slightly below it. This beam moves slowly back and forth from its source at the separation point, which acts as a kind of pivot.

Dowsing indicates that plus and minus energy is not generated within the earth - nor even in our visible universe - it is archaic and a relic of forces that exist outside our universe. The minus element is a remnant of the force that brought the present universe into being, and the plus element comes from a source where the universe will meet its destruction and subsequent reconstruction. This supports the view, held by certain astrophysicists, that the universe is not a one-trip experience, but that it is cyclic in nature and undergoes numerous 'deaths' and 'rebirths'.

The theory of a cyclic universe requires it to be positioned between two branes (membranes), which can collide - ending one cycle and beginning another. This event would cause a great explosion, another Big Bang, throwing huge amounts of matter back into space. The collision between the matter and the branes would result in some debris from the damaged brane becoming entangled with the basic components of observable matter - and consequently it could still be detectable to us today when we dowse.

This model of creation lends support to the emerging theory that our present existence is not a one-off event, but that it is part of a cyclical process which could, theoretically, continue ad infinitum.

This does not, of course, answer the obvious question, as to how the two large opposing forces came to exist in the first place, or indeed, how the cycle began, but maybe we can leave that to the theologians for the time being!'

Stars made of string?

'Another problem that has yet to be properly explained by science is how matter accumulated into clumps, or at least how it developed into the stars, planets and galaxies, and not all come together like a large clump of grapes, as would be the case if gravity were the sole force to cause their formation.

Robert Woodrow Wilson, American astronomer and 1978 Nobel Laureate in physics, who with Arno Allan Penzias in 1964 discovered the cosmic microwave background radiation expressed the following view:

". . .there is a suggestion that galaxy and cluster formation might take place by accretion around "cosmic strings." Cosmic strings, long strands or loops of mass-energy, are a consequence of some theories of elementary particle physics. They are envisaged to arise from phase transitions in the very early universe in a fashion analogous to the way faults can occur in a crystal that suffers dislocations because of imperfect growth from, say, a liquid medium. The dynamic properties of cosmic strings are imperfectly understood, but arguments exist that suggest they may give a clustering hierarchy similar to that observed for galaxies. Unfortunately, the same particle physics that produces cosmic strings also produces magnetic monopoles (isolated magnetic charges), whose possible abundance in the universe can be constrained by observations and experiments to lie below very low limits. Particle physicists like to explain the absence of magnetic monopoles in the Cosmos by invoking for the very early universe the mechanism of inflation. The same mechanism would also inflate away cosmic strings."

The problem with this theory lies in how the cosmic strings are formed in the first place, and then sustained long enough to create galaxies. However, this concern only applies if we see our universe as an entity existing alone, in a void. If, as I suggest above, there were two opposing forces, or branes, then they would produce energy forms, spirals etc., similar to those that emanate from all matter, and what we dowse as earth energies. They would penetrate the space in which the developing universe is travelling and may be sufficient to cause the clustering of particles, which could subsequently form the various heavenly bodies.

This line of reasoning has some resonance with the theory that evolution may be brought about by the nature and pattern of energy on the face of a planet - and that the shape and structure of that material world is contained in the form of that energy. In other words, <u>creation and evolution is influenced by a blueprint supplied by natural forces and basic information</u>, which I believe exists in all matter, a little bit like DNA in living organisms.

Eventually we get some stabilisation, as the form that energy develops is determined by the relative positions of one mass to the other. As gasses turn into mass, a slowing up of the change in energy forms would occur and a more stable condition would develop.'

For a reader new to this field, some of these concepts may seem strange, even alien, to our everyday understanding of the world around us. However, they are no stranger than the similar ideas being developed by theoretical physicists.

The only real difference is that while the scientist seeks to find the physical process predicted by advanced and theoretical mathematics, Billy seeks to understand and interpret the energy phenomena he senses and 'sees' through his practical dowsing.

I find it astonishing and very exciting to appreciate that these two, very disparate, ways of researching the nature and origin of the universe actually seem to be dovetailing.

Subtle Energies and the Evolutionary Process

The survival of Darwin

'The theory of evolution, put forward by Charles Darwin in 1859 in his book *On the Origin of Species*, has stood the test of time better than most of its contemporaries.

It has two main strands; natural selection and survival of the fittest. The over-riding assumption is that we have got where we are merely by chance and good fortune. Over the years, scientists, through the use of better methods of observation and the development of suitable tools, have found much evidence to support Darwin and they have overcome some of the arguments that have been put forward in contradiction of the theory. Few would radically challenge what Darwin postulated 150 years ago.

Charles Darwin

In broad terms, I would not disagree with most of what is contained in the Theory of Evolution, nor with the evolving philosophy of Neo-Darwinism that has developed out of it. However, there are still unanswered questions and unfilled gaps in the reasoning:

Darwinism demands that evolution is a gradual and continuous process. Any progress that has taken place has occurred by trial and error - that is, simply by chance. A multitude of changes take place, but only a few prove successful and continue into future generations. From these, further changes occur and from another large selection of mutations again, only a few are 'fit for purpose' and survive. This suggests that there was great instability within the genes of those primitive organisms.'

Some limitations of Darwin's work

'However, it has been discovered that some types of archaebacterial species appear to be as old as life on Earth. They have not evolved very far in almost four billion years.

Firstly, this suggests that change does not take place for change's sake alone. A need for change must have existed in the cases where change occurred - and, if the environment within which the organism finds itself remains stable, then little change will take place.

Secondly, the entire explosion of life, which took place during the Cambrian geological period (about 570 million years ago), took only five to nine million years. All kinds of multi-celled creatures, in astonishing variety, seemed to develop out of nowhere, all around much the same time.

It is possible to estimate mathematically the likelihood of the creation of a new gene. However, the mathematics breaks down if the creation of the new gene happens purely by chance. The number of potential variations required to develop a new gene quickly approaches the theoretical maximum, so the proposed evolution mechanism does not increase the probability of arriving at a wholly new gene by chance within the available timeframe.

For the discovery of additional processes, which add new meaning to the equation, the maths as it stands doesn't work. A model, which deals with pure chance alone, without some external guidance to give focus and narrow the field, will not succeed.

As I come from a farming background, I have observed animal behaviour down through the years. There is no doubt that survival of the
fittest is a fact, and I have seen this in action on many occasions where
the fit animals in a herd or pack attack those who are weak and pursue
them until they are dead. It appears to be within the instinctive
behaviour of animals, other than some humans, to kill those that show
any sign of weakness, or those that are significantly different from the
main body of the pack.

Evolution is totally dependent on change taking place within a species,
or no development would take place at all. Development therefore must
be slow enough so that the changes per generation are almost unobservable - or the pack would attack those that are different and eliminate
them.

The amount of progress that a species can attain in any given period of
time depends, to a large degree, on the length of the reproduction or
generation cycle. Insects and very small life forms including bacteria
can reproduce in a matter of days, and sometimes hours, after birth.
This means that they can have thousands, if not millions, of opportunities to advance and develop in a 100 year period. Humans and larger
animals like elephants, even at their most prolific, will only have five or
six generation spans in that time.

Those species with short life spans can adapt much more easily to
sudden and unexpected changes in our living environment. As we have
already noted, the medical profession is fully aware of the ability of a
'Smart Bug' to quickly reinvent itself - and to become resistant to
whatever is thrown at it.

We know that the dinosaur became extinct as the result of perhaps just
one catastrophic event. Meanwhile, smaller and simpler life forms
survived that experience in sufficient numbers to again flourish and
repopulate the earth. Could it be possible that a species, in a crisis
which threatens its very existence, temporarily sets aside the instinctive
fear of change - reducing the urge to kill those that are slightly different
and facilitating more rapid evolution?

Survival of the fittest is satisfactory to explain progress and advancement within a particular species, but the hypothesis is less convincing when it comes to the evolution of new species. The weakness lies in Natural Selection, which according to Darwin, must run in parallel with change.

The instinct within all life forms is to select a mate that is compatible and has similar characteristics. If one follows through the logic of this trait, then it is apparent that this will lead to the purification of that species - which would tend to make reproduction more clone-like. This, in turn, would minimise any differences that may be exhibited. Those that are different would have more difficulty in acquiring a mate - and males that are dominant will produce most of the offspring. The species would therefore become more and more homogenous.

If all life has developed from a single cell organism, first appearing millions of years ago, into the great biodiversity that we have today - and there is a lot of solid evidence to support this - then new species must have developed over time. Scientific research has demonstrated that although that period of time is very long, the explosion of life as we know it today has only happened in the latter stages of that development.

According to Darwin, the evolution of new species must originate from a mutation taking place within a species - and there must also be significant numbers of that mutation produced at a given time. Additionally, the mutated group must survive in significant enough numbers to breed within itself, and so stabilise the changes that have occurred, to cause a new species to be established.

A further complication in this line of reasoning is that often a mutation has a reduced chance of reproducing due to infertility. Coupled with survival of the fittest and natural selection, mutations very often do not survive - and usually the purity of the species is maintained. Therefore, it would be difficult for a new species to become established unless some other factor enters the equation.

Scientific research suggests that significant changes in biodiversity, especially the extinction of old species and the creation of new ones, appear to correspond with earth-wide catastrophes due to events such as asteroid impacts. These can cause earthquakes, floods, large changes in temperatures and, in extreme cases, changes to the topography of the earth itself. Additionally, tectonic plate movement is constantly changing the face of the earth - albeit very slowly.

However, evolution also happens slowly - and often spasmodically. Could it be that the ongoing changes taking place in the earth have had an important part to play in the evolution of life found on it - and also in the diverse ways that it displays itself? Certain species are to be found only in certain habitats, dictated by the specific conditions found at that location.

Comparatively small changes to the local habitat would result in the extinction of that species.'

Other Darwinian considerations

While neo-Darwinism continues to be the bedrock of our understanding of species evolution, there are many apparent flaws in the simplistic application of Darwin's theories:

'Artificial selection and breeding programmes, as carried out in livestock farming, never produce wholly new characteristics; they only refine the characteristics that already exist. This is why livestock breeders are currently anxious to introduce genetic engineering, to overcome this obstacle in nature. Without the input of new genes, there is no evidence that natural selection introduces new characteristics either.

The notion that mutation and recombination can compose new genes is therefore implausible.

There is scant evidence that mutation and recombination can compose functional new genes that differ from any known predecessor by more than, say, a dozen essential nucleotides.

Evolution does not appear to be gradual, contrary to Darwin's firm prediction. There is now a lot of evidence to show that for many thousands of years the diversity and development of species remained largely unchanged - and then, within a comparatively short period, great changes took place.

The standard theory cannot explain why the coordinating genes - those that control the development of embryos and major features - are often very similar across totally different species. This is termed Convergent Evolution - and it is something of an evolutionary surprise, which is not explained convincingly by neo-Darwinism.

Convergent evolution, which has been observed since the time of Darwin, is the name given to apparent coincidences in evolution, such as the physical similarity between fish and mammals, or of birds and mammals. Examples of convergence also appear at the molecular level, as in similar antibody proteins carried by camels and nurse sharks. It has been observed that the more scientists research this topic, the more examples of convergence they find.

Macro-evolution - evolutionary change on a grand scale, encompassing the origin of novel designs, evolutionary trends, adaptive radiation, and mass extinction - is not accounted for by neo-Darwinian micro-evolution.'

Beyond Darwin

'To understand where evolution is heading - and what is driving it - I think we need to look beyond Darwin and the evolution of species - and to look at the yet unanswered question as to where life came from in the first place.

For the religionists, the answer is simple; God created life, as he did everything that exists, and he placed man on earth as the most advanced lifeform, we are told in his own image, to have dominion over everything else. Therefore we have every right to feel superior, and to exploit everything that God has placed before us for our use. Scientists do not find the answer so simple, and the argument continues unabated. The idea that has held sway for many years is that life was spawned in a sea of 'prebiotic soup', with some spontaneous reaction, such as violent electrical storms, triggering the production of amino acids essential to life. This theory assumes that this was a one-off occurrence, at one location on the surface of the earth; that all subsequent life evolved from it, and subsequently spread across the face of the earth.

However, since then, other ideas have been put forward.'

Panspermia

'Panspermia, which means literally "seeds everywhere", is the proposition that the seeds of life came from Cosmic sources - possibly from the remnants of comets and meteorites that have bombarded the earth since it was first formed.

This is not a new proposal. Its earliest recorded advocate was the Greek philosopher Anaxagoras, who influenced Socrates. However, Aristotle's theory of spontaneous generation came to be preferred by science for more than two thousand years. Then on April 9th 1864, the French chemist, Louis Pasteur, reported on his simple, but elegant swan-necked flask experiment disproving spontaneous generation, as it was then held to occur. These experiments not only put to rest the organic life-from-non-life idea, but also set the foundation for the law of biogenesis: life only comes from life.

In the 1870s, the British physicist Lord Kelvin and the German physicist Hermann von Helmholtz supported Pasteur's work - and went on to suggest that life could have come from space.

In the first decade of the 1900s, Swedish chemist Svante Arrhenius suggested that bacterial spores, propelled through space by light pressure, could have been the seeds of life on Earth. However, it did not overthrow the theory that that life was spawned in a sea of 'prebiotic soup'.

In the 1970s, British astronomers Fred Hoyle and Chandra Wickramasinghe rekindled interest in panspermia. By careful spectroscopic observation and analysis of light from distant stars, they found new evidence, traces of the building blocks of life in the intervening dust.

They also proposed that comets, which are largely made of water-ice, could carry bacterial life across galaxies and could protect it

Fred Hoyle

from radiation damage along the way. One aspect of this research programme - the contention that interstellar dust and comets contain organic compounds - has been continued by other scientists.

It is now generally accepted that space contains the 'ingredients' of life. This development could be the first hint of a huge paradigm shift. But mainstream science has not as yet accepted the concept of a modern panspermia - that whole cells seeded life on Earth.'

Seeds of immortality

'However, even if it were eventually to be fully accepted, it only pushes back one step further the question as to where and how and when life began.

In 1995, two scientists at California Polytechnic State University showed that bacteria can survive, without any apparent metabolism, for at least 25 million years. This was a remarkable finding as it suggested that to all intents and purposes, life forms as complex as bacteria are probably immortal.

There was a further strengthening of the case in 2000, when a team of biologists and a geologist announced the revival of 250 million year old bacteria.

Anecdotally, it is well known to farmers and gardeners that certain weed seeds can lie dormant for 50 or 60 years until the ground is disturbed and the correct conditions for their growth are provided.

Even if panspermia were to be the reason behind the beginning of life on earth, it still requires conditions to be right for those 'seeds of life' to take hold and to survive.

Clearly, the seeding need not be a one-off event; in fact it could still be occurring. The development of those seeds into a recognisable life form could take a very long time, and we need not be aware of it happening. Chandra Wickramasinghe has suggested that the recent advent of new strains of virus could indeed be evidence of this happening in our present time.

Those of us who are familiar with the sowing of seeds in

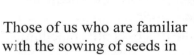

Chandra Wickramasinghe

fields and gardens, their subsequent survival, and their growing into whatever they grow into, know one or two basic facts. Firstly, if we want to grow cabbages we must sow cabbage seed. If we want to grow turnips we must sow turnip seed. To you or me, looking at cabbage seeds and turnip seeds out of the packet, we could not tell the difference between them. The difference does not lie in their outward appearance, but in what is inside the seeds. Again, if we split them open we would not recognise any difference. The difference is not in the appearance but in the information that is contained in the germ within the seed. It is this that allows the one to grow into a cabbage or the other into a turnip - provided the conditions are right. Therefore the seed must have the ability to become aware of the necessary change in conditions, usually an increase in heat and light, to allow it to burst into growth. This suggests a primitive form of intelligence in the seed, in that it can receive information and respond to it.

In today's world, we all appreciate the importance of information. Architects design buildings, plans are drawn and builders follow those plans to construct the end product. Education is totally dependent on the passing of information from the teacher to the pupil. Every teacher knows, that no matter how good the system is, there are many things that can interfere with the outcome. Our very existence is dependent on the successful transfer of information within and throughout our bodies.

We would not be what we are without the information contained in our DNA. Did the information contained in our DNA come about as the result of evolutionary processes or did the information within the DNA come from an archaic source and predates the life form? What is the chicken and what is the egg?'

Mind and body

'Information flows endlessly throughout our bodies. Our autonomic nervous system works flat out to keep us alive by regulating our heart rhythm, respiration, body temperature, blood pressure, the chemical balance throughout the body, and many more critical activities - day in, day out - without us even being aware of the process until something goes wrong.

It is considered that the brain is the powerhouse of our nervous system, and the controller of all communication within the body; that electrical activity within the brain sends impulses via the nervous system to the main components of the body and regulates their behaviour. Whilst that is patently so in the gross sense of the word, there is another - more subtle - transfer of information. We are all dependent on inter-cellular communication - where no system of nerves exists.

Medical science is becoming more aware of the mind/body-body/mind relationship. The mind and the body interact in powerful ways that affect a person's health. The digestive system is profoundly controlled by the mind; anxiety, depression, and fear dramatically affect its function. Most people, on the basis of either intuition or personal experience, believe that emotional stress can cause or alter the course of physical diseases - even major ones. The pathways and mechanisms by which the brain and immune system interact are only just beginning to be identified. It is remarkable that the brain can alter the activity of white blood cells and thus an immune response, because white blood cells travel through the body in blood or lymph vessels, and are not attached to nerves. Nevertheless, research has shown that the brain does communicate with the white blood cells. For example, depression may suppress the immune system, making a person more susceptible to infections, such as those brought by the viruses that cause the common cold.

The mind-body interaction is a two-way street. Not only can psychological factors contribute to the onset or aggravation of a wide variety of physical disorders, but also physical diseases can affect a person's thinking or mood. People with life-threatening, recurring, or chronic physical disorders commonly become depressed. The depression may worsen the effects of the physical disease and add to a person's misery.

The concept of mind over matter is something that intrigues the imagination - and scientists working in the fields of sub-atomic and quantum physics are becoming acutely aware of the problems caused by the human mind getting in the way of experiments that are being carried out at these levels. Much convincing research has been carried out on telepathy and related phenomena.

Less work, if any, has been done on the reverse side of the coin - the effect of matter over mind. However, it is well-recognised that our immediate environment can impact on our wellbeing and on our health. This is well described in the earlier chapter titled 'Detrimental and Beneficial Energies'. If this is so then we must ask the following question: Can our environment at a less local level also impact upon us, and if so, in what way?'

. . . on a planetary scale

'In the early 1970s, the British chemist and inventor, James Lovelock, proposed the theory that life controls the Earth's environment - to make it suitable for itself. The theory, which he called *Gaia*, has gained a small but growing following.

James Lovelock

It proposes that the earth is a self-regulating living organism, which can adapt and facilitate change over time. The planet is not therefore in a state of steady decline - and creatures that improve the environment for their own survival do better than those that damage it. Lovelock suggested that Gaian processes are necessary for higher forms of life to emerge and to succeed on any planet.

This again suggests a two-way process is taking place. If life forms act in a way that is kind to the earth systems that support them, then the earth will provide even more favourable conditions for those life forms. It is a self-perpetuating process.

Earlier, I described experiments that I carried out some time ago, and which I have repeated many times. I demonstrated that certain natural radiations that emanate from the earth, that are detectable by dowsing, can be shown to be detrimental to humans. They can lower our ability to perform certain simple tasks - such as resisting downward pressure on an outstretched arm.

Refining these experimental techniques allowed me to show that this

222

effect came about as a result of interference in the transmission of information, through the nervous system, from the brain to the arm - the quality of the information being reduced and becoming incoherent. The results gained from the experiment in themselves are not earth-shattering. However, it clearly demonstrates that matter - in this case the earth or at least radiations that emanate from the earth - has the ability to interfere with the natural communication system of the human body.

There are many other subtle energy emanations, which are not currently considered to be detrimental, but that originate in all the matter that makes up the earth - such as hills, mountains, trees and boulders - the landscape around us, the topography of the earth. Because this topography is far from uniform, no two places are identical. Therefore, the pattern of natural subtle energy emanations at any given place is unique.

Additionally, imperceptibly slow plate movements, together with rapid, localised, cataclysmic events, will also result in changes over time to the subtle radiations of any given place.'

Energy emanations

'I feel it is necessary at this stage to explain further what I mean when I refer to 'energy emanations'.

As I said earlier, I believe that the word "energy" is misleading as there is no evidence that the subtle radiations that we dowse contain any energy that is recognizable within the electromagnetic spectrum. However the term energy is so ingrained in the vocabulary of dowsers that it would be confusing at this stage to use something else. You may have noted that many times I have used the word 'radiations' as I feel that it is more accurate. No matter which is the best descriptive term to use, the fabric of subtle energies can be divided into two components.

Firstly, there is the network of earth energy lines and grids, which we covered in detail in the first part of this book. These will vary according to local circumstances. This network can be likened to the electrical wiring in a house, or the fibre-optic cables that carry our broadband signals - or possibly the electromagnetic carrier waves that distribute radio signals through space.

In the case of the subtle energy network, it would appear not to be electromagnetic as such. However, in my opinion, it does have the capacity to transport basic parcels of information - information of a timeless nature, which goes back to the beginning of time, and played a large part in the creation of the structure of the universe that we have today.

Secondly, I have carried out experiments to demonstrate the changes in non-detrimental energy emanating from an object of modest mass, such as a stone. By moving the object to a new location, I have been able to observe the changes in its energy display. Importantly, it was not only the object that was moved that was affected, but also all of the other objects in the vicinity as well. Sometimes the changes are slight, but in other circumstances they are considerable.

It is quite easy to demonstrate the impact of detrimental energy on the neurological system (by muscle testing, see Appendix A). However, it is not possible to use the same simple procedure with other types of radiation - of which there is a much greater amount. It is, however, reasonable to suggest that it, too, will have an impact on the energetic environment one way or another - and that such changes in radiation will either improve or interfere with the transference of information to, from or within, whatever life forms exist in its vicinity.

As stated above, the form and nature of the subtle radiation in any given location is unique to that location. Therefore, the amount of inter-ference or enhancement in the transfer of information within a life form, whether animal or vegetable, at any place would also be likely to be unique.'

The impact on the origins of life

'Assuming this to be the case, let us look at the potential impact on the evolutionary process.

If life began on earth in a pond of 'prebiotic soup' and gradually spread then, as life extended outwards, it would be influenced by the changing circumstances it encountered. That, in turn, might assist in bringing about changes in the life form itself. It may not be enough, in itself, to bring about the changes in genetic make up that are necessary to produce a new and different species - but it could perhaps facilitate the refining and improving of a species, which could allow that species to adapt to gradually changing circumstances.

However, if we consider panspermia - the possibility of the continuous seeding of the earth from space - then the impact of local topography and the subsequent unique earth energy conditions may lead to new species developing from different seeds. We are what we eat (or absorb), and we reap what we sow.

My dowsing indicates that information is attached to the amino acids necessary to foster life at these levels. What that information contains is likely to be determined by the original clustering, and be further tempered - and censored - by the subtle radiations present at any one location. This increases the chances of different species appearing. It could possibly reduce the number of attempts necessary for a species to overcome new problems and it would certainly help to make the maths add up.

New evidence would suggest that certain parasites not only have the ability to respond quickly to changing circumstances, but can also pre-empt an event and be ready to take action. An example of this is the Trypanosome, a small eukaryotic parasite in Africa that causes sleeping sickness in humans and some animals. The animal responds by producing special protein molecules - antibodies that bind to the coat of the parasite and stop its growth. However, when the antibodies have almost gained control, parasites with a different coat make their appearance. When the new antibodies are produced, the second wave of parasites disappears, and yet another kind emerges, with coat molecules different from the first two.

The study of this phenomenon has uncovered amazing organisation in the parasite's DNA. Radioactive probes have revealed that at least a hundred genes are devoted to coat variation - each gene specifying one kind of coat molecule - yet only one is active at any given time.

One possible conclusion that could be drawn from this evidence is that there is freely available information within the environment; that this information can be evaluated and addressed in a less-than-random fashion, and that suitable changes can be made or a line of action taken to cope with the site-specific conditions.

This would provide a more comprehensive explanation for the diversity of life that we find throughout the earth than the current neo-Darwinian model.'

Growing out of it

One last connection between evolution and earth energy is the way that certain types of organism cope with detrimental energy. We assume that just because detrimental energy is generally harmful to humans - and that is why we call it detrimental - that it is also harmful to other earth-bound animals. However, Billy's visual dowsing has unearthed some surprising evidence to the contrary.

Again, visual dowsing provides us with information here that would not be readily available to even the most intrepid conventional researcher.

'For some while, people have been saying that cats seem to be attracted to energy that would be detrimental to humans. Dowsers have remarked that quite often they are found sitting directly over an upshoot of detrimental energy.

Our cats like to sit on the window sill in the lobby, by the back door. One day I saw that there was a little stream of detrimental energy rising up through the sill where the cats were in the habit of sitting. The next time that I saw them seated there I had a look to see what was happening. They were not avoiding the rising spout of energy in any way, but sitting right on it. However, when I looked a bit closer, I found that the energy line split just below the cats, went all around them and joined up again above their heads. The cats were sitting in a nice little cocoon of good energy - and were not absorbing, or being disturbed by, the detrimental energy at all. It was the same situation as I had observed with a few people who did not respond to muscle testing as described on page 168.

I think this was the cats throwing out their own protection - but I don't think they went through any kind of a ritual to do so! It is something that has been acquired through the evolutionary process.

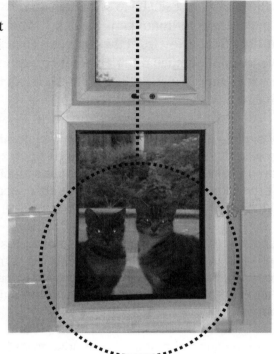

Line of detrimental energy diverted around

As mentioned in the section relating to detrimental energy, I would estimate that the ability of humans to be immune to detrimental energy could be up to 1% of the population. I put it down to the length of time that we have been evolving. If a generation has a span of, say, 20 years, that means we only have about 50 chances in 1,000 years to evolve and change. If I am correct in asserting that detrimental energy only started to become a real problem with the advent of settled agriculture, the clearing of rocks from fields and the felling of trees in large numbers - say, about 10,000 years ago, then we have only had around 500 evolutionary cycles since that time. This is nothing compared with the cat, which can breed within a year of birth, and would therefore have had about 10,000 opportunities to change in that same time. When you look at more basic life forms with a life cycle of a couple of days, then the mathematics speaks for itself. They have had many millions of opportunities to evolve. Many of these very basic life forms seem to be immune to the effect of detrimental energy - and they may even thrive on it.

As the energy just seems to separate naturally around them, their impact on the energy environment is minimal. They are just keeping the harmful effect away from themselves. To achieve the same effect, we have to employ much more elaborate procedures, which has an effect on the wider energy matrix that might even extend all the way across the universe.'

This may explain why not everyone seems to be affected by detrimental energy to the same extent. On the one hand, studies have suggested that some types of illness can be linked to the location of houses, such as in those dwellings directly under overhead power lines. However, it also seems that other people, living in similar places, are quite unaffected by their presence.

Billy's discovery that cats have a special power may add some credibility to the belief, long-held in some quarters, that cats have mystical powers. Cats are considered to be lucky, to have nine lives and to be associated with witches. Maybe there is more than a little fire behind the smoke of this particular superstition.

There are many lines of research that arise from Billy's visual dowsing work, and the concept that we may be gradually evolving a mechanism to cope with at least some of the detrimental energy we seem to be generating is yet another. It is quite possible that this could grow into a whole new field of study on its own.

Templates in the Ether

Following on from the potential impact of earth energy matrices on the evolutionary process, we finish this chapter with a short introduction to yet another possible portal that Billy's open-minded approach to dowsing has revealed.

If images can be created through natural energy emanations - with or without the help of the observer - does this mean that there are energy patterns 'out there' that could influence the form that subsequent matter, and subsequent life, might take?

'I met a computer simulation expert called John Evans at a seminar in England. John had done quite a lot of research into energy forms. He was of the opinion that the appearance of energy preceded the emergence of matter, forming a type of template in the ether. The form (the matter) only developed at a later stage of the process. His book *The Silent Sound* makes interesting reading.

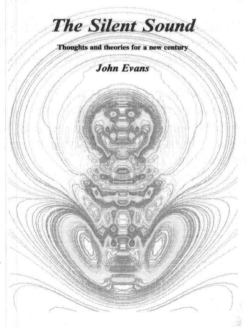

Certainly, this could apply when it comes to evolution. Where you get a lot of humanoid energy forms of one particular type, this could encourage the development of matter in a certain format. In turn, that could influence the production of life forms that conform to the underlying energy template.

Where you have an egg, there is an energy pattern that seems to be in a form similar to that of an embryo, even before the chick starts to grow. It could even be argued to some extent that the chick grows to fit the energy form that is there.

The line of reasoning would be that this is why the chick grows into a chicken and not in to something else. It may even help to explain mutations and malformations, which could be derived from damaged or incomplete energy templates. It's only an idea at this stage - but it's an interesting idea!

It would imply that the underlying energy pattern would tend to support the development of energy into matter - and subsequently into life in a certain form at a certain place. Again, we are coming back to the power and significance of information as a starting point of the whole information-energy-matter-life chain of development. I certainly feel that the information comes first - and that the energy pattern conforms in some way to the information footprint that is already there.

Every cell of our body contains the template for the whole body in all its complexity. There is a lot of medical scientific evidence to support that contention - and it seems to be how DNA causes us to be what we are.

The issue that has yet to be understood is that, if all the information is there in every cell, how does one cell know to grow to be part of a finger and another a nose . . . but I don't have all the answers . . . yet.'

This section has described some of the work that Billy has undertaken. Some of it is an extension of the application of his individual visual dowsing technique. Much of it has not appeared in print elsewhere.

Yet even while he has been at work in rural Northern Ireland, largely separated from the rest of us, others have also been working on some of these themes. It is yet another indication that ideas are being drawn out simultaneously, but quite discretely, from the information background - which is an idea we will investigate in the third part of this book.

MAKING SENSE OF

THE SERIOUSLY

SPIRITUAL

The Impact of Intent

Reading through the assembled work of Billy Gawn, it would be easy to come to the conclusion that he has little, if any, interest in the intervention of intent. While there are many facets of his life and work that do set him apart from other dowsers and researchers, a marginalisation of the value of intent really would put him in a very different camp. However, this is not the case.

Billy certainly emphasises the contribution of the physical placement of objects in changing and healing the energy of the earth above anything more esoteric. In that sense, he places himself much closer to the scientific end of the spectrum.

But there are other, more subtle, aspects to his approach:

> 'The reason why most of my focus has been on the manipulation of subtle radiations by physical means simply comes from my early interest in megalithic sites and from my attempts to understand the 'whys and wherefores' of their construction and placement.
>
> It was the accidental discovery that a small stone in my garden, which I had placed over the crossing point of two underground streams, had the ability to attract and earth detrimental radiation for some distance around it. That set me on the pathway I have travelled.
>
> I am quite aware and accept without question that subtle radiations do respond to human intent when properly focused. It is impossible to take any action without intent. However, it is also possible to take action without considering the outcome resulting from it. In that case, the intent is entirely focused on the mechanics involved in carrying out the action. I believe that in cases like that, any intent does not influence the result. Most experiments that I have done were carried out in that way, and I was not at all interested in what the result may be. It was only when the experiment was set up that I observed through dowsing any changes that had occurred and I accepted them at face value.

Therefore, I feel there are two aspects to intent. There is the intention inherent in doing something physical as described above - and there is pure intent, where we express the intent with a specific outcome firmly fixed in our mind, but do nothing physical. That is the difference between the spiritual and the non-spiritual aspects of dowsing - and that is where the debate really arises.

I have no doubt that employing intent with an outcome in mind but without physical action will certainly have an impact on the energies in an area, and possibly the desired impact as well.

It could well be that that was why the building of massive megalithic structures ceased. Prayer, in the sense that we know it today, probably was not well developed much before the time of Christ. Prior to that, prayer was not the big thing - it was more about ritual and sacrifice. Some of the aspects of the old religion that the early Christians tried to do away with were blood sacrifice, and an over-reliance on ritual. To replace it, they used supplication and prayer. It may have been a gradual realisation that you did not need to keep moving 60-ton boulders here and there, and that you could do much the same thing with prayer - if you did it properly.

Personally, I find that changing earth energies by prayer or intent does not have quite the same effect as doing it physically - and it does not last as long. Perhaps that is due to me not concentrating on the method of pure intent as I am a great believer in that practice makes perfect.

However, I feel the two methods are quite complementary and which-ever one is used is the choice of the individual concerned. If you are seeking to bring about change in any way, whether it is by pure intent or by physical means, it is better to understand the mechanics of what you are doing.

If you took a 50-ton stone and put it in a field, there are a thousand places that you could put it where it would not have any impact whatsoever on what you are trying to change. However, there could be one place where you could site it, where it would have an immense impact. Similarly, if you are attempting to have a particular outcome with intent, it is necessary to be absolutely clear as to the wording of the request to enable the outcome to be accurately targeted.

It is so important to ensure that your intent is properly expressed. Our subconscious mind takes what we say quite literally. It does not seem to be able to interpret or translate our intent very accurately, unless we spell it out clearly. It is exactly the same problem that we have with the Dowsing Question. If you are doing things with intent, you have to be absolutely clear what you have in mind.

One of the things that we were very aware of in the early days of Earth Energies Group is that just as you can do beneficial things with good intent, the opposite is also possible. Dowsing needs to be in the hands of people who are seeking to do things for the common good. Sadly, there are a lot of people about who have other motives. What is good for you or me as individuals in the short-term is not necessarily for the long-term common good.

While developing the sensitivity of the brain for dowsing purposes, through repetitive action, can open up portals to a better future, it can also open up opportunities to negative influences.

This is where the need for psychic protection comes in to play. I think the need for that protection is certainly there, but I do not think we have to ask for it on every occasion. We should always have the default protection system in place. That way, it is automatically activated when we get into sticky situations. I do not think you have to go through the ritual of setting it up every time.

I can see the reason why intuitive processes were sometimes the pre-serve of secret societies or closed guilds - and time alone will tell if dowsing is forced back down that path in time to come. The problem with all secret societies is that, over time, the inner circle of priests, priestesses or whoever, who originally knew what they were doing and why, are replaced by others who have not had any direct access to the source. The whole operation of the group just becomes a performance of ritual, without an understanding of the reasons behind it.

I feel I have demonstrated quite clearly that the effect of the placing and removing of stones, and other objects with mass, has an effect on the surrounding energy environment - with or without the intent of man. However, even then, it could be argued that once the outcome of an action is known (for example when we repeat an action such as the deliberate placement or removal of an object) then the agent is using intent - and perhaps even dowsing in an intuitive manner.

Human intent can be involved in all dowsing activity, particularly when it comes to influencing outcomes at the subatomic level. Man can, and does, have a part to play in the ongoing development of the world around us, but it is necessary to bring that part played by man down to size. The human race is a relatively new innovation. The world revolved and evolved quite successfully for millions of years before we came along.'

For Billy, the implementation of intent is real - but when it comes to making beneficial changes to the energy matrix, you can't beat plonking a huge boulder in just the right place.

However, Billy not only follows his own intuition on this issue, but he is very supportive of the studies of the practical impact of intent as described by Lynne McTaggart and others. Just as dowsing works, so intent can work too. He fully acknowledges the ability of many people to effect healing, either in person or at a distance. For Billy, the ability to use intent may be an indication that we all have a spark of the divine in us - but it's only a spark.

For many, the successful and beneficial application of intent to information gleaned through dowsing is as close to understanding the meaning of life as you are likely to get - which is especially the case for those involved in the field of health. However, as we have seen, Billy has come to this aspect of the subject through a very different route - and for him, intent is just one arrow in his quiver.

'Every hour of every day of every week there are people throughout the country with JCBs and excavators moving earth about the countryside without any intent. They are disturbing energies, sometimes detrimentally, sometimes beneficially. You just have to live with that.

The nature of the intent depends on the person involved.   The developer's intent is usually to move quantities of earth from one place to another to landscape an area. The dowser's intent is to improve the quality of the energy in that area.

One factor that causes the lack of intent or awareness to be not quite so crucial as it might otherwise be, is the distribution of the location of critical points - earthing or reversal points. While they are numerous, they are not found everywhere - and there is a reasonable chance that a developer may miss them altogether. So, with a bit of luck, you could do quite a large development, and not hit a significantly large reversal point.

Additionally, some of the reversal points only affect the few metres around, and you could effectively forget about them, unless, of course, they are under your bed!

What I would say is that when I'm carrying out that type of experiment, I don't concern myself with what the answer is going to be. I just do it; I attempt to keep my mind clear of the end result and I just accept whatever answer I find. Whether that totally removes intent or not, I do not know.

I have even found random boulders that have tumbled down a hillside in times gone by which have ended up on a spot that has removed detrimental energy for an area around it, which adds further weight to the positioning being more important than the intent.'

In terms of measuring the impact of intent on earth energy systems, I could refer you to the work carried out by Hamish Miller and myself at the Merrivale complex, on Dartmoor in Devon in recent years - and indeed any number of other well-documented examples. However, given Billy's upbringing, perhaps we should conclude this chapter with a brief summary of a piece of work carried out by Earth Energies Group member, Jan Spence, which Billy enthusiastically included in a 1999 edition of Earth Energy Matters.

A survey was carried out daily at, or as near as possible to 9am each morning, on two energy lines which ran through the grounds of Fishbourne Church in Sussex. This meant that the Sunday dowsing check took place after the first of three services.

The decision to carry out a daily check was as a result of having previously discovered a big variation in the width of the mean energy line running eastward from the church when dowsed at irregular intervals. I used a Y rod and asked for the near and far edge of each line before crossing it. The results showed that the width of the line increased, apparently as a consequence of the weekend service, but diminished as the week goes on - unless a funeral or wedding is held. It clearly shows that there was an interaction between earth energy lines and human activity, especially of a spiritual nature.

'I would rate this as a first class example as to how a survey should be carried out. It demonstrates dedication, and therefore the results are significant and worthy of consideration - WAG *Editor.*'

And Jan's work again, included in Billy's Earth Energy Matters magazine in 2001 - this time at St David's Cathedral in Wales:

Walking around the cathedral . . . revealed that three main lines of dowsable energy ran through the building from east to west. Another set of three lines ran from north to south. The lines were first dowsed on Friday 15th May 1998, again on Monday 18th and every day after that for two weeks, except for Saturday 23rd.

The first week was an ordinary one for the cathedral, in that most religious activity took place on the Sunday. During the second week there was a musical festival, with daytime rehearsals and evening performances, as well as the usual services. The area at the font was also dowsed to determine the quality and strength of the energy.

My previous survey at Fishbourne Church showed that the width of the lines increased in accordance with the amount of worship. There was an immediate increase due to the Sunday services and a steady decline through the following week unless there was a baptism, wedding or funeral.

This trend is consistent with what was found during the first week at St David's, but was reversed in the second week with the increased activity of the musical festival.

This clearly demonstrates that human activity of a religious and joyful nature has an effect on the size, strength and quality of earth energy lines.

In conclusion, for Billy, intent works, but it's not the whole story. The marriage of mind and matter is a dedicated partnership.

Consciousness, Dowsing and
the Red Socks Syndrome

As we have seen right through this book, dowsing is at - and perhaps a little beyond - the leading edge of 21st century scientific and philosophical research. With any concept like this, which is still just over the horizon of the current scientific paradigm, yet has an abundance of supporting evidence, there is a well-worn model for the process of acceptance.

Firstly, the existing establishment, feeling threatened by a new idea that might sweep away a lifetime of personal investment and development, denies that the new idea exists at all. With so many practitioners around the world, using dowsing in so many varied ways and with such a high level of success, this stance is gradually becoming increasingly untenable.

The second phase is to ridicule the idea - and to attempt to disprove the concept, by fair means or foul. We are moving through this part of the model at the moment. With more new researchers finding interesting and novel aspects to dowsing, this is also starting to make the ill-informed hecklers look a bit ridiculous themselves.

The third stage is to reach the point of accepting, however grudgingly, that the emerging research is producing interesting results, but then to ask the killer question - OK, how does it work, then?

Off-the-wall ideas such as gravity, electricity and heavier-than-air flight have made their way steadily through this maze, and are now so firmly established that it's difficult now to imagine how previous generations could have considered them to be anything but obvious.

Relativity and quantum physics moved through the process of acceptance in the last century, but the best brains on the planet are still trying to get to grips with how much our view of the reality we know and love will have to change to accommodate them.

As dowsing has developed as a professional modern skill, and has moved away from its previous niche as an ancient and anachronistic oddity, it, too, has entered the third phase. Certainly, there are still plenty of determined dowsing denyers - and any number ready to pour scorn on the use of a couple of bits of bent wire to reveal the wonders of the universe - but this is all starting to seem a bit old-hat.

Dowsing is part of an incoming tide - one that is going to require a rewriting of the textbook (or should that be e-textbook?).

The Newtonian model doesn't accommodate the phenomenon. In the current conceptual matrix, dowsing shouldn't work. Standing behind the two-way mirror, the spiritual worldview uses language that fails to resonate with modern rationalist thought. It has become so hidebound with ancient texts and dogmatic practices, that any assistance it could provide in explaining the inexplicable is lost in the undergrowth.

However, Einstein (who himself is on record as regarding dowsing as a very matter-of-fact process) explained that a problem cannot be solved using the same building blocks that brought it about. To get an appreciation of what lies at the heart of the conundrum, it is necessary to 'think outside of the box' - indeed, to realise that there is no box.

To date, even those who are immersed in the world of dowsing have tried to make sense of it in terms of physics, chemistry and biology. Yet, it is now apparent that the next level of understanding lies beyond the physical world altogether.

Dowsing clearly has a sort of physical manifestation, and therefore some sort a physical explanation - but the rapidly evolving field of quantum physics is leading both science and spirituality towards the need to comprehend consciousness.

Whilst the most prominent thinkers in the land are using some of the best-equipped laboratories to tease out the issues, the thinking-person's tractor driver has been on the case for some time:

To be, or not to be?

'Consciousness is poorly defined and little understood. The more it has been studied, the clearer it has become that it is a very complex subject. The current view is that consciousness is considered to be a function of the mind; the mind being directed and controlled by the brain - and therefore substantially under the control of the individual. Therefore, the conscious state of every person is an individual experience - and there is no trespass of one individual's consciousness upon another's. Because of this individualism, no two minds sense the same picture and we all see the world from our own unique perspective.

However, there is a standardisation of experience through the learning processes that we all go through. We are taught, that things are as they are, and for us that is the way that it will remain, unless we determine it differently for ourselves. We recognise colours because we are taught at an early age that red is red and green is green. There is no way to prove that the hue that I see is identical to the hue that others see.

Most of what we understand within our conscious state is determined by how others have described their experiences. These, in turn, were moulded by the experiences of their forebears. As humans, we look upon ourselves as the supreme species; we assume that all other species are less intelligent, and therefore experience consciousness at a much lower level. However, when we come to fully examine the available information, this assumption is open to doubt.

Generally, those involved in the study of psychoanalysis only acknowledge two states within human consciousness, namely the fully conscious state and the unconscious state.

The fully conscious state can vary in degree from being very aware to being vaguely aware of our surroundings. Beyond the conscious state most now acknowledge the existence of the subconscious, which operates at a subliminal level mainly without our overt knowledge. The heightened or super-conscious states, which connect us to our spiritual dimension, and are usually entered into through an intermediary, are currently only acknowledged by a minority of researchers. There are no clearly defined boundaries between these states. An individual may never experience some of them - and even if they do, they may not acknowledge that experience.

The term subconscious is looked upon as a layperson's term and has been condemned by many psychoanalysts. To quote Sigmund Freud:

"If someone talks of sub-consciousness, I cannot tell whether he means the term topographically, to indicate something lying in the mind beneath consciousness - or qualitatively, to indicate another consciousness, a subterranean one, as it were. He is probably not clear about any of it. The only trustworthy antithesis is between conscious and unconscious."

Sigmund Freud

The term subconscious is therefore often treated with suspicion as being a New Age invention. This generally makes it a taboo subject amongst those involved in the mainstream of medical science. However, there are some who do accept the possibility that our consciousness is not confined to our brain; and that the mind, where consciousness is believed to exist, has no physical location. It could be thought of as being a little bit like the concept of 'cloud computing'.

Some consider that, through the subconscious, we can connect with what Carl Jung termed the 'Collective Unconscious' - the sum of all the conscious states that have ever existed. This leads on to the bold hypothesis that consciousness, like the all-pervading information matrix, exists universally - and it is not the prerogative of the human race.

Carl Jung

This raises a somewhat thorny issue. If one accepts that consciousness does exist ethereally throughout the cosmos, because consciousness and intelligence go hand in hand, it throws a very large spanner into the works of the theoretical backbone of many scientific disciplines. It shakes a bedrock assumption, namely that 'creation' has arrived at where it is today by chance alone - and that it has not been given a guiding hand, even though each culture might describe or visualise such assistance. Such virtual earthquakes are not welcomed.

In some quarters, such hypotheses are considered to be Pseudo-science, which is the polite way of casting all who express slightly offbeat opinions into the 'loony bin' of science.

Worse still, mainstream thought will give little or no consideration to any other suggestions or ideas that such proponents may make from that time onward. Understandably, this is usually sufficient to make most professionals with any ambition within the scientific fraternity, carefully avoid the debate altogether - at least in public.'

Intelligent plants?

'One who did step over the line was Cleve Backster (born 1924). He is best known for his experiments with bio-communication in plant and animal cells using a polygraph machine which he undertook in the 1960s. This work led him to develop the theory of primary perception. Backster began his career as an Interrogation Specialist with the CIA, and went on to become the highly respected Chairman of the Research and Instrument Committee of the Academy for Scientific Interrogation.

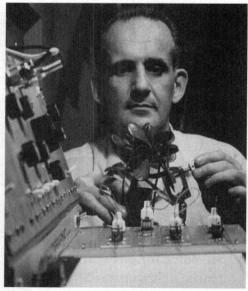

Cleve Backster working on one of his experiments

His life changed course in the 1960s, when he reported observing that a polygraph attached to a plant leaf registered a change in electrical resistance when the plant was harmed or even threatened with harm. This drew him to postulate that plants could potentially perceive human intentions. As Backster investigated further, he also reported that other human thoughts and emotions caused reactions in plants - and that these could also be recorded by a polygraph. He termed the plants' sensitivity to thoughts 'primary perception', and published his findings in the International Journal of Parapsychology. The article resulted in strong criticism of his research methods. However, other researchers became interested in Backster's work, and he later expanded his experimental range to test for primary perception in other life forms, such as yoghurt bacteria, and human cells.

In his book *The Secret Life of Your Cells,* Cleve Backster, made the following remarkable statement:

"Your plants know what you are thinking. The cells of your body, even when removed and observed at a distance away, know what you are thinking. The cells of your brain, with which you think, know more than you think they do. And if other primary perception phenomena that have been studied under laboratory conditions for twenty years prove out, the world may never be the same".

What Backster was really demonstrating was the existence of not just a primary perception at the plant cell level, but of a primary intelligence at the plant cell level. What this implies is that any living cells have the ability to gather information, to process it and to take considered action on the strength of it - in much the same manner as the amalgam of cells we call humans.

The website of the Alaska Science Forum carried an article by Larry Gedney in 1986 called *Do Trees Communicate for Mutual Defence*? The article was provided as a public service by the Geophysical Institute, University of Alaska, Fairbanks - in cooperation with the UAF research community. Larry Gedney was a seismologist at the Institute and the following is an extract from this article:

245

"According to an article by Jeanne McDermott in the December 1984 issue of Smithsonian Magazine, researchers have found that trees can actively defend themselves against serious insect attacks, even to the point of communicating a warning to other trees in the vicinity.

This startling suggestion was first made in the spring of 1979 by chemist and zoologist Davey Rhoades, who was working at a field site outside Seattle. Rhoades took two groups of willow trees, infested one with caterpillars, and left the other alone as a control. Two weeks later, he plucked leaves from the trees, which had been infested and fed them to caterpillars in the laboratory. He found that these caterpillars grew quite slowly. The surprising finding was that a diet of leaves from the non-attacked control trees nearby also caused the caterpillars to grow slowly.

Both groups of trees had apparently flooded their leaves with an unsavoury chemical that discouraged the insects' growth. Rhoades concluded that the attacked trees had slipped the control group a danger signal, and that this must have been done by releasing a chemical into the air."

More recently, Victoria Gill, a science reporter with BBC News posted an article on 14th July 2010 entitled *Plants Can Think and Remember*. She stated in that report:

"Plants are able to "remember" and "react" to information contained in light - according to researchers."

Scientists from the Warsaw University of Life Sciences in Poland, have shown that plants transmit information about light intensity and light quality from leaf to leaf, in a very similar way to our own nervous systems. These electro-chemical signals are carried by cells in the flora that act as the 'nerves' of the plants.

They recorded how light shone on to one leaf caused the whole plant to respond. Furthermore, the response, which took the form of light-induced chemical reactions in the leaves, continued to have an effect even if the plant was later placed in the dark. They concluded that the plant appeared to 'remember' the information encoded in the light.

Professor Stanislaw Karpinski, who led this research, presented the findings at the annual meeting of the Society for Experimental Biology in Prague, Czech Republic:

"We shone the light only on the bottom of the plant and we observed changes in the upper part. The changes proceeded even when the light was off. This was a complete surprise."

In a previous experiment, Professor Karpinski had found that chemical signals could be passed throughout whole plants - allowing them to respond to, and to survive, changes and stresses in their environment. But in this new study, he and his colleagues discovered that when light stimulated a chemical reaction in one leaf cell, this caused a cascade of events, which was immediately signalled to the rest of the plant via a 'bundle sheath cell'.

Stanislaw Karpinski

The scientists measured the electrical signals from these cells, which are present in every leaf. They likened the discovery to the finding of the plant's 'nervous system'.

Even more strangely, Professor Karpinski found that the responses of the plants changed depending on the colour of the light that was being shone on them:

"Plants perform a sort of biological light computation, using information contained in the light to immunise themselves against diseases. There were characteristic changes for red, blue and white light."

He suspected that the plants might use the information encoded in the light to stimulate protective chemical reactions, so they examined this more closely by looking at the effect of different colours of light on the plants' immunity to disease:

"When we shone the light on the plant for one hour and then infected it with a virus or with bacteria 24 hours after that light exposure, it resisted the infection, but when we infected the plant before shining the light, it could not build up resistance. So, the plant has a specific memory for the light which builds its immunity against pathogens, and it can adjust to varying light conditions."

He said that plants used information encrypted in the light to immunise themselves against seasonal pathogens:

"Every day or week of the season has… a characteristic light quality, so the plants perform a sort of biological light computation, using information contained in the light to immunise themselves against diseases that are prevalent during that season."

Professor Christine Foyer, a plant scientist from the University of Leeds, said that the study 'took our thinking one step forward', when speaking on BBC News:

"Plants have to survive stresses, such as drought or cold, and live through it and keep growing. This requires an appraisal of the situation and an appropriate response - that's a form of intelligence."

A Morphic Field?

'Another researcher to step over the line is Rupert Sheldrake. He is an English biochemist and plant physiologist, who has proposed an un-orthodox account of morphogenesis as part of his research into para-psychology. His work has led him to propose the theory of morphic resonance, and covers topics such as animal and plant development and behaviour, memory, telepathy, perception and cognition in general. Sheldrake's ideas have often met with a predictably hostile reception from some scientists.

Sheldrake proposes that there is a field within and around a living entity, which organises its characteristic structure and pattern of activity. He terms this phenomenon 'The Morphic Field'.

According to this concept, the morphic field underlies the formation and behaviour of living entities and can be set up by the repetition of similar acts or thoughts. This has echoes of our previous discussion on the use of intent and even the establishment of visual leys. The hypothesis is that a

Rupert Sheldrake

particular form belonging to a certain group, which has already established its (collective) morphic field, will tune into that field. The particular form will read the collective information through the process of morphic resonance, using it to guide its own development. This development of the particular form will then provide, again through morphic resonance, a feedback to the morphic field of that group - thus strengthening it with its own experience and resulting in new inform- ation being added. Sheldrake regards the morphic fields as a universal database for both living organisms and abstract, mental forms.

Sheldrake's theory gained acceptance in some quarters, as it fits in well with the idea of the collective unconscious, proposed by renowned psychiatrist Carl Jung.

Sheldrake's work is also complementary to the concept of akashic records, a term used by the writers of the Indian Vedas to describe the library or, more accurately, the database of all human experiences and memories, as recorded by their physical lifetime.

It is possible that these can be related to morphic fields, since one's past is a mental form, which consists of thoughts as simpler mental forms (all processed by the same brain). A group of similar or related mental forms also have their associated morphic field. In Sheldrake's view, these memory traces are "non-local" - not located in the brain.

While Sheldrake's concept has gained little support in the mainstream scientific community, this is largely because the idea is currently unfalsifiable (is currently impossible to determine one way or the other) and is therefore outside of the scope of scientific experiment.'

Memory in water?

'Dr Jacques Benveniste (1935 - 2004) was in the vanguard of scientific research into the ability of water to retain 'memory', and more recently, with what he termed 'digital biology'. Benveniste was at the centre of a major international controversy in 1988, when he published a paper, in the prestigious scientific journal *Nature*, which seemed to support the concept of homeopathy.

Dr Jacques Benveniste

Biologists were puzzled by Benveniste's experimental results. He demonstrated that molecules of water, devoid of molecules of the original antibody with which they had been in contact, remained in the homeopathic solution. Benveniste concluded that the configuration of the molecules in water was biologically active; a journalist coined the term 'water memory' for this hypothesis.

Much later, Benveniste also asserted that this memory could be digitised, transmitted via the internet or via CD, and reinserted into another sample of water, which would then contain the same active qualities as the first sample.

As a condition of publication, *Nature* asked for the results to be replicated by independent laboratories. The controversial paper, published in *Nature,* was eventually co-authored by four laboratories worldwide - in Canada, Italy, Israel, and in France.

After the article was published, a follow-up investigation was set up by a team including physicist and *Nature* editor John Maddox, illusionist and well-known sceptic James Randi and fraud expert, Walter Stewart. The team pored over the laboratory's records, and oversaw seven attempts to replicate Benveniste's study. Three of the first four attempts turned out somewhat favourable to Benveniste; however the *Nature* team was not satisfied with the rigor of the methodology. Benveniste invited them to design a double blind procedure, which they did, and conducted three more experiments. Before fully revealing the results, the team asked if there were any complaints about the procedure, but none were raised. These stricter procedures turned out negative for Benveniste. One significant difference with the latter process was that to record the procedure, equipment was used that produced high electromagnetic fields, which could have invaded the area in which the tests were carried out. The possibility that this distorted the results was not considered.

The purpose of scientific experiment is to carry out planned experiments, using well-defined criteria, to test the validity of a hypothesis. If it cannot be demonstrated, then it is usually discarded. However, if it can be shown to stand up when the experiment is repeated, ad nauseam, then it can be supported. However, even if a hypothesis has not been substantiated in the first instance, it is sometimes wise to revisit the scene.

Further experiments were carried out into Benveniste's theories by a team led by Professor Madeline Ennis, Professor of Immunopharmacology BSc, PhD, of Queens University, Belfast, and an article, published in *Inflammation Research* in 2004, brought new media attention to the issue.

Following up on a study they had published in 1999 in the same journal, the researchers concluded that an effect did exist. Some of the researchers had not been involved in homeopathic research before, while others had, such as former Benveniste collaborator Philippe Belon, Research Director at the homeopathic company Boiron. It was Madeline Ennis who received the most attention in the media. Ennis led the activities at the British lab, with other labs in Europe running a variation of Benveniste's water memory experiments. Ennis states that she began the research as a sceptic, but concluded that:

Madeline Ennis

" *The results compel me to suspend my disbelief and start searching for rational explanations for our findings.* "

Can you do that again, please?

'One of the problems Cleve Backster and others have found has been the difficulty in replicating results. While there have been some successfully replicated experiments, other teams who looked for consistent repeatability failed miserably. This has kept Backster's work in the shady side of scientific research.

However, what Backster discovered early in the experimental process was that plants and cells under test appeared to be able to differentiate between real situations and contrived situations such as structured experiments. In other words, the plant or animal organisms under test displayed a degree of intelligence and considered it unnecessary to react in a contrived situation. To get the subject to respond, Backster and others who achieved positive results, had to build in a measure of surprise into their actions - such that the organism had no advance knowledge of what was about to happen.

Clearly, this is an even more difficult concept to accept, as it implies capabilities in plant samples and single cells that are very similar to the type of intelligence displayed by humans - even though the plant doesn't have a brain, as such. If we grasp the nettle, and we accept the findings at face value, this lends credence to the idea that the mind is independent of - and outside of - the brain. A brain would not then be a pre-requisite for some aspects of communication, information processing and intelligence. <u>If communication, and the gathering and processing of information, is a function carried out in the field of consciousness, rather than just being confined to the individual brain, then the presence of a universal consciousness becomes a credible reality.</u>'

The nature of consciousness

Consciousness has troubled scientists and philosophers alike since the dawn of reason. Is it a mental state, another dimension, the presence of the divine or the real human condition hiding behind the façade of matter? Everyone from the ancient Greeks to the new age community has had a swing at explaining what it could be.

As ever, Billy not only has his own ideas, but underpins them with a scrupulously scientific approach:

'I feel that consciousness may also be a type of subtle energy, although a lot more research work needs to be undertaken in that particular field.

Where I feel the current scientific paradigm is incomplete is that it leaves out the input of packages of information. I think they are only infinitesimal vibrations in the ether, if we can call it that, and they are all vibrating at different 'rates'. What we understand as reality depends on how all this information comes together.

How that information comes together determines the shape and form of energy, matter and life. That, in turn, depends on how and <u>why</u> the little packages of information combine. Only at quite an advanced stage of development does the combination of the packages of information enable something more complex - something that we can understand, let alone detect, to evolve in a particular way.

I feel scientific research should be directed to investigating this possibility. However, if they do that, they could end up bringing God, or at least the intelligent universe, back into the equation - which would be an unwelcome concept in some quarters!

An understanding of the nature of consciousness is one of the biggest missing strands of science. It's something that's been totally ignored up to now. Because it doesn't seem to have a mass, an electrical charge or a monetary value, it doesn't seem to exist. It's a bit like Einstein throwing out the ether, because he didn't need it in his equations.

At the end of the day, there's no such thing as nothing. You can get to a level where there are things that we can't observe, but that's not the same as confirming that they don't exist.'

Consciousness clearly exists; it has some physical content - and if energy and consciousness can interact, they must in some form be on the same spectrum. If they were present in the same place, but were totally unalike in form, they wouldn't interact. Therefore, I feel that consciousness must be part of the same holistic process as the environment that surrounds us, and of which we are a part.

The nature of reality

'To gain a little clarity in an increasingly murky pool, we need to widen the discussion to take a brief look at reality itself.

Just what do we mean by reality - and are there any absolute truths? These are two fundamental questions that have come to the fore with the advent of quantum physics in the new century.

They were given even more relevance by the seemingly absurd proposition by the renowned, American born physicist David Bohm (1917-1992), of the University of London, that there is no such thing as reality - and that what we observe around us is nothing but a gigantic phantasm, an illusion. While Buddhism and other eastern philosophies have considered this assertion to be blindingly obvious for millennia, it is still shocking to hear it espoused, in the cold light of the lecture theatre, by a leading physicist.

David Bohm

To add weight to this hypothesis, Alain Aspect and his team from the University of Paris discovered that, under certain circumstances, sub-atomic particles such as electrons appear to be able to communicate instantaneously with each other - regardless of the distance separating them. It doesn't seem to matter whether they are 10 feet or 10 billion miles apart - somehow each particle always seems to know what the other one is doing. There is, of course, a serious problem with this remarkable feat - it appears to violate Albert Einstein's long-held tenet that no means of communication can travel faster than the speed of light. But if the information was available to both particles from a common source . . .

In the age of Sir Isaac Newton and his colleagues, reality started and ended with material objects. Between them was just empty space. If we could not touch it, feel it, smell it, see it or hear it, then it did not exist.

The wind of change in the perception of reality began with the work of Max Planck and those that followed him. In 1874, Planck (1858-1947) was advised against taking up a career in physics by his Munich physics professor, Philipp von Jolly, who felt that "in this field, almost everything is already discovered, and all that remains is to fill a few holes". He was to later to discover that this was a very long way from the truth.

Planck was not interested in experimental physics, and instead concentrated on trying to understand the known fundamentals of the field. Through his work came the birth of quantum physics - with all the uncertainties that it has uncovered. Einstein followed on to devise the theory of relativity, which demonstrated that there are very few absolutes - and showed that even time and length altered according to circumstances dictated by speed. The only thing that Einstein considered to be constant was the speed of light. Today, even this is thought to be changeable under certain extreme conditions.

At the end of the 1920s Bohr, Heisenberg and Pauli worked out the Copenhagen interpretation of quantum mechanics. However, it was rejected by Planck, as well as by Schrödinger, Laue, and Einstein. Heisenberg has probably had the most impact on our changed perception of reality through his work on the 'Uncertainty Principle'. He postulated that it is impossible to know both the exact position, and the exact velocity of an object, at the same time.

In practical terms, the effect of the Uncertainty Principle is minute, and consequently it is

Niels Bohr

only noticeable on a subatomic scale. But at the subatomic level, <u>Bohr, and others, demonstrated that the observer affects the object observed</u>. This breakthrough resulted from a series of experiments based on Young's 'Double Slit Experiment'. Young first carried out this experiment in the early 1800's. It was designed to demonstrate that light was a wave and not a particle. This had profound implications for emerging science, in that this conclusion prevailed for most of the nineteenth century.

Young's work was designed to determine that if light exists as a series of individual particles, the intensity of light beams passing through two slits in a metal plate will be the sum of the intensity from the individual slits. However, if light exists as waves, then the light waves will interfere with one another under the principle of superposition - creating bands of light (constructive interference) and dark (destructive interference). Each time the experiment was repeated, it produced bands of interference - forcing Young to the conclusion that light must propagate as a wave. However, things are never that simple.

The experiment was performed again at a later date, after the death of Planck. By then, the concept of quantum physics had emerged, which considered that light was not a continuous wave, but a rapid series of very small parcels, called quanta.

These experiments were subsequently refined, using ever-improving scientific technology, to the extent that it became possible to produce a light source that was set up in such a manner that it could emit just one photon at a time - a photon then being considered to be an elementary particle. The outcome of the experiment matched Young's version identically - with alternating light and dark bands, seemingly resulting from wave interference. In theory, this should not have happened, as the photons were being emitted individually. Interference can only occur as the result of a collision of elementary particles, so there was no opportunity for wave interference to take place. However, the resulting image on the sensitive film showed that collision must indeed have occurred. The only rational hypothesis that would allow this phenomenon to occur was that light could behave with the characteristics of both a wave and a particle - and that it could change, in some way, from one form to the other.

Scientists were keen to know when and how the transformation from a photon to a wave took place - and they set up experiments through which they could observe the occurrence using a detector. The results were even more confusing. With the detector in place, the bands of interference disappeared - the photon behaved as a particle. From this surprising result, it had eventually to be concluded that the very act of observation had changed the outcome of the process. <u>In other words, the input of the observer had affected the outcome of the experiment</u>.

Another mystery that arose from these experiments was that at times both waves and photons disappeared completely, and then reappeared unpredictably somewhere else.

Over the years, the experiment has been conducted in a number of different ways. In 1961, Claus Jonsson performed the experiment again, but this time using electrons. The results conformed with Young's original particle behaviour, creating interference patterns on the observation screen.

The experiment has continued to be performed using photons, electrons, and atoms. Each time the same result ensues - something about the measurement of the position of the particle at the slit eliminates the wave behaviour. Many theories exist to explain why this should be the case, but so far much of it is still conjecture.

The notion of the observer becoming a part of the observed system was fundamentally new in physics. In quantum physics, the observer is no longer external and neutral, but through the act of measurement they become an integral part of observed reality. This marks the end of the neutrality of the experimenter. If, in an exact science such as physics, the outcome of an experiment depends in some small part on the view of the observer, then what does this imply for other fields of human knowledge?

It would seem that in any field of science, there are different interpretations - and often several different interpretations - of the same phenomena. Quite frequently, these interpretations conflict with each other. Does this mean that ultimate truth is unknowable? Or does it mean that there are as many answers as there are observers - and that all have equal value as far as truth is concerned?'

And so, back to dowsing

'However, I believe that we can learn a lot about this apparent contradiction from dowsing, and from the uncertainties that it often throws up - especially from the multitude of inconsistent results that dowsers achieve.

In this context, I would refer the reader to the section on page 270, entitled 'Red Socks Syndrome'. A very brief summary of this section is that I believe we are all restricted in our ability to see beyond the far horizon by barriers that we place around ourselves. Some of these barriers have been constructed by others, through assumptions that they have made in the past, and we have allowed these assumptions to be accepted as fact. I feel that similar conceptual restrictions exist in the field of science, in that certain tenets are considered to be absolute.

As with most seemingly insoluble problems, the answer can be decep-tively simple. The assumption that a photon is an elementary particle of light is, I believe, to be at the root of the problem. The use of the word 'elementary' implies that it is not possible to break it down into smaller parts.

However, if I am correct in that the behaviour of earth energies is similar to what is being observed by quantum physicists; then we may be well on the way to an understanding of the apparent contradiction. When I have disassembled energy lines, I have found that they can be reduced down into two basic forms (as discussed in pages 153). The type 1 form can display itself as anything from a straight line to a single dot, or any other transitional manifestation, including a wave. The form that is displayed at any given time is totally dependent on local circumstance.

If I am also correct in saying that Dark Matter is unassembled matter, and that matter - as recognised by physicists - is several stages up the ladder of reconstruction, then a photon or electron is not an elemental particle at all, but an intermediate component on the energy/matter spectrum. If subtle energy lines and basic matter behave in a similar fashion, as I feel they do, then a photon or an electron would be a group of tightly wound up wave forms. Changing circumstances could cause them to unwind, and possibly to break down into smaller components.

If I am correct on a third count, in that matter displays both fractal and holographic tendencies, then the smaller components would reflect all of the characteristics of the larger unit.

If the Double Slit Experiment is carried out with that possibility in mind, much of the mystery evaporates.

If the particle remains intact - i.e. it is tightly wound - then it will only go through one slot. As there is no other particle with which it could collide, there will be no interference pattern.

However, if the particle is made to unwind into a wave form, before it collides with the slotted plate, then it would be more fragile and it could be broken up into several smaller parts. Those smaller parts would retain the characteristics of the original whole particle. Each of them would have an equal opportunity of passing through either of the two slots, and may possibly collide. In the process of colliding, interference patterns would be formed.

If the disintegration of the wave form was complete then the component parts, as they pass through the slots, would become unobservable as they briefly go beyond the electromagnetic spectrum. Because of their continued chaotic movement for a short period after passing through the slots, some would re-assemble themselves and revert back into an observable state. I do not believe that it is necessary to invent parallel universes to explain the mysteries of the one that we frequent.

The phenomenon of the observer affecting the result is certainly not new in the field of dowsing. It is, however, not fully taken into consideration - as I discuss in more detail elsewhere.

If we accept the possibility of the existence of a universal consciousness - and that it is possible to merge our own conscious state into that of universal consciousness - then the practice of dowsing becomes a highly credible means of bridging the gap between the two.

I am aware of at least a few researchers in the field of quantum physics who are starting to indicate that even if dowsing didn't already exist, then the predictions of the emerging worldview are that it ought to be possible! So, it seems that in some respects the ancient art of dowsing is already producing more tangible results than some of the theoretical work undertaken by the physicists!'

Dowsing in historical times

'Most of this book has focused on earth energy dowsing, as this is the area of the subject that I have spent much of my life researching. As we have seen, this is a relatively recent strand of the discipline. However, the art or practice of dowsing is on record as having been used in one form or another for hundreds, if not thousands, of years.

In the middle ages, dowsing (or divining, as it was more commonly called) was employed in the pursuit of minerals and underground water. In 1556, Georgius Agricola published his work 'De Re Metallica' which contains a woodcut clearly showing dowsing activity taking place. One dowser is shown cutting a branch from a tree, whilst two others are shown in the act of dowsing using forked twigs, whilst surrounded by miners digging.

Shortly after this publication, during the reign of Elizabeth I, German miners were employed in England to locate the zinc ore necessary to blend with the Cornish copper to make bronze for the armaments of the realm. J. W. Gough relates in his *The Mines of Mendip* how '*great faith was placed in the virtues of the divining rod*'.

However, those who practised the 'art' during the last five centuries of the last millennium did so at their own peril, due to persecution that took place under the various Witchcraft Acts that were passed between

Woodcut from Georgius Agricola's *De Re Metallica*

1542 and 1735. Dowsing was treated as severely as any other practice of a mysterious nature - many times resulting in the burning of the dowser at the stake. Those who think that these laws were only invoked in the dim and distant past, should be made aware that the last convictions took place as recently as the 1940's and 1950's, just before the acts were repealed. Admittedly, the convicted were not burnt at the stake in the twentieth century - but it was still regarded as a criminal activity.

That is why divining was only practised in out of the way rural areas - and even then confined to the finding of underground water for local consumption.

The word divining has spiritual connotations, which can be confused, in the minds of some people, with rituals practised by pagan traditions. This made it unpalatable to members of all religious groups. Dowsing practitioners themselves were often looked upon as practising the 'art of the devil' - well outside mainstream religious practice - and occasionally we are seen in this light today!

In the twentieth century, the use of the descriptive term 'divining' declined in favour of the more secular word 'dowsing', which just means to search. One picture that may spring to mind, when some try to visualise a dowser, is that of an uneducated rustic with a twig in his hand and a straw in his mouth. I admit to being an uneducated rustic, but I have long since thrown the twig away - and I do not like the taste of straw. Those days, if they ever existed, are long past. Today, dowsers can be found in many professions and disciplines, and they come from all walks of life and sections of society.

In Russia, and in other eastern European countries dowsing, or 'biolocation' as it is called there, is widely practised by many university professors, and heads of departments. It is an ability that is used openly and in various circumstances.

As we mentioned at the start of this book, the British Society of Dowsers was formed in the year that I was born, 1933.

The first President was:
Colonel A. H. Bell, DSO, OBE, MRI

Colonel A. H. Bell

He was succeeded by:

Colonel K. W. Merrylees, OBE, MI Mech. E

Major-General J. Scott Elliot, CB, CBE, DSO

Dr Arthur R. Bailey, PhD, MSc, FIERE, MIEE

C. B. Thompson, Dipl. Arch, RIBA

Sir Charles Jessell, Bt.

Major-General W. F. Cooper, CBE, MC

Clearly, these men were no local yokels. It is apparent from the list above that dowsing was accepted in at least some quarters of the armed forces, and in particular by the British Army. It was used extensively to find water supplies for the allied armies during the first and second world wars.

One officer who carried out this type of work was Colonel H. Grattan CBE, whose story is told in *A Successful Feat -Practical Dowsing,* published by G. Bell and Sons in 1965. His dowsing resulted in the saving of considerable expenditure on new water treatment plants for the British Forces stationed in Germany.

Additionally, there are many, many water dowsers who, between them, have marked the location of thousands of wells around the world - with a proven success rate in excess of 90%. If, after all that, you feel the need for more reassurance about the effectiveness of dowsing, there are plenty of written accounts of the exploits of modern dowsers - including my own.'

So, how does dowsing really work?

'I believe the reason for many of the inconsistencies in dowsing results could be more easily explained if we had a better understanding of both the mechanism of dowsing and of the physiological barriers in the mind of the dowser.

How dowsing actually works is equally confusing to dowsers and non-dowsers alike. There have been many different models of how it might work proposed down the years. The differences in the explanations tend to depend on the perspectives, viewpoints and motives of those who are putting forward the explanation. Those currently on the table include:

The strictly scientific viewpoint

'This approach would suggest that the movement of the dowsing tool is caused by the hand and arm of the dowser coming into contact with some form of radiation or flux of energy, not yet determined, which in turn brings about an involuntary muscle movement in the lower arm and wrist - causing the dowsing tool to move in a way that is meaningful to the dowser.

This explanation has some appeal, in that there is both a cause and an effect - the backbone of scientific reasoning. However, the weakness of the reasoning is that it can only apply to on-site dowsing, where the dowser is directly over the target. Those who are experienced in dowsing will know that it is not necessary to be on site or directly over the target. It is quite possible to dowse using maps, photographs, diagrams, or even a visualisation of the target area, to be able to successfully find the object of a search, such as underground water.

I have personally heard the renowned American dowser, Terry Ross, describe how he successfully directed a non-dowser at the end of a phone more than a thousand miles away to find the location for very high yielding boreholes to provide water for ranches in South America from his home in Florida. He achieved this on a number of occasions. I have tried this 'third party' dowsing with students on some of my advanced dowsing courses, and I have found that most people could do it successfully, once their disbelief was overcome.

Therefore, if there is only one model for explaining how dowsing works, it cannot be this one.'

The spiritual model

'In this scenario, we are guided by a spirit that channels information from a higher intelligence, or from the deity of their tradition. The dowser is just the supplicant - and has no more responsibility than to ask a question and await the answer.

This theory also has a certain amount going for it, in that it overcomes the problem associated with off-site dowsing. However, it would seem to fall down in that utterly non-spiritual people are also able to dowse perfectly successfully.

Therefore there must be another explanation that can cope with both on-site and remote dowsing - while encompassing both the spiritually minded and those with a non-spiritual outlook.'

The third way

'An alternative explanation proposes that an information field of universal consciousness holds information about everything in creation - now, in the past, and everything that is yet to come. This field permeates everything, space and matter - even Dark Matter. As we humans are composed of nothing more than matter, and if the information field permeates all matter, the information within the field is also within us.

It is possible that DNA molecules, as well as acting as a store of genetic instructions for cell replication, may also contain the key to connecting to this additional information source. Recent work by Chinese researchers has suggested that certain sections of the DNA molecule, which are not part of the human Genome, may be associated with intuitive abilities, such as dowsing, and may be the gateway into the field of universal consciousness.

This explanation bridges the gap between all viewpoints and would allow both the seriously scientific and spiritually minded dowsers to work side by side - with only a review of the terminology used by each required to bring them together. Furthermore, if the terms 'Higher Intelligence' and 'Universal Consciousness' are considered to be the same thing viewed from different perspectives, then the gap is substantially bridged.

However, the information field does not resonate with the current paradigm of mainstream physics - and will not be likely to convince the hardened sceptics that dowsing is a real phenomenon. While it may be a vital part of the explanation, it still has unproven elements, which need to be addressed.'

The holographic universe

'A fourth approach stems from the work of the physicist David Bohm - the father of the concept of a holographic universe. In essence, he suggested that what we believe to be reality is nothing more than a mirage.

The concept of holography is well understood, as it is used widely in the field of photography. It is perhaps less well known as a cutting-edge method of data storage, where it is being developed to allow huge amounts of information to be stored in a physically minute medium.

The use of holography demonstrates that all the information required to form the complete picture is contained in every small part, every pixel of the whole. The work of Bohm calls into question the concept of the space-time continuum, which was sacrosanct to Einstein's Theory of Relativity. A holographic universe does not require distance or time to process or convey information.

Coupled with this, work undertaken by Karl Pribram led to the Holo-nomic Brain Theory, which described a different concept of cognition. He developed this line of research independently from Bohm, but they later collaborated when it became apparent that their work dovetailed. Pribram studied the location of the storage of memory in the brain. He found that the removal of large sections of the brains of rats did not deplete their ability to recall - and they could continue to carry out tasks for which they had been trained prior to their partial lobotomy. This astonishing breakthrough implies that information is not stored in a specific part of the brain, but is fully available in every small part of it. Interestingly, this also appears to corroborate the work of Backster, which we described earlier. You will recall that Backster found that every single cell of a leaf appeared to carry information about the whole plant.

Bohm stated very clearly - the concept of a holographic universe suggests that all information about what is, what has been, and what will be, is present in every basic particle of existence. It is there to be accessed because everything is interconnected - no matter how great the apparent separation in time and space.

Karl Pribram has produced strong evidence that suggests our brains work using holographic principles. All we need to do to access memory is to create electrical activity within the brain - in a similar manner to the way laser beams create the interference patterns of holographic photography. Promoting the appropriate type of electrical activity is dependent on the thoughts that we generate within the brain.

Every day, new technology places more strain on our ability to differentiate between the 'real' world and imaginary worlds. The introduction of the humble T.V. into our living rooms brought us into contact with a world that sometimes appears to be real, while at other times imaginary. The apparent reality of this experience has developed rapidly over recent years with larger screens and higher definition pictures. The advent of the three-dimensional format makes our experience seem even more realistic, in that it creates the illusion of bringing the foreground of the picture out of the screen, actually in our living space. We almost feel that we could reach out and touch it. I believe that the possibility of fully holographic television is just around the corner.

At that point, most of the action would be fully projected into our living space. Instead of being a distant observer, we would be encapsulated in the scene, and would become an active player in it. The next step would be to create the illusion that the holographic images are solid - so that we could feel them and touch them as we would any other solid object. Whilst this may seem like science fiction, the ability to develop seemingly solid holographic images is not far away - and may well become science fact in the lifetime of many who are alive today. If, and when, that does occur, our ability to differentiate between our perceived impression of reality and a type of reality imposed upon us, would virtually disappear.'

How does all this relate to dowsing?

'Experienced dowsers understand the importance of an unambiguous Dowsing Question - a question with a clear yes/no answer. It needs to be formulated in the brain, so that we are absolutely clear as to what we are seeking. According to Pribram, this process will search through the database of universal information that is already in every brain cell - at a speed that would put even Google to shame. It will extract the requested information and will make it available within our own field of consciousness.

Unfortunately, dowsers often make things more difficult for themselves. Many allow it to be necessary to have instruments of a special kind, to convey the message into their conscious state for them to understand it - when, with sufficient practice, direct cognition would suffice.

My own experience over the years of using deviceless dowsing techniques - using my eyes and my hands - in the study of earth energies has allowed me to virtually 'see' and 'feel' the shape and form in which the lines of energy, or perhaps more accurately the lines of radiation, display themselves. When sensing them with my hands, they feel like solid objects - and my eyes allow me to see their exact position.

I am aware that this impression is also illusory, but I am convinced that the existence of such energetic forms is not purely down to my presence - but is the sum of everything that is in the environment in which I find myself.

Taking a lifetime's practical dowsing experience into consideration, I therefore consider that this fourth scenario - the holographic universe - is indeed the correct one. As well as satisfying my personal beliefs through modifying the terminology used, it can accommodate all dowsing viewpoints.

Perhaps even more importantly from the viewpoint of credibility, it unveils an independently formulated framework that happens to embrace dowsing.

It is also meshes in with the direction of travel of quantum physics, to which mainstream scientific researchers can relate. If accepted, some of the turbulence in the debate might abate, and the serious collaboration could begin.'

Red Socks Syndrome

'If the holographic universe, accessed through the holographic mind, is a cosmic database, which contains the universal information on everything, then why is it not more readily accessible to all?

I believe that the answer lies in the 'Red Socks Syndrome'. Some years ago a certain dowser proclaimed that when he wore red socks he could no longer dowse. He believed that the colour red had an insulating effect on the radiations coming out of the earth, which in turn caused the dowsing rod to fail to move in his hands. Some other dowsers, when told about his experience, also found the same thing happening to them - much to their consternation. From this, it could be argued that this theory as postulated is valid, if the anecdotal evidence is taken at face value. However, we all know that the logic is false. It can easily be shown that if the dowser is not aware of the colour of socks that he is wearing, it is likely that he will still be able to dowse on all occasions. If a dowser is not able to dowse for some reason, it is just as likely that the colour of his socks is something other than red!

On another occasion, I read an article which claimed that we could be insulated from what the author referred to as 'the dowsing signal' using anything made of rubber. This person when standing on a rubber mat could not get a dowsing response; when previously standing on the same location - without the rubber mat - they did get a reaction. They also stated that the same would occur when wearing rubber-soled boots or wellingtons. I was sufficiently intrigued to try the experiment for myself. It was a dry day, but I donned a pair of wellington boots and I went into a nearby field where I knew there was an abundance of veins of underground water. I walked across the field and, lo and behold, I couldn't get any dowsing responses at all. I retraced my steps with one boot removed and very soon the dowsing rod dipped as I approached underground water. I put the boot back on again and the dowsing response stopped. In my mind at that time, I felt that the writer was correct in what they had stated.

A number of days after that, on a showery day after working in the garden, I decided to check out something routine through dowsing. I gathered up the rods and successfully went about my task. It was only when I had finished dowsing that I realised that I was wearing wellington boots - the same boots I had worn previously. Rubber boots need have no effect on your dowsing, it is only the belief that stops us getting a reaction!

Amongst dowsers, one of the most common examples of RSS is the belief that one type of dowsing tool performs better for one task and another type is best used for something else. You may find one tool more comfortable than another to hold, but the tool plays no intrinsic part in the process.

Also high on the RSS list is the perceived need to transfer the responsibility for dowsing onto a third party, by asking 'Can I?' or 'May I?' before starting to dowse, rather than accepting that the validity of the outcome lies entirely within ourselves.

The need for these dogmatic, ritualistic procedures prior to a dowsing session I feel is essentially RSS. Yes, there is a need to calm the mind; yes, there is a need to be clear about what we are going to do and yes, we need to formulate a precise dowsing question, but then it is over to us - and nobody else. If we fail, we should not blame anything or anybody other than ourselves - and we must remember to learn from our mistakes, rather than hastily sweeping them under the carpet.

From these lessons, I grasped a fundamental trait that the human mind - and the beliefs we have all accumulated down the years - can determine our inability to extend our consciousness beyond self-limiting parameters. These parameters are the Red Socks within our minds, many of which have arrived there through association with the Red Socks of everyone else with whom we have ever come into contact. Our upbringing, our schooling, and our religious outlook (including atheism) all make their mark. No matter how broad-minded we claim to be, we are still in the clutches of these restricting influences.

This phenomenon has been recognised by those involved in medical research. The area of the brain that is involved is the reticular formation. It is a part of the brain that triggers actions such as the waking/sleeping cycle, and the filtering of incoming stimuli. It is believed that the reticular formation can act as a blocking mechanism to information that is not in line with our belief system. This is not confined to dowsers. It is present in all people, including scientists, unless they have taken deliberate action to clear away the obstructions.

Most people who become aware of the concept try to reduce the impact of these self-limiting influences. However, it is not sufficient just to wash your socks a few times in the hope that the red dye will eventually disappear. All that happens is that the virtual colour becomes a little paler, but the self-limiting influences remain - albeit, maybe in a little less dominant form. If we are to make any serious progress, then we must get rid of the Red Socks altogether - to cast them into the waste bin of self-doubt. If that occurred, then dowsers would spend less time debating about unimportant issues - and scientists and others, who claim to live in the real world, would at least listen to the views expressed by those outside their discipline.

To conclude this section, I would like to quote Dr. Wayne Dyer, PhD, who is an internationally renowned author and speaker in the field of self-development. He has written over 30 books, has created many audio programmes and videos, and has appeared on thousands of television and radio shows.

His book *Excuses Begone!* is self-explanatory. In *The Power of Intention* he states that intention is a force in the universe, and everything and everyone is connected to this invisible force. Lastly, in the title of a later book, he turns the old axiom you will believe it, when you see it on its head - and it reads *"You'll see it, when <u>you</u> believe it"*.

Red Socks Begone!'

Dowsing, Science and Spirituality

In the eclectic world of dowsing, religious and spiritual beliefs - and the lack and denial of them - come in all forms and formats. Perhaps as a reflection of the wider world, there are dowsers of every inclination and denomination. There are a few who have deep-seated views, both in support of or in opposition to the spiritual worldview. In general however, dowsers tend to be a very open-minded bunch.

Most of us have been drawn to take up the arcane art through sheer curiosity - and most of us have had to change our previous worldview considerably to accommodate the evidence of our own enhanced senses. Billy and I are no exceptions.

It is very pertinent to an understanding of how Billy came to consider the various possibilities, and the conclusions that could legitimately be derived from them, that his upbringing and his subsequent worldview were very different from that of most of us in the 'next generation'.

While dowsers may come from a vast spread of backgrounds, and often support a bewildering range of philosophies, I have only encountered a few who could be ticked off as card-carrying churchgoers, in the conventional sense of the word. Even amongst those, the active 'Believers' I have met on courses and at meetings, tend not to be what you would call regular churchgoers. Some prefer to term themselves Celtic or Spiritual Christians - leaning towards the pre-Roman version of the church, with its emphasis on the deeply personal relationship with the divine.   Billy, however, as a root and branch Northern Irish Presbyterian, by both heritage and inclination, comes from a minority, within a minority, within a minority. While we are all unique - some of us are uniquer than others!

Against this strict backcloth of primary colours, Billy's views and discoveries weave an even more dramatic tapestry. His understanding of the non-physical world has doubtless led him to mull over the teachings of his tradition, but you get the impression that they have informed, enhanced, and even clarified his worldview.

It is therefore fascinating to hear what someone who has approached the esoteric from a seemingly oblique angle, has to say when reconsidering many decades of intermittent contemplation:

Religion, science and magic

'In many ways these three disciplines are incompatible. Religious beliefs are usually cast in stone and not open to question. They are right because they say they are right - and anyone who suggests otherwise is a hypocrite, or worse.

Scientists, too, whilst questioning the truth of other people's work, are often reluctant to accept that their own conclusions also require regular scrutiny. They claim to work and live in the 'real' world, and they reject anything that cannot be proved using their own rules and procedures.

Magic, on the other hand, exists in the unreal world, and defies the rules, or so it seems. Anything that cannot be explained in scientific terms could be described as magic and that takes in most, if not all, of what today is termed esoteric. Magical concepts are mysterious in their own right - and perhaps because of this, they can generate a large and dedicated following, even in this modern and enlightened world.

The last vestiges of traditional magical practices can be glimpsed amongst the cultural remnants of aboriginal peoples around the world - in Australia, native North America and parts of Africa.

In the West, there are those who glory in mystery, sometimes seemingly for its own sake. At times, I believe they prefer to ignore a rational explanation of a phenomenon, to protect their own personal position.

In the scientific field, the same mindset is at work. This may be because certain aspects of new thinking could remove the platform on which an individual has stood for most of their career. In an article in *Science News*, Benveniste asked the questions " Why are scientists so opposed to the evolution of science? Do these advances appear to threaten their all-too-fragile certitudes?" His frustration is understandable, given the criticism that he suffered from his peers for daring to shake the foundations of the accepted order.

On the other hand, there appears to be a growing openness and in- quisitiveness developing in the wider population. More and more people are taking an interest in the skill of dowsing - and in what lies behind it. Thankfully, enough people wish to know the truth, and they will welcome research and knowledge from whence it comes.

When a new line of thought is brought forward it is often felt necessary to demolish and demonise much of what existed before it. The new orthodoxy can demand a clean sweep of the accumulated wisdom of generations. My experience tells me that this is not always the best way forward, and it is certainly not my inclination. Instead, I feel we can make more positive progress in developing our current outlook by building bridges - and by bringing together as many views, opinions and diverse lines of thought as possible.'

The new picture

'It is a matter of fitting as many of the pieces of the information that are available to us - together with a few additional elements - into a new jigsaw puzzle picture. To make any sense of our new worldview, I feel the first requirement is that we must acknowledge that all things are indeed part of a greater whole - and that every piece of knowledge must, and will, fit into the jigsaw, if we look carefully enough.

To do so, may require us to step back from our work, so that we can see, and accept, that nothing within creation is separate - that all things are interactive with, and interdependent on each other.

I feel it is this holistic outlook that is most likely to allow us to increase our understanding of how mankind fits into the overall matrix of nature.'

When I started dowsing about twenty years ago, it was not uncommon to face outright hostility from those who practised their religion in a traditional manner. At that time, the scientific establishment also dismissed the idea of manifesting information, without using the five sense organs that could be dissected in the mortuary, with blunt ridicule.

In the intervening period, something subtle, yet seismic, has happened. It is a change that has taken dowsing from being regarded as a music-hall sideshow, to being a valid, even important, line of research.

The first wave of late twentieth-century earth energy dowsers - including John Michell, Guy Underwood, Sig Lonegren, Hamish Miller, and Billy Gawn - has largely been responsible for that change. They have surfed the wave rebounding from the wall of fundamentalist materialism and found themselves at the forefront of a new, exciting and enlightening worldview. They have done so - not by rejecting the essence of religion or the breakthroughs of science - but by realising that both schools, in their radically different ways, bring something important to the table.

John Michell

This is not to say that either tradition has a complete picture, or that by merely combining the two, the whole panorama would be revealed. What these researchers sense is that dowsing is one entry point to an all-embracing loop of understanding, which includes both spirituality and logic. The work of Jim Lyons, Ron Pearson and others is further developing that understanding.

The great thing about dowsing is that just about everyone can do it - regardless of whether we are working in Anatolia, in Antigua or in Antrim. It helps to be open to it, and practice is the key to being good at it, but it's a slit-window view on the higher realities that the greatest minds and the more reverent gurus approach from other directions. It has led many to ponder the nature of human consciousness and the very validity of our received view of reality. The builder from Ballyclare is no exception.

Given the extensive research that Billy has carried out into the building and application of megalithic structures, it is not surprising that he has developed his own ideas on the evolution of science and the relative dissolution of spirituality:

Wisdom of the ancients

'I have been aware of the notion that mankind, in ancient times, had some kind of super-knowledge. This romantic idea has been the subject of a whole raft of books. One of the best-known exponents of this view was the late John Michell, author of the seminal *The View over Atlantis*. He drew attention to the 'ley' system of alignments of significant sites throughout Britain, rediscovered by Alfred Watkins (1855-1935), and also to similar features in other parts of the world. He also produced impressive research that suggested that many ancient structures have solar, lunar, planetary and stellar alignments built into them.

There is good reason to believe that Neolithic man, and woman, had much the same brain capacity, and therefore much the same intelligence, as ourselves. Although they lived what seems a long time ago; 6,000 years is only 300 generations. There is little positive proof that our ancestors had a super-knowledge that we have now lost.

There is a distinct difference between knowledge and ability, and I believe that it may be the latter that has been eroded. The ability to which I am referring is one of awareness, of being in close contact with the more subtle elements of mother earth. This erosion could be the direct result of the advancement of new technologies, the earliest evidence of which can be seen in the late Neolithic and Mesolithic periods. A classic present day example of this decline in specific abilities is the widespread use of electronic calculators in recent decades, which appears to have eroded our ability to carry out reasonably simple mental calculations.

It does not mean that we are any less intelligent, as much intelligence comes from the knowledge of how to source information efficiently. It is impossible, and unnecessary, for anyone to know at first hand all the information that is contained in our libraries and databases. All we need to know is how to access that information. The main obstacle for the advancement of ancient mankind was that they had not yet developed the tools to support their intelligence.

However, throughout the world, there is archaeological evidence that ancient man did carry out mammoth tasks of construction - some of which display what could be interpreted as an advanced knowledge in such scientific disciplines as astronomy, geometry and mathematics.

Could any form of ability have compensated for the lack of super-knowledge, and have enabled pre-technological man to build these structures, which undoubtedly embody the geometry of lunar, solar and stellar alignments?'

Parting of the ways

'In early civilisation, it appears that there was no clear distinction between what we now term science and what we choose to call religion. However, the earliest writings of our ancient forebears only date back to about 2000 years BCE. For information about earlier periods we have to rely on myths and folklore that have been handed down through the centuries, complete with the embellishments they have accrued over the centuries.

It is obvious that, when these stories were being first told, there could not have been any physical communication between the people and the races of these geographically remote areas. Yet, a common thread woven into all of these myths and legends is that people everywhere believed in a spiritual world that existed beside the 'real' world.

Mankind could, apparently, communicate easily with this spirit world and, from what we are told, these spirit beings roamed around freely on the surface of the earth. However, their home was within the earth and they were reputed to live in an 'otherworld'. This spirit world was not the exclusive preserve of humans but was present in everything. It was recognised as a sign of He or She who created mankind, our environment, and all that was to be found in the heavens above.

Although called by various names, this universal spirit was identified in all cultures either as 'God' or a 'Supreme Being' that had overall control and to whom we were all subservient. However, as this spirit was present everywhere and pervaded everything, most civilizations paid homage, not to one God, but to a hierarchy of Gods.

There is considerable evidence of the reverence for certain locations and topographical features such as mountains, which were believed to house these lesser Gods. Consequently, these places were deemed 'holy' or 'sacred' - and it was here that many ancient structures were built for what archaeologists have classified as places for the performance of ceremony and ritual.

It could be said that science and religion are basically seeking the same goal - namely, a better understanding of life and creation. Although, in our modern world, where the emphasis is on a shorter-term and more tangible profit, commercial interests divert science at times from this task.

Whilst in ancient times, there did not seem to be any clear distinction between science and religion, this has changed over the last two thousand years, with the advent of modern religious groups. Most of these appear to be static in their approach to understanding. They believe that the revelation of all truth was given, usually to one person, at the time of the birth of that religion - and that it is sacrilege to seek any greater understanding of the basis of their existence. Alongside this stasis, science continues its long and gradual path of uncovering the secrets of the world around us. Whilst at times scientists are certainly reluctant to let go of long-held beliefs, nothing is totally sacrosanct, and everything remains under scrutiny.'

The development of science

'The seeds of modern science were sown during the two thousand years prior to the advent of Christianity. However, some of the disciplines that exercised the minds of those early scientists have, perhaps temporarily, been cast aside - and they are currently considered to be purely superstitious or magical in nature.

Science grew out of philosophy, and it took centre stage within the religion of the day. The rigid parameters that now exist within religion had not been firmly set in concrete, and questions could still be asked. These early philosophers began to see that many things within God's creation behaved in a regular way and that many were the result of circumstance. From this, the first simple laws of physics were observed and recorded.

Philosophical discussion appeared to be focused on a few topics. First and foremost was knowledge of the world of nature. There are many regularities in nature that mankind had to recognise for its own survival since the emergence of *Homo sapiens* as a species.

They observed the Sun and the Moon periodically repeating their movements. Some motions, like the daily "motion" of the Sun, were simple to observe; others, like the annual "motion" of the Sun, and that of the Moon, were far more difficult to document. However, all of these movements correlate with important terrestrial events.

It was apparent to these early researchers that the basic relationship between the movement of the Sun, the presence of mankind and the environment in which we live had a great influence on our everyday existence. It was these cycles that created the seasons, which allowed agricultural crops to be grown. They provided a seedtime and a harvest that was essential for survival. It was, therefore, reasonable to assume that lesser influences, such as the movements and positions of the planets and stars, would also have an effect on our well-being. To that end, the discipline of Astrology was born. However, two schools of opinion developed within this discipline. Some confined their interest purely to the movements and the mathematics of the planets and the stars. They dismissed the view that the stars could control our destiny - and, from that conflict, the seed of modern Astronomy was sown.

The opinion of the Astrologer declined in popularity, but never completely disappeared. Even to the present day, it has stubbornly refused to go away. As we saw in an earlier chapter, my own dowsing work on the presence and influence of planetary grids on the surface of the earth implies that there is more than a little fire behind the smoke - and that all heavenly bodies might indeed have a subtle influence on what happens to us, and to our planet.

From early times, it must have been obvious that in order to gather data and information it was necessary to have the ability to measure and to count. There is much evidence to show that the study of mathematics was practised in ancient Mesopotamia. There, the system of degrees, minutes, and seconds was developed, which was to provide the basis of geometry. More advanced forms and uses of mathematics developed - and ultimately these went far beyond the requirements of daily business and survival.

However, did ancient man have a sophisticated knowledge of advanced geometry several thousand years before the time of the Greco-Roman scholars, as is sometimes suggested? Hippocrates of Chios (5th century BC), Theudius and Euclid, (c. 300 BC) are credited with laying the foundations of modern geometry. Euclid, in particular, was a first-class teacher of mathematics (his textbook has remained in use, practically unchanged, for more than 2,000 years!). This scientific discipline survives surprisingly intact to this day. Non-Euclidean geometry and the use of modern technology have speeded up the process of calculation, but few of the building blocks that were put in place thousands of years ago have been found to be substantially in error.

It is difficult to put an exact date on when science, as we know it today, was born. By this, I mean the science of Physics rather than that of Chemistry. Chemistry dealt purely with the materials of life and their chemical properties. The study of Physics dealt with 'being' and 'existence' - on which were two opposing viewpoints - Materialism and Idealism.'

Philosophy in practice

'The simplest form of Materialism is found in the statement that only matter exists. The hypothesis that human thought could in any way

influence matter - or that matter could influence thought - was completely ruled out.

Idealism believes that all of existence is essentially composed of spirit,
or at least is penetrated by spirit. Gottfried Leibniz (1646-1716) was
born in Leipzig, and a contemporary of Newton. He asserted that '*the
true atoms of nature were monads or souls; at bottom nothing existed
except minds*'. George Berkeley (1685-1753), who was born in Ireland,
claimed that '*sensible things have no existence without the mind; there
are spirits that experience, including an infinite spirit, and there are the
contents of their experiences, but there is no independently existing
world of matter*'.

These opinions did not hold sway. It was the mechanistic view,
postulated by many, but brought to fruition by Isaac Newton (1643-
1727), which came to the fore. It is more accurate to say that the
mechanistic view evolved gradually over a few thousand years, but it
was not until after the time of Newton, who is looked upon as the father
-figure of this viewpoint, that the last traces of religion, magic and
alchemy were removed from the scientific scenario.

One of the main goals of alchemy was the pursuit of the creation of gold
by chemical means. The possibility of achieving this was not con-
clusively disproved scientifically until the 19th century. Rational as he
was, Newton thought it worthwhile continuing to experiment with this
in mind.

An equally important activity in alchemy was the search for an elixir
that would give everlasting life. As many of the potions contained
arsenic and other poisons, quite often the impact on those who imbibed
them was the opposite of that desired! Therefore, this line of research
went out of favour.

Another factor in the weakening of interest in the achievement of
immortality by chemical means - and thus in one of the mainstays of
alchemy - were the promises made by several of the emerging religions
at that time.

The Christians, perhaps, led the way by guaranteeing everlasting life,
not in this life but in the hereafter, to all true believers. Having seen the

failure of alchemists in achieving this aim in the present, it is not surprising that the new option was more attractive to the populace.

Great care has been taken by scientists over the last three hundred years to remove all vestiges of what could be described as 'magic' - defined as 'that which cannot be explained in a mechanistic and rational manner'. However, it is now apparent that science is not as simple as that.'

More recent developments

'Albert Einstein (1879-1955) proposed revisions to the laws that govern the behaviour of the universe and developed the Theory of Relativity in early decades of the twentieth century. It was not long before the advent of quantum physics further muddied the waters. Certain concepts, which had previously been regarded as absolute facts, had to be revisited and reconsidered.

The greatest problem with any gradual uncovering of knowledge is that the more we come to know, the more we realise how little we do know. Every answer raises a multitude of new questions. New knowledge can raise doubts about the 'absolute truth'.

In recent times, even the most sacred cows of physics, namely that the speed of light is constant and that nothing can travel faster than the speed of light, have been cast into doubt. They may have to be reconsidered, in the light of experimental evidence announced towards the end of September 2011. Numerous experiments, involving the beam-firing of neutrino particles from CERN, near Geneva, to a receiver at a laboratory in Italy 454 miles away - recorded that the particles arrived 60 nanoseconds faster than the speed of light. As one swallow does not make a summer, this does not provide conclusive evidence of faster-than-light travel. The experiments will need to be repeated by other laboratories elsewhere, to see if the same result is observed consistently. However, if other results do confirm these findings, I believe that it need not be shocking - and perhaps they ought to have been predicted.

A neutrino is an electrically-neutral, weakly-interacting elementary subatomic particle with a small but non-zero mass. Being electrically neutral, it is able to pass through ordinary matter almost unaffected. Neutrinos are similar to the more familiar electron, with one crucial difference: neutrinos do not carry electric charge. This means that the electromagnetic forces that act on electrons do not affect them. Neutrinos, as well as electrons, are considered to be elementary particles, and to be slightly beyond the threshold of what is termed as baryonic matter. Baryonic matter is composed mostly of baryons, which include atoms of any sort. It therefore includes nearly all matter that we are likely to encounter in our everyday lives.

As I have stated previously, I believe there are several stages of existence for particles beyond this - at non-baryonic levels - before they reach their true elementary form. Any such particle is beyond the electromagnetic spectrum and would not be restrained by the electro-magnetic field. It is not surprising that they may not obey the laws of classical physics, and not be restricted to the speed of light.

I am of the opinion that particles of primitive sub-baryonic matter sit within all ordinary matter, and that they produce the lines of subtle energy that we dowse. If it is eventually proven that neutrinos can exceed the speed of light, this would support the view held by many dowsers that subtle energy, and the information carried by it, is not restrained in any way by other matter, or restricted to the speed of light.

Also back in the melting pot is something that has, until recently, been unthinkable - that human consciousness and thought can have an effect on material things and bring about change within them.
The search is on for what may be described as a new 'Holy Grail' - a unified force field from which everything derives. There is an increasing feeling that this field is composed of 'energy', rather than solid matter - and that energy (or perhaps information) is the more fundamental building block of the real world.

Science has nearly turned full circle. A new realisation is dawning that, by using slightly different terminology, many of the ideas described by both religious groups, and those involved in magic, can indeed be expressed and explained in scientific terms. Even if they are not fully explicable using current scientific paradigm, they are again back on the radar.

Within some religious groups, this interaction between the material and the spiritual is not a new thought. In many cases, it is the backbone of their existence. The power of prayer, spiritual healing, and the belief in a universal spirit that pervades the human condition, is freely and unquestionably accepted. Many religious groups demand that these poorly understood facets of our existence are accepted by faith and without question.

Clearly this approach contradicts the view of those scientists, who insist that everything must be reduced to 'nuts and bolts', before we are allowed to accept that anything exists at all. If we cannot do that, then, in the opinion of those scientists, we must deny the possibility of other, more subtle, ingredients that contribute to life and support our existence.

There are currently many individuals, groups and societies that are attempting to bridge the destructive divide between the dogmatic stand taken by most modern religions, on the one hand, and the hard-line stance of much of mainstream science on the other. Sadly, there is a tendency amongst many in the scientific community to group the views of all those who sense this middle ground as 'pseudo-science'. This, in my view, is a way of rebranding it 'magic' - ideas off the beaten track and not worth considering. I feel that we should all be a little more discerning - and that we should be prepared to carefully examine the emerging evidence before dismissing it.'

So, what is magic?

'When we turn to the Oxford Dictionary it is not particularly precise. I quote:

Magic - Pretended art of influencing events by occult control of nature or of spirits, witchcraft; mysterious agency or power

According to Merriam-Webster's Colligate Dictionary the definition of Magic is:

1 a: the use of means (as charms or spells) believed to have supernatural power over natural forces. b: magic rites or incantations

2 a: an extraordinary power or influence seemingly from a supernatural source. b: something that seems to cast a spell

3 a: having seemingly supernatural qualities or powers b: giving a feeling of enchantment

All of these definitions suggest that there is indeed a belief in a two-way communication between the material world, which includes mankind, and an encompassing spirit world - a world of consciousness. To take the line of thought one stage further would mean that not only can the mind influence matter, but also that matter can influence the mind. As we have seen, my research shows categorically that this is indeed the case.

I gave earlier my own definition of magic as 'that which cannot be explained in a mechanistic and rational manner'. It seems that this definition is possibly more accurate than those given in the two quoted dictionaries, in that it is more in line with what people actually think. To make it even more precise, I would add the words 'at this moment in time'.

Phenomena that may be inexplicable, and viewed as incredible today, may be accepted as normal in the future. My grandfather would have classified as magic the ability to sit in his favourite armchair and, by simply pressing a button, see what is happening almost anywhere in the world on a small glass screen just a few milliseconds after it happens - or by the flick of a switch, light up a room. The 'miracle' of the computer would also fall into this category. Writing in the autumn of 2011, it seems it will not be long until the keyboard will be a thing of the past - and I understand that Microsoft are considering the possibility of computers being controlled by thought in the foreseeable future. Consequently, much of the work of those who are at present cast into the mould of pseudo-science may eventually be taken on board by mainstream science - and may become not only respectable, but even the new orthodox!

Anthropologists squarely place religious belief and practice in the magical arena. In *The Golden Bough* (1890), Frazer developed an evolutionary scheme for magic and religion. He saw them as *'belonging to different stages in the development of human thought'*. Magic came first, because it seemed to him to be logically simpler. He assumed (erroneously, as it turned out) that the Australian Aborigines, an example of an archaic people, believed in magic but not in religion, and he felt that magic formed a substratum of superstition, even in advanced societies.

According to Frazer:

'Individuals in the earliest cultures must have come to realise the inefficacy of magic and the powerlessness of men to control nature; from this they postulated the existence of omnipotent spiritual beings who required supplication in order to direct nature as men wanted.'

Consequently, in Frazer's view, religion came into existence.

The final stage in this schema began with the recognition of the existence of empirical natural laws, aided by the discoveries of alchemy and then of science proper. With this final development, religion joined magic as superstition.

Merriam-Webster's Colligate Dictionary does not treat Superstition any more kindly than Magic.
It states:

1: a belief or practice resulting from ignorance, fear of the unknown, trust in magic or chance, or a false conception of causation

2: a notion maintained despite evidence to the contrary

In this context, magic and religion are treated as being the same.

Modern religions rigorously defend themselves by denying any magical tendencies. They pin the stigma of magic firmly on pagan religions, indigenous tribes and aboriginals such as the American Indians (with their shamans), and the African tribes (with their witch doctors). Magic is generally looked upon as a thing of the past, practised by ignorant and ill-informed people. Could it be that those who are most ill-informed are the very people who ridicule and criticise it - and fail to examine the evidence to see if any understanding can be gained from it?

The problem remains the same. There is a tendency to place every belief that cannot currently be fully explained into the one basket or the other - religion or magic. Therefore, firmly held beliefs, and myths handed down from the mists of time, are dismissed without proper examination of whether they in any way equate with, or even add to, modern knowledge.'

The way ahead

'There is a responsibility on everyone not to accept anything as true unless there is adequate evidence to support it - to maintain a healthy scepticism. However, there is a corresponding responsibility not to dismiss anything as untrue unless there is conclusive evidence to show that this is indeed the case.

Discussion and debate should not be suppressed, simply because we do not understand something, or because it does not fit into the current paradigm. The lesson of history is clear - even though something does not fit comfortably into our accepted worldview today, we ridicule and dismiss it at our peril.'

Looking Beyond the Far Horizon

Despite the length and depth of this book, it could only ever have been a brief précis of the sheer practical effort and the many hours of thought that have gone into a lifetime's work. We could easily have produced a much longer and even more comprehensive tome - but, at the end of a long day, it's important that a wider audience actually gets to read about the themes and the concepts that have been introduced here. You have to draw the line somewhere.

Such is the depth and scope of the material - and the potential avenues that open beyond it for ongoing research - that, at times, I feel even Billy himself has struggled to come to terms with the magnitude of its implications.

One aspect that has caused both of us to struggle with the presentation of the content is that he has reached a level where all of the various themes are gelling together - inter-weaving into a dense web of insight. It has been difficult to introduce one thread without referring forward or backward to other aspects of the wider picture. It has been a process of trying to provide structure to a seamless loop of understanding.

Billy broke through into that loop, quite unintentionally, through dowsing - the virtual bridge - and he has left, quite literally, a paper-trail for others to follow. Perhaps it was the very nature of this trail that has enabled him to remain firmly rooted in the soil of Ulster, whilst appreciating the infinite possibilities of reality.

Billy has always been very clear in stating that while his personal dowsing technique has enabled him to take his insight to a higher level - it is something that is available to all of us. Most people can dowse at least some of the time - but just about everyone who can dowse can also aspire to be a deviceless dowser too. From there, the whole of reality can almost be 'seen' on another plane.

Despite the great strides that have been made through his research, Billy is very aware that he has only opened a few doors - portals, if you like - through which others can follow. I have sought to point out some of the starting points for the next stages of this epic journey as we have gone along, but there are so many new vistas that spring from this research.

As with all breakthroughs, it may take time for the significance of his work to be grasped by the wider academic and scientific community. However, at least it has now been collected in one place, for others to use. When they do, I sincerely trust that the source of that wisdom is acknowledged. Billy may not seek praise or congratulation, but he does deserve to get the credit for carving a new and valuable niche in the unfolding story of human endeavour.

By way of a final emphasis, Billy is keen to clarify and summarise some of the basic principles of the physics and mechanics of earth energy, as he has described them at greater length in this book.

1. 'There is no evidence to show that earth energy lines contain any energy as we know it within the current scientific paradigm.

2. These dowsable radiations are not confined to the earth.

3. They are a phenomenon relating to all matter - from those with the smallest mass, such as atoms, right up to the largest groupings of bodies of mass - galaxies.

4. They can be contained within mass, but are generally radiated out from it in the form of lines.

5. These lines can be in any form, from perfectly straight, to curved, convoluted, or even rolled up into a small ball.

6. They exhibit themselves in three-dimensional form except for the straight line, which is linear - and can be horizontal, vertical, or at any angle.

7. Where a pattern or form could be described as geometrical, geo-glyphical, or archetypal - or any other overlapping pattern - these are formed by a single unicursal line, which starts at the source and eventually returns to that source.

8. The lines of radiation are, in most cases, susceptible to outside influence. They can alter in response to lunar, solar and planetary cycles, natural changes in the local environment, or changes brought about by all kinds of activity, human and otherwise - with and without intent.

9.   This susceptibility to influence is more significant when the source objects emitting the lines of radiation are placed in certain geometric relationships.

10.   All matter is interconnected through the web of subtle radiation that is an inherent part of it.'

No dowser alive today has travelled further down this particular line of research into the essential nature of earth energies.

Additionally, as we have seen, Billy has found that many megalithic structures appear to have been originally located, designed and built specifically to eliminate the harmful impact of detrimental earth energies - and he has demonstrated that this effect can be replicated very effectively today.

As a by-product of this work, not only has he confirmed that astronomical alignments are present in most megalithic structures - but that they appear to be naturally inherent in the design.

In addition to the energy templates that may have determined the shape and form of the megaliths, his academic dowsing has led him to appreciate that there are many energy patterns in the ground, or in 'the ether', that may act as a blueprint for the shape, form and very presence of life itself.

This train of thought has brought him as close as you can get to a practical confirmation of the concept - as many disparate philosophies have implied over the millennia - that we, and everything in our environment, are all profoundly and critically interconnected. He has described this both at the level of energy and also of its precursor, information. In a very real sense, we are all, indivisibly, one.

It is an exciting time to be alive, and an exciting time to be an earth energy dowser. The increasing awareness in human society is pushing out the scientific paradigm into areas previously reserved for spiritual contemplation. At the same time, fields abandoned for centuries as mere superstition are being given renewed focus and credibility. Billy's work has been part of this momentous dovetailing process.

It may have taken a lifetime, but getting beyond the far horizon has been a very worthwhile undertaking - and I consider it a great privilege to have been a Sherpa on the final ascent.

Billy marking out the position of stones for a proposed stone circle, using deviceless dowsing, at an EEG workshop at Bury St. Edmunds in 2008

APPENDICES

APPENDICES

Appendix A

Deviceless Dowsing - Why?

'Why would you want to convert to deviceless dowsing if you are already dowsing quite satisfactorily using a device of your choosing? After all, deviceless dowsing will not make you any better as a dowser, or enable you to get more accurate answers - so, why bother? Quite simply, it takes your dowsing to another level.

The main benefits of deviceless dowsing, using the methods that I describe, are:

1.   Speed - it is possible to gather as much information in a few minutes as would take perhaps an hour or more using tools.

2.   Detail - using the eye method allows for one to stand away from the target and observe in much greater detail, than when directly over the target. Three-dimensional dowsing is made easy.

3.   Discretion - when dowsing in public places. Using dowsing tools in public places can make those   who do not understand dowsing uncomfortable. We should strive to avoid this at all times.

4.   The bigger picture - not only can the deviceless dowser 'see' over a much wider area, but using my deviceless techniques I can detect energy forms that the conventional dowser would be unlikely to come across at all.

5.   The holistic approach - the conventional dowser is always restricted to dealing with one aspect of a search at a time. The deviceless, dowser using my 'visual' method, has the ability to see more of the inherent inte- relationship of a number of factors and elements in any given investigation.

There are many different forms of deviceless dowsing. Over the decades that I have practised dowsing, I have developed several methods which allow me to dowse without the use of tools. The one that I use most often for site dowsing is to ask that my eyes be directed towards the location of the object of my search. I then lock my eyes on that location and walk quickly towards it.

When using this method I re-programme my mind, so that the involuntary muscular movement is transferred from the arms (as used in conventional dowsing) to those muscles that control my neck and eye movements. Instead of the dowsing rod being pointed towards the target, my eyes are directed to the precise location of the object of my search.

I believe that the reason why the involuntary muscle movement is primarily found in the arm muscles is because we are usually taught to dowse by holding a dowsing tool. As I emphasised in this book, our minds are easily influenced by suggestion, and we will accept most things we are taught without question (see 'Consciousness, Dowsing and the Red Socks Syndrome' on page 240).

Another method that I use to find a target is to use my arms and hands without holding any tool or device. The hands should be held well apart, slightly wider than the body, with the palms of the hands facing forward at about 45 degrees to the forward path. Walk towards the target area with the expectation that when reaching it that the arms will be pushed apart until parallel with the body. At that point you should be directly over the target. To speed up getting started, it is a good exercise to initially find a target using your usual device and mark it. Then, approach it without the device, and encourage your arms to be pushed apart as you get close to the target. You will find that this action will soon happen without any encouragement on your part.

For more detailed dowsing, I use my hands to feel the outline of an energy form, both horizontally and vertically. By raising the sensitivity of the hands, the target starts to feel like a spongy object with real shape and mass.

I use my outstretched finger to follow and trace out a line of energy, which allows me to look at it in great detail. Again, this requires the re-programming of the default mechanism, so that the finger will feel as if it is stuck in a groove and it will follow the line of energy.

For dowsing at a distance I use visualisation dowsing. For this, I visualise the target area - and the desired target in my mind, and 'see' the answer as a grayscale, or black and white, picture with lines running across it. Even if one has never visited the dowsing site, or has scant information about it, it is possible to do this. First of all, try to visualise a rectangle, large enough to contain the area of your search, with you standing at one of the edges. Look for your desired target within this area. It is good practice to do this experiment with an area that is close to you, but which you have not previously dowsed, and then go to it and check it out.

To obtain 'yes' and 'no' answers to dowsing questions, I have again re-programmed my default mechanism - this time, so that my head will nod for a 'yes' answer or shake for a 'no' answer.

All of these methods require the formulation of the ever-important, unambiguous question, - generally called the Dowsing Question - that focuses the mind on the object of search. Without the Dowsing Question, no one can dowse successfully.

It is universally accepted that the movement of a dowsing tool is dependent on the dowsing process in the mind, which causes involuntary muscle movement to occur in the muscles of the arm and hand holding the tool. This, in turn, causes it to move in a meaningful way, which allows the dowser to gather the information that he or she is seeking. To change to any other method, which requires other muscle groups to be involved, it is necessary to re-programme the default mechanism so that the correct muscles respond. You only have to ask that this be so.

So, how does one start? First of all it is essential to have a belief in your ability to be successful at whatever you attempt to do - and that it is well within your ability to dowse devicelessly by whatever method you chose. To start with, it is perhaps wise to attempt to find a flow of underground water, rather than an energy line, as there are perhaps dozens of energy lines for every stream of underground water.

To use the 'eye' method, stand where you have clear sight over an area of ground. Cast your eyes over the area, and ask that they be focused on the surface of the ground where there is a flow of underground water. Speed is of the essence. Immediately allow your eyes to be locked on to a chosen spot, and walk quickly to the place indicated. Have something in you hand ready to mark the spot. Then, walk ten to fifteen paces away from the mark, take up your dowsing tool, close your eyes and walk toward the mark until you get a dowsing reaction, again searching for the same water. When you get a reaction, open your eyes and see how close you are to the mark.

Naturally, all underground streams have a width. So, using the dowsing tool, (or if you are sufficiently inspired, your hands) find both edgelines of the flow closest to the mark. This will allow you to see if the place you have selected devicelessly is within the edgelines.

If at first you do not succeed, try, try, again. In a short time, I am sure you will become successful. Continued development of any technique depends on repeated practice, and that much at least is within the control of every dowser.

I find that my method of dowsing is particularly useful when dowsing for energies that radiate from the earth, as they are usually three-dimensional in form. I can detect the path that they take as they rise from the surface of the ground. - I do not 'see' what they are, as they are invisible to the human eye, but rather I observe where they are. I know that what I am observing is the result of the dowsing question, which has focused my mind on the desired target.

To be able to follow the flow of energies as they rise from the earth is important, as they do not always rise vertically. Sometimes they rise at an angle or only emerge for a small distance above the ground.

Some of this radiation, especially that associated with flowing underground water, is considered to be detrimental to human health. To show the significance of this assertion, especially to someone new to the concept, it is important to have some means of demonstrating that this is indeed the case. I have found that when most people are exposed to detrimental energy, it causes interference with their normal brainwave function. It lowers the coherence of the signal generated in the brain, as it passes through the neurological system. If the signal is intended to be sent to a muscle in the arm, the muscle will not respond as requested, and will appear to be weak when put under pressure.'

Confirmation by muscle testing

'A simple but effective test, which I use to determine the presence of detrimental energy, is derived from the field of kinesiology. I feel that both dowsing and kinesiology are important tools in providing evidence for research into earth radiations; into their effect on our neurological system, and consequently on our well-being.

However to use muscle testing effectively in this way, it has to be carried out in a manner that prevents suggestion interfering with the achievement of accurate results. It is therefore important that the person under test is unaware of the expected result. It is also important that the person carrying out the test is fully aware of where the detrimental energy is rising upward, and that it rises higher than the head of the person under test. As there is a great variation in the amount of detrimental energy from one location to another, and there are certain areas where no detrimental energy rises from the earth at all, it is essential that its presence is verified by the dowser prior to attempting muscle testing. Before any testing is carried out over detrimental energy, it is also essential to test the subject when he or she is exposed to beneficial energy. In this manner, a baseline can be established as to the muscle resistance offered in normal circumstances.

The illustration at the top of page 302 shows a muscle test being carried out directly over a crossing point of the edge-lines of two flows of underground water. Where this is at a location that allows, or causes, detrimental energy to rise out of the ground, then the result is a lowering of muscle resistance - and the arm will be easily pushed down if the subject is positioned so that the rising line of detrimental energy passes through their head.

When setting up a test, it is essential that the dowser is clear as to where the detrimental energy rises, but that the subject does not know. After the initial test I would then get the person initially to stand about one foot away from where the detrimental energy rises, and with their back towards it. In this position the arm should test strong. I would then move the person backwards a few inches at a time and repeat the test. In this manner the subject will be unaware as to when they are being subjected to the detrimental energy, and this totally removes expectation from the experimental outcome.

If, and when, they are positioned so that the detrimental energy passes through their brain, then the arm will be easily pushed down. The difference in resistance is unmistakable to both the subject and the tester. In many cases the arm can be pushed down using only one finger placed on the arm above the wrist. Pressure should be applied just above the wrist in order not to risk damage to the wrist when the subject is not over detrimental energy.

The illustration overleaf shows where the test is being carried out at a seemingly similar location. However, in this instance the radiation does not rise vertically, but is angled to the left, and consequently it misses the head of the subject. The person under test is standing directly on the location where this radiation emanates from the ground, but due to the influence of some local feature - natural or manmade - it is deflected from the vertical. The result of this is that there is no lowering of muscle resistance. However, if the person is made to move sufficiently to their left so that the line of radiation passes through their head, then the arm would again be easily pushed down.

More interesting information can be discovered when the same test is carried out at a place where a very narrow line of this type of radiation, about the thickness of a pencil, is rising from the chosen location. This enables very accurate targeting of the line as it passes through the body. From this experiment, the parts of the brain and body that need to be affected to give a weakening of the arm muscle can be detected and identified. These are *the primary motor cortex*, responsible for generating the neural impulses

controlling execution of movement. The *cerebellum,* which acts as a co-ordinator and administrator of the muscles. The *thalami*, or midbrain through which most sensory messages pass. Finally, the nerves passing through the shoulder and upper arm.

Another series of tests can then be undertaken, with the person standing to the side of the chosen location. This time the outstretched arm is positioned directly over the line of ascending radiation, with it passing through the arm, between the hand and the elbow. The first test shows muscle strength to be normal. Next, the test subject is moved an inch at a time closer to the line of radiation and subsequent muscle tests applied. It is only when the line of radiation penetrates the arm above the elbow that the arm is easily pushed down. This would indicate that when the nervous system, which carries the message from the brain to the muscle, is subjected to this type of radiation the muscle resistance is lowered. (See diagram at top of next page).

A further, more refined, series of tests can be carried out to demonstrate more accurately the areas of the brain and the arm that need to be affected in order to bring about a lowering of muscle resistance (see previous page). The person under test is asked to stand at least a metre

or so away from where a line of detrimental radiation is rising from the earth. This experiment is best carried out indoors on a level floor. The end of a length of flexible wire is then taped to the ground directly above rising detrimental energy. The cable needs to be two to three metres in length - long enough for the other end to reach the head and arm of the person under test. An initial test for resistance is carried out, to provide a yardstick against which further tests can be evaluated. Then, the free end of the cable is placed against the head of the person so that the radiation flowing through the cable is directed precisely to certain areas of the brain. A sufficient number of muscle tests are then carried out, with the end of the wire at a different location on the head each time pressure is applied. The locations where a lowering of muscle resistance occurs can then be noted.

It can be seen that the areas of the brain affected are directly involved in both voluntary and involuntary muscle movements taking place throughout the body. Therefore, it is not surprising that when these critical parts of the brain are subjected to detrimental earth radiation that it can be demonstrated through a lowering of muscle resistance.

Muscle testing can be effectively used to demonstrate methods by which detrimental energy can be successfully earthed.

This is undertaken with the subject standing exposed to ascending detrimental radiation rising from an edge line of underground water. The first test will show a greatly reduced level of muscle resistance (see the photograph on the left). A second test is then carried out at the same location but with an object, such as a small to medium-sized stone, placed on the same edge line of the underground water - a short distance from where the person is standing. The result, this time, will be a return to normal strength (see the photograph on the right). The object appears to act as an earthing pin, and causes the radiation to be pushed back into the ground around it. The distance earthed depends on the mass of the object. To find the correct location to place the object without the ability to dowse would require a lot of time, but with dowsing the most effective place can be found in a few seconds.

These are all simple, repeatable experiments that can be replicated with 100% certainty - once the technique and expertise is fully understood and the procedure carried out correctly.'

Appendix B

Technological Advances in Design and Construction of Stone Circles

'Ever since mankind became dissatisfied with his lot, and tried to improve on what nature has provided, we have undertaken a similar, familiar, process: a problem is observed, an answer sought, and then a possible solution is put in place. Quite often that solution appears to work well in the first instance. However, in the longer term it is found that either there are several additional problems caused by the original action - or that the solution only works intermittently. In both situations, the choice is either to abort the original action taken, or to improve upon it, taking into consideration the shortcomings that have been observed.

In the great sweep of human history, I feel that there have been three significant processes that have had a particular impact on the state of wellbeing that we enjoy today. The first happened in the distant past, perhaps 10,000 years ago, with the introduction of farming. This required the clearance of large areas of land to make it suitable for agriculture. It paved the way for the settling down of populations, and for the establishment of towns and cities. The second, which started during the 18th century, but only came to its zenith in the 19th century, was mechanisation and the industrial revolution that followed on from it. The third originated in the late 20th century; it was the move beyond mechanisation, into the world of electronic engineering and Internet Technology.

In recent times there has been a realisation that, marvellous as all these advancements have been, there is also a downside to them. Significant harm is being done to our environment in a subtle manner that is difficult to observe. As a result of this appreciation, we are now trying to manufacture goods, construct buildings, manage houses, and adjust our lifestyles in ways that achieve a zero carbon footprint. In the many cases where this is unachievable - or only achievable at excessive cost - other actions can sometimes be taken to offset this shortfall that can effectively cancel out the carbon debt. By doing this, it seems that it may be possible to continue with something like our current lifestyle without causing irreparable damage to our planet for the foreseeable future.

Beyond the Far Horizon

In the 21st Century, we are of the opinion that this realisation of the subtle damage inflicted on our planet by human intervention has only became apparent in recent years - but I believe that may not be the case. I am convinced that at least some people, shortly after the commencement of farming and the clearance of large areas of land of trees and boulders, became aware that a subtle change was occurring in our living environment. They realised that it was to our wider detriment - and they took action to reverse the situation. The subtle change I refer to was a significant increase in a form of radiation or energy, which was detrimental to the wellbeing of humans, - and also to that of all other forms of life in the areas affected.

The action taken was two-fold, and mirrors closely what is being considered today with respect to our physical biosphere. Firstly there was a need to contain the situation: then they had to reverse, or offset, the harm that had already been done. The primary intervention was to erect structures of timber or stone, of a particular design and type. These caused whatever harmful radiation was present to be driven back into the earth, and away from the environment in which we live. The secondary line of action was to ensure that any new or existing structures, set up for purposes other than earthing detrimental energy, would enhance the subtle energetic environment - or at the very least be neutral in that respect.

However, as with most things, it is not always possible to get a solution that works effectively everywhere all of the time. Therefore, ongoing innovation and modification is required to adapt a generic plan to meet unique local conditions. I believe that this was what the stone circle builders in ancient times had to contend with. I also believe that they looked, listened, learned, and solved many of the difficulties that they encountered. The diversity of design that we find from one structure and location to another was what they found necessary to implement in order to overcome the unique problems they came across.

I want to revisit a significant problem, which I believe the ancient circle builders became aware of - one which I believe they were able to address in the majority of cases. On pages 84 and 85 I explained, with the help of diagrams, that a problem arises as the result of an interaction between the earth and moon as they orbit the sun, in addition to the tilt of the earth. These planetary mechanisms cause the lengthening and shortening of daylight hours, and result in the onset of summer and winter in those latitudes north and south of the tropics. Those of us who have studied subtle energies over the years, as they are displayed on the face of the earth, have noted that they change in a manner that relates to the solar and lunar phases.   There is likely to be planetary interference as well, although it is not so noticeable.

There is a significant change that takes place for about two days around the time of each new and full moon. I have observed that the energy vortices present over the intersections of the edgelines, and in some cases the centre lines, of flows of underground water alter shape and take on the form of energy cylinders. Where a standing stone has been erected or a stone circle built, using stones of a reasonable size, there is little or no problem for about nine months of the year, because the diameters of the energy cylinders do not expand significantly, and consequently they remain in contact with the whole stone. This keeps the detrimental energy firmly earthed.

However, after the September equinox, the days shorten. At each new and full moon, the girths of the energy cylinders grow larger and larger until they eventually lose contact with the stone. Detrimental energy is then no longer earthed for a period of a few days. This situation has its greatest impact at the new or full moon that is closest to the winter solstice. During this period, detrimental energy can be present - no longer earthed by the stone - for up to a week. There is a similar event at the time of the summer solstice, although here the impact of the leaking detrimental energy only lasts for a couple of days.

As the occurrence of this phenomenon is aggravated by the change that takes place in the length of the day - due to the angle of tilt either away from or towards the sun - it is therefore more noticeable in latitudes well north and south of the equator. As the earth is a sphere, these increases in the girth of the energy cylinders are not gradual from the equator to the poles, but, exponential. Therefore, the effect is greater, and more noticeable, the further north or south from the equator that one travels. For example, there is a significant difference between what happens in the south of England and the north of Scotland - where at the time of the winter solstice the sun only rises for a short while each day. The opposite happens at the summer solstice, where in the further reaches of the northern hemisphere the sun barely sets. Therefore, a solution to leaking detrimental energy that could work well at one latitude would not necessarily suffice at another.

So, what potential solutions were available for the ancient stone circle builders to use?

In some latitudes, the use of sizable stones would, in itself, suffice. If not totally eliminating the problem, it would reduce it to an insignificant level.

However, where this approach does not prove adequate, a short-term solution can be found by taking one or more appropriate actions. Human activity in the form of certain types of ceremony (including drumming, dancing or chanting) can cause detrimental energy to retreat into the earth, at least whilst this activity is being carried out. The random scattering of pottery shards or cremated bone, or the lighting of fires, may also eliminate detrimental energy for a short period of time.

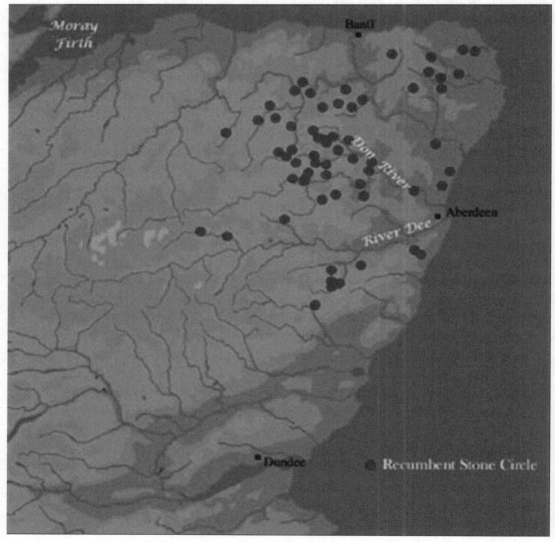

Map showing the density of recumbent circles in Aberdeenshire, Scotland.

There is historical and archaeological evidence that these activities may have been used, perhaps in combination, at certain locations.

However, all these interventions require ongoing effort. I believe that a more permanent solution was investigated - and achieved - in the more northerly areas, where the problem was most severe. In the northeast of Scotland, there are a number of stone circles that have unique characteristics - they are known as The Recumbent Stone Circles of Aberdeenshire. Recumbent stones, i.e. stones that are lying flat on the ground rather than upright, can be found elsewhere. However, they are not the same as those found in Aberdeenshire, and they may well have fallen down, or were possibly never erected in the first place. The Aberdeen recumbent stones are unique in that they were deliberately positioned between two upright pillar stones. The remainder of the stones comprising the circle are upright, and are more or less in the same format as can be found in stone circles elsewhere.

As a starting point, it is interesting to consider the findings of professional archaeologists:

"Recumbent Stone Circles (RSCs) are found in the Grampian region of northeast Scotland, where over one hundred have been identified. They are particularly concentrated in the rolling hills around Bennachie, a singular peak dominating the Aberdeenshire countryside. These are the best and earliest examples of the type, dating (on the basis of pottery finds) to about 3000 BC. Over the course of the following centuries, the tradition spread to some of the peripheral areas to the north, east and south - the latest dating to about 1500 BC.

The circles are smallish - perhaps 18-25 metres in diameter - and are usually made up of ten or eleven stones, graded in height, with the tallest pair set in the south western quadrant flanking a much larger stone lying on its side (the recumbent).

While only a small number of workers - perhaps fewer than a dozen - would have been required to transport and set up most of the stones in the circle, the recumbents tend to be much larger and heavier. The one at Old Keig weighs over 50 tonnes and came from a source over 10 kilometres away. Dragging such an enormous block to the site would have needed the effort of at least a hundred people."

Several people have suggested that the recumbent stones were used for sacrificial purposes, with animals or even humans stretched out on them, and killed as an offering to whatever gods they worshipped at that time. Another theory is that the top of the recumbent was used as a surface over which the heavens could be viewed. However, from the following evaluation these do not seem to be very satisfactory answers.

"At many of the sites, the upper surface of the recumbent is actually more of an edge - too narrow to support an outstretched body or sacrificial animal - and therefore not really suitable as an altar although it is tempting to imagine it as such. The setting is far too broad to have been much use for sighting solar events or the appearance of particular stars. The most convincing alignment involves the lunar cycle of 18.61 years and the majority of recumbents lie on the arc between the major rising and setting of the moon at these latitudes - roughly south-southeast to southwest."

Old Keig recumbent stone.

As you will recall, the stones in any authentic circle that I have dowsed appear to be related to the underground water flows that I have found there. I have also emphasised the need to be able to differentiate between water coming from blind springs as opposed to that from downshafts. After dowsing a number of recumbent circles, a distinct pattern began to emerge in my findings which show a common feature - the two pillar stones and the length of the recumbent is over a centre line of an underground flow from a downshaft. There is another similar underground flow crossing this at the mid point and at approximately 90 degrees to it. See diagram below.

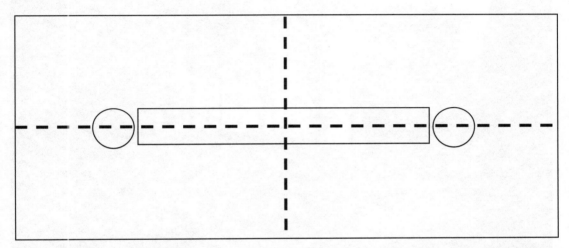

There is a vortex of energy at all intersection points, as I have described elsewhere. It is this vortex that would be influenced by the lunar and solar phases, changed into an energy cylinder and expanded greatly at the time of the winter and summer solstices. The pillars and recumbent stone create a sufficiently wide structure to contain this expansion and continue to earth detrimental energy in the area of influence of the circle.

The exception to this general rule is at Midmar Kirk, which is located beside a church. It is well known that this circle has been altered in recent times with several of the stones being repositioned. I believe that the two pillar stones and the recumbent may have suffered this fate. Burl politely says that this circle has been *"interfered with"*. That is, landscaped and probably rearranged.

The stones at Midmar Kirk are not sufficient to effectively earth rising detrimental energy at critical periods, and a much longer recumbent would be required than the one in place at present.

If we look at the recumbent stone at Midmar in the photograph on the below, it can be seen that it does not match the situation observed by archaeologists at other circles. I quote:

"Apparently it was important that the upper side of the recumbent was horizontal and parallel to the ground."

If that is the case, then why should it be so, if it was not intended to be used as an altar or a sacrificial table? I have carried out a few relevant experiments that suggest an answer to this question - and it is an answer that fits with the observations on site. Understandably, these experiments were not carried out using stones weighing 50 tonnes or more, but with a small plank of wood that was easily handled, in conjunction with a suitably sized spiral containing detrimental energy. As the plank was uniform in thickness, and it was placed on a level floor, this allowed for reasonably accurate measurements to be made.

I found that an object ceased to effectively earth the detrimental energy when the breadth exceeded the height by more than about 6%, unless the top was reasonably level. The critical point at where the object loses its effectiveness is when the top surface exceeds 3 to 4 degrees off the horizontal. (This angle of between 3 and 4 degrees seems to be critical in many of my research findings. It keeps cropping up at different places and in various applications.) If we look at the picture of the recumbent at Midmar Kirk, it is far from level on the upper side. My dowsing indicates that for the Midmar Kirk configuration to be effective, using my scaled down model as a guide, the pillar stone standing towards the church would need to be much closer to it - and nearly touching the headstones - while the pillar stone to the right would need to be moved about its own breadth further to the right. The recumbent stone then would need to be about 50% longer to fill the gap.

In all the other recumbent circles that I visited, the stones as they are positioned at the moment would successfully overcome the fluctuations in energy vortices that occur at the solstice periods.

The written reports of excavations that have taken place at several of the recumbent circles has revealed that preparatory or adjustment work was carried out, either before, or some time after the original circle was built. In the case of the stones at Tomnaverie it was found:

> " . . . that the earliest feature detectable at the site was a cremation pyre, its area, identified by magnetic measurements, was found to contain a scatter of small cremated bone fragments. The first structural phase of the monument was the construction of a cairn, or platform, of stone rubble, which levelled the site. The stone circle was constructed next, enclosing the original cairn. The last activity detectable at the site was the digging of a cremation pit into the centre; this is thought to have occurred around 1000 BC.

> The discovery that a ring cairn predated the circle construction completely changed ideas of how these monuments had evolved and were constructed. This finding was of such importance that further limited excavations were carried out at the RSCs of Cothiemuir Wood and Aikey Brae in 2001, to see if the same sequence of construction could be found at those monuments. Sure enough, both of these investigations returned similar findings."

However, we find another report that, at least as far as Aikey Brae is concerned, is contradictory of the above.

> "Aikey Brae Stone Circle

> The usual pattern was for these circles to fall out of use within a few hundred years, then for later generations of residents to use them as cremation cemeteries, eventually building a cairn in the centre of the circle. It is not

clear whether that happened here, because although the circle itself is relatively undisturbed, the same cannot be said of the area within it. A dig in the centre of the circle by Charles Elphinstone-Dalrymple in the 1800s revealed little of value and probably removed any evidence that might be available to later archaeologists."

A report on the Nine Stanes at Mulloch Wood is interesting in that excavations exposed a central ring cairn, but the conclusion was that it was added later.

"A central ring-cairn was added later. The site was excavated in 1904 and a pit, which contained charcoal and cremated bone, was found at the centre. Another four deposits of cremated bone and one of charcoal mixed with pottery were also found around the pit."

Easter Aquhorthies recumbent stone circle is unique in several ways.

"It is almost perfectly circular and consists of 9 erect stones, the recumbent, two flankers plus two massive blocks which form a reserved area in front of the recumbent, almost at perpendicular to it. The stones are graded in height from the 2.25m high flankers to the 1.7m high stones on the circumference opposite. The stones are unusually broad and are of pinkish porphyry, with the stone next to the east flanker being of glowing red jasper. The flankers are grey granite. The recumbent is reddish granite, whose outer face has been smoothed carefully. Some evidence indicates that a ring cairn was situated inside it although no traces can be seen. The interior has a slightly hollowed area towards the centre. Keillar (1934) referred to a cist, which 'had been covered with a capstone'. The low stone bank surrounding the circle has been added to in recent times."

All of this demonstrates clearly the unique nature of each construction, and the way that it was tailored to meet the requirements of the site. It also demonstrates that there was an ongoing process of research and development, which took place. Modifications were made accordingly, to improve the functioning of the structure and overcome any deficiencies.

The work that I have undertaken at my own circle and cairn, and the effects achieved through the introduction of quartz and bone, would appear to provide a reason for the way that ancient stone circles developed over the two or three thousand years during which they were constructed.'

Appendix C

Underwood and Thom Revisited

Guy Underwood

The name of perhaps the first earth energy dowser, in the modern sense of the word, Guy Underwood, makes several appearances in this book. For some years his seminal work, *The Pattern of the Past,* has been regarded with a mixture of scepticism and derision. Whilst Underwood certainly didn't get everything correct, the unfolding research is showing that he might have been much closer to the truth than it has been realised.

'Guy Underwood said that standing stones etc. were placed on spirals. I would agree with this statement as spirals are found where centre lines of underground water from downshafts cross. However, he did not indicate that the spirals he referred to were due to underground water. I do agree with his findings that the chambered cairns seem to have been placed over spirals (and then charged to boost beneficial energies).

He was decried (by myself and others) for showing that energy lines marked out the positions of the fallen stones at Stonehenge and elsewhere - and for drawing the conclusion that they had been placed in that way deliberately, sometime in the distant past.

However, we have to remember that Underwood was working in a field with little academic precedent - and what he recorded was what he found. In fact, he was closer to the mark than most of us thought a few decades ago, in that he probably dowsed where the energies were at the time he was doing his research, and that showed that objects of mass tend to attract energy around them.

In the experiment with the flowerpots on the patio, I showed that a line of energy can be bent or attracted to an object by the judicious placing of it and other objects. Fallen stones, especially those of great size in an energetically charged location, could have much the same impact.

So, with hindsight, his work was surprisingly solid - it was just his conclusion that was incorrect. He should be posthumously commended for it. It was a sound platform to stand on (and the rest of us are still standing on it!)'

Alexander Thom

Another name closely associated with the positioning of megaliths and their associated geometry, is that of Professor Alexander Thom. He believed that the ancient civilizations, who constructed stone circles, had an advanced knowledge of mathematics, geometry and astronomy which they used to establish the design and layout of these structures. Thom was given a hard time by contemporary archaeologists, who felt his ideas on the methods of construction and use of stone circles were preposterous. He is best known for the discovery of the measurements, found at many archaeological sites, that he termed the Megalithic Yard (M.Y.) and the Megalithic Rod (M.R.). However, for all his insight, Billy takes Thom to task when it comes to the way he carried out some of his work and the conclusions that he drew from that research.

'The stone circle that I built in my garden incorporates a measurement, which conforms very closely with the Megalithic Yard and Megalithic Rod, as defined by Alexander Thom. If it had been an ancient circle, it would have been in the top three or four circles in terms of conformity - when compared to over a hundred others that he described in his work.

I did not use any complicated geometry, or measure the stones into position after drawing a detailed plan. I dowsed for their location by marking the precise position of the major intersections of the edgelines, and in some cases the centre lines, of the numerous large underground flows crossing at the selected site. This is something that is always present at an authentic stone circle. Several major energy lines will usually be found to cross there as well, but the stones do not necessarily need to be placed to correspond with them. If these characteristics are not present at what Thom called 'stone rings', then they are not stone circles, but the remains of some other ancient circular structure.

I dowsed the locations where the stones should be placed, by standing somewhere near to the centre of the proposed circle, eyeing out the intersection points and quickly walking to them and pushing a peg into the ground. The complete operation only took about twenty minutes. In carrying out this operation I did not for a second consider the completed shape of the proposed circle. The pegs were not inserted in order around the circle, but at random as my dowsing dictated. It was only when all 19 pegs were in place that I stood back and looked at the complete picture. I had no idea of the total number of stones that would be required until my dowsing told me that they were all in place. I could see that the pegs did not form a perfect circle and that the form was egg-shaped or elliptical. The stones were placed with the intersection points as near to the centre of the stones as possible, but not precisely so.

Sometime after the stones were in position I marked on the top of each stone, with a piece of chalk, the exact position of the edgeline intersection of the underground water over which the stones were placed. I hammered in a fencing post close to the centre of the circle and put a nail in the top of the post on to which I could secure the end of a long steel tape. I then measured from this nail to all the chalk marks on the stones. I added these together, found the average value, and multiplied the result by two to give the mean diameter. This was then compared to the value of the Megalithic Yard. The results are shown overleaf.

The next task was to find an accurate perimeter measurement. At first glance this may appear not to be too difficult. If it were a circle, one simply needs to multiply the diameter by 3.14159 to get an accurate result. However, when we are measuring something not circular, or rectangular in form, difficulties arise.

Thom was aware of these difficulties and devised systems of complicated geometry to arrive at a solution. This produced arcs, which in the main corresponded with the position of the stones. However, in some cases a stone, or several stones, lay outside or inside the arc. The lengths of these sections of arc were added together to give a perimeter length.

In his book, *Megalithic Remains in Britain and Brittany,* Thom listed many of the difficulties that he encountered during this process. His first observation was that that there is little or no correlation between the size of the stone, the size of the circle and the spacing of the stones around the perimeter. He also felt that several factors had been responsible for moving some of the stones away from their original positions, thereby altering the respective diameters. He went on to give several examples of how this might have happened.

Soil Creep: Over a long period of time, even a one degree angle of slope can produce what is termed as solifluction. He used the Cumbrian megalithic complex of Long Meg and her Daughters as a typical example. It is built on a slope of 3°, which he believed to have been responsible for stones having moved because of soil creep. His survey plans suggested that some of the stones had moved down the slope to the north. In his opinion, this explained why the original geometry now appears to lie in some disarray.

Trees: Stones can become entwined in the roots of trees. If the tree falls, the stone is uprooted with the tree. In time, the wood rots away, leaving almost no trace, and the stone position has consequently been changed from its original placement.

Frost: Wet earth lifts under heavy frost, which can exert considerable force on a stone. Over many winters, the positions of stones may change by a few inches.

Farm Animals: He also reckoned that there was some movement of stones due to farm animals using them as rubbing posts.

Thom dealt with errors as follows:

With small errors, where the sample was large enough, there are usually as many negative errors as positive ones, and they tended to even themselves out. In this situation he took a mean value. He was of the opinion that very large errors did not occur very often. Where they were encountered, he believed them to be the result of human action - people moving stones either through malice or by re-erecting fallen stones without fully considering their previous location.

At sites that were badly damaged, with several stones missing, he took another approach. Sometimes he was able to establish the original position of a missing stone by locating the socket, as it was almost impossible to remove all traces of the hole where a stone or post once stood. When that failed, Thom attempted to assess the original position of a missing stone by averaging the spaces between adjacent stones. The position of a fallen stone was similarly 'guestimated' by averaging within the implied geometry of the adjacent or neighbouring stones.

Having identified the difficulties in establishing a perimeter measurement in *Megalithic Remains in Britain and Brittany* Thom warns that, '*It is only in exceptional circumstances that we can expect megalithic stones to be accurately in their original places*'.

I would agree that there is indeed the possibility that a few stones have moved slightly from their original location over the years. However, I believe we are entitled to ask the question: Have all the stones that did not conform to the geometry that he imposed on the sites actually moved, or are most of them still in the position that was originally intended for them, and were his expectations over ambitious?

With my modern circle, none of the above reasons for any of the stones not being in their 'proper' place applied. The stones are exactly where I required them to be according to my criteria. As I said previously, it is not a true circle and I am aware that two of the stones in particular would not conform to any arc that I can apply to the structure. Not having a theodolite to assist in the measurement, I had to resort to other means that would provide a reasonably accurate result.

I measured the perimeter in a series of straight lines, using the chalk marks on the stones that indicated the intersections as reference points. This was carried out carefully, with the minimum of error. I took Thom's view that any errors that present in the 19 sections would cancel each other out.

As a straight line is the shortest distance between two points, it is therefore clear that an arc measurement must be slightly greater. The amount of that additional length is not dependent on the radius, but on the distance apart in degrees of the two points on the circumference. If the two points are less than 5 degrees apart, the additional value is so small that it could be safely ignored. With 19 stones in my home circle the average spacing is just less than 20 degrees. The adjustment value used to convert a straight line measurement to an arc measurement is the multiple, 1.005.

I, further, converted the calculated perimeter measurement to Megalithic Rods and found that my home circle is very close to conformity according to Thom. He held the view that the circle builders intended the diameter, where possible, to be a multiple of M.Y.s Where this could not be achieved, half and quarters were allowable. The perimeter to be expressed in M.R.s or fraction thereof. See Page 61. Line four in each of the calculations, in brackets, is Thom's target measurement.

Mean Diameter = 68.6925 ft. or 824.31 ins.
1 M. Y. = 2.72 ft. or 32.64 ins.
68.6925 ÷ 2.72 = 25.2546 M.Y.
(25.25 M.Y. = 824.16 ins.)
824.31 - 824.16 = 0.15 ins. diameter error

Perimeter = 217.666 ft. or 2611.99 ins.
1 M. R. = 2.5 M.Y. = 6.80 ft = 81.6 ins.
217.5 ÷ 6.80 = 31.985 M.R.
(32 M.R. × 6.8 = 217.6 ft. or 2611.20 ins.)
2611.99 - 2611.20 = 0.79 ins. perimeter error

Since then, I have had the opportunity to measure one of the other circles that I designed and built - the one in Askeaton, Limerick - again using the same method for setting out. Here, too, it is close to conforming with measurements in Megalithic Yards and Megalithic Rods.

Mean Diameter = 39.58 ft. or 474.96 ins.
1 M.Y. = 2.72 ft. = 32.64 ins.
39.58 ÷ 2.72 = 14.55 M.Y.
(14.5 M.Y. = 473.28 ins.)
474.96 - 473.28 = 1.68 ins. diameter error

$$\text{Perimeter} = 125.71 \text{ ft or } 1508.52 \text{ ins.}$$
$$1 \text{ M.R.} = 2.5 \text{ M.Y.} = 6.80 \text{ ft} = 81.6 \text{ ins.}$$
$$1508.52 \div 81.6 = 18.487 \text{ M.R.}$$
$$(81.6 \times 18.5 \text{ M.R.} = 1509.60 \text{ ins.})$$
$$1509.60 - 1508.52 = 1.08 \text{ ins. perimeter error}$$

I am not saying that a Megalithic Yard does not exist in the design of ancient stone circles. Quite the converse, I am a firm believer that it does. However, I feel that it is inherent in nature, and not contrived by man. I am making the case, derived from my own personal experience, that the stones in stone circles were placed according to an existing blueprint in the ground. This blueprint was the result of natural forces, which caused underground water to be present where it was - and that the stones were placed at the intersections of the edgelines of those water flows, to earth detrimental energy that was rising into the environment.

The natural forces that I am referring to are contained in the hubs of attraction that are located in mountains and hills and the lines of attraction that run from them. These lines criss-cross each other as they transverse the landscape. As a result there are locations where several cross at the same place. I have mentioned that at the location of authentic stone circles there will be crossing flows of underground water and major energy lines. I have found that where these are present there will, of necessity, be several lines of attraction crossing there as well. I believe that it is the attractive power at the crossing of several of these lines that causes the underground water and energy lines to exist at that place. The only other factors which determine the location and format is the geology of the earth beneath, and the ability of the various types of strata to hold underground water.

Whilst it appears that the two circles referred to above conform closely to the M.Y. and M.R. measurements, it may be over-ambitious to expect every circle to contain the same degree of accuracy. There are likely to be locations where the geology determines another outcome.

What concerns me about Thom's work is that, although he states that his measurements were accurate to a fraction of a millimetre, using the best theodolite available, to have a truly accurate measurement, you must have something to measure from - and something to measure to. He had something to measure from, which was the centre as he defined it, where he set up his theodolite - but where did he measure to?

Typically, you're talking about the breadth of a stone with a diameter of maybe half a metre, sometimes a little more. Where on that half metre of granite, or whatever, do you put the point that you are measuring to?

When I was doing the measurement of my circle, I put a chalk mark on each stone on the precise point of the intersection of the edge lines of the underground water flows, so I had a point that was accurate to within one or two millimeters to measure to. I therefore feel that Thom's measurements cannot be regarded as sufficiently accurate. They are supposed measurements to a superimposed arc that has been drawn over the circle.

Thom assumed that any point on the top of a stone indicated an intended point. Any stone which was not on the arc, was probably the result of sloppy construction methods, or of some movement to the stone over time.

However, leaving the accuracy of his work aside, he did identify the possible presence of a standard measurement, which he called a Megalithic Yard, at a large number of stone circles. That I do not dispute. What I do question is whether those who designed and built these ancient structures were aware of this measurement, and if they understood the complicated geometry that Thom felt was necessary to construct the circles that remain to this day.'

Appendix D

Useful Dowsing Exercises

No matter what we aim to do throughout life, the knowledge that we can carry out whatever task that we set ourselves successfully increases our confidence, and thus our ability to achieve more. This is doubly so with dowsing. With some aspects of dowsing, such as marking a suitable position for a well, or borehole, feedback on the accuracy of the dowsing will usually come quickly. It is similar when attempting to find lost objects. Generally, the more positive the feedback, the greater the improvement in accuracy.

However, in many of the disciplines in which dowsing is now used, the verification of results is difficult to achieve. Earth Energy dowsing is one of those, as here we are dealing with the unseen. I believe it is important that those who are interested in this field of dowsing should find ways of providing verification, as it is one of the sections that attracts most external interest. However, there are certain exercises that can be used to give some indication of the dowser's level of success. I believe that if a dowser can achieve a high success rate in one discipline then they are more likely to do so when they take on other tasks.

Below, I outline several exercises that will improve skills. If practised regularly, they will help the dowser to reach an acceptable level. While some dowsers feel that certain aspects of the skill are only for the more expert, in my experience I have often found that it is easier for a relatively new dowser to take on new and seemingly difficult tasks. Those who have been dowsing for some years can sometimes be hesitant of attempting to work outside their comfort zone - so I would encourage you all to have a go, and you may well surprise yourselves.

Most of the following exercises may be best carried out with two people working together. Whilst they are directed towards those wishing to learn the skill of deviceless dowsing, nearly all of them can also be undertaken using standard devices.

Exercise 1:

This exercise is best carried out on a large area of ground, which is reasonably flat and free from obstacles.

Place a straight piece of wood, such as a brush handle, on the ground about 15 to 20 paces away from where you intend to start the exercise.

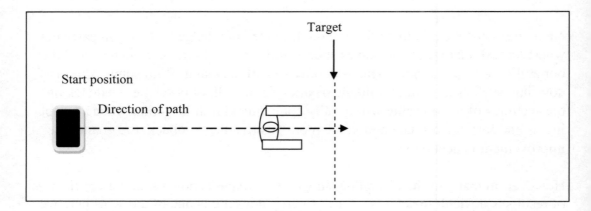

At the start position, face down the area of ground. Close your eyes, and walk slowly towards the object with the intention firmly in your mind that you will get a dowsing reaction that will cause you to stop directly opposite the end of the piece of wood. When a reaction is felt open your eyes and see how close you are to being in line with the target. (see diagram above)

Exercise 2:

Most dowsers find an underground stream or an energy line by intersecting it, either once, or at several points. However it is useful to be able to follow a line, whether it is an edgeline of underground water or an energy line. It is only by doing so, that the true course it takes, and its profile, can be observed. If a dowser is serious about investigating earth energies it is essential to be able to follow a line at walking speed. Plenty of practice with eyes open, as well as with eyes closed, carried out regularly, will soon improve this skill. At first, energy lines may seem straight and continuous, but when dowsed carefully, and with the intention of observing the detail, they may seem different. This ability needs to be developed to a high degree of skill before moving on to the more complex aspects of dowsing.

Exercise 3:

This exercise requires two people, and a good area of level ground over which neither of them have dowsed previously. It involves searching for streams of underground water, or energy lines.
Ask your dowsing partner to mark out an area of ground about 30 paces by 20 paces, by putting in a stake at each corner of the selected area.

This should be done out of your sight, so that you do not know the exact position of the selected area.

Take a sheet of A4 paper and draw a line about one inch in from the edges to form a rectangle. This rectangle will represent the selected area of ground. Decide where you will be standing on the designated area of ground. Close your eyes and envisage the rectangle in your mind. Ask that you be shown where streams of underground water are present within this area. Have confidence in your ability, and mark lines on the drawing where you believe streams to be. Confine yourself to a maximum of three lines.

Go to the area of ground and stand where you had visualised. Relate the orientation of the piece of paper to the area of ground. Then, dowse the actual area to see how closely that corresponds with what you marked on the drawing. You could also ask your dowsing partner to dowse the ground for the lines of underground water, and see how their work corresponds with your own drawing. The exercise can be repeated with major energy lines as the target. Make sure it is major energy lines that you aim for, as there will be many, many, smaller energy lines, which could render the results of the exercise useless. This exercise could also be carried out with the target being rooms or buildings where you have not dowsed previously. Repetition will assist greatly when you attempt map dowsing, or visualisation, prior to visiting a site.

Exercise 4:

Map dowsing, and the dowsing of photographs, is often carried out successfully, using various methods involving tools. However, if visualisation dowsing is used instead, it opens the way to successfully dowse images on a computer or on a television screen. With the advent of modern technology, images can be frozen on the screen, which makes dowsing more practical as the scene in real time may only last for a few seconds. It is possible for anyone who adopts this method of dowsing to examine landscapes to determine the quality of the earth energies, or the presence of underground water anywhere, as live TV images now come from all over the world. Another good source amenable to this method of dowsing are those produced by Google Earth. This allows us to focus in on almost anywhere we wish, and for many locations the detail is excellent. It is exceptionally helpful that with Google Earth it is possible to navigate around the screen. Consequently, the dowser can follow either water or energy lines back to their source, or on to where they terminate.

Exercise 5:

Although this is a much more ambitious exercise, you may be surprised at your level of success, if you approach it casually, but with confidence. As in the previous exercises, two people and a large area of level ground are required.

Both participants need to stand at the mid point of one edge of the area. Person (1), who is directing the operation, should stand with their back to the area of ground. Person (2) should stand beside the person (1), but facing towards the selected area.

Person (1) then directs person (2) to a position where they are over a sizable stream of underground water. The first instruction should be to ask them to walk forward in a straight line for not less than 20 paces and then stop.

Person (1) then evaluates the situation and determines whether person (2) needs to walk straight on, or to turn 90 degrees to the left, or to the right. Person (1) also determines how many additional paces person (2) will need to take.

If person (1) is happy that person (2) is directly over underground water, then they should be told to stand still until instructed otherwise. If it is felt that more adjustment is required, then more instructions are given. When person (1) gets an affirmative answer, through dowsing, that person (2) is standing on the correct location, they are told to stand where they are, or to put a marker into the ground.

An even more ambitious way of directing the person to the target can be by both parties being some distance apart and out of sight of each other - but in contact by mobile phone. This opens up the possibility of carrying out such an exercise at any distance, no matter where they are in the world, provided phone contact can be made.

Checking the accuracy of the dowsing can be undertaken in two ways. The first method is to go directly to person (2) and to dowse for the presence of underground water. Both edgelines should be found to establish if the person is over the water, to one side of it, or possibly nowhere near it at all!

An alternative method of checking can be by person (1) turning around to generally face the area of ground. However, instead of walking directly towards person (2), they aim at an angle of about 30 degrees to their right or left. Then they walk, with their eyes closed, and ask to find the edgeline of the underground stream that person (2) is standing over - or, if they are not over a stream, the one closest to them.

When a reaction is felt, still with eyes closed, turn to face your target. Detect where the edgeline is, and follow it towards your target. During this exercise person (2) should remain silent. It is only when person (1) is about to bump into them or into something else (or that they are so far off course and in danger of disappearing into the distance!) that person (2) can speak. Those of you keen enough to try this out, may be delighted by your results. Even if you do not succeed, it is all good fun - and you may have better success next time.

Exercise 6:

This exercise, which employs visualisation dowsing, can be carried out when you call in at a service station to fill up with fuel. As you get out to work the pump, allow a number to come into your head, which will be the expected amount required to fill the tank - in either litres, or in money terms. If a round figure is selected then there is room for a small degree of error. When the pump cuts out, the handle should be pushed again in case there is an airlock. Persistence with this will soon provide you with some surprising results, which are much greater than you would achieve by chance alone.

It is important that dowsers develop their skills to a high level - and achieve consistent and reliable results - before launching themselves onto the general public in the expectation of a financial reward.

Appendix E

The Golden Mean and Three Bricks

'Some time ago I observed that when three objects were placed in positions relative to each other the individual energy fields of the objects interacted in various ways. When placed in alignment, and at certain distances apart, the three circular fields disappeared. Instead, a straight line of energy was formed with radial lines going away from each object. The energy dowsed in these lines is mainly detrimental in nature.

I also observed that, when three objects were set in a certain triangular formation, interaction again took place - with the individual energy lines disappearing and straight radial lines of energy coming away from the objects. However, in this case it dowsed as being mainly beneficial. I subsequently wondered if the shape or geometry of the triangle had any significant impact on the outcome. Therefore, I carried out the following experiment to see if that were the case.

I placed two bricks (A & B) at random on a reasonably level area of concrete. There were energy fields to be observed around both bricks. I then placed a third brick at random in a position that created a triangular form. There were individual energy fields around all three bricks. I then moved brick (C) until I observed the disappearance of the individual energy fields and there were straight lines of energy dowsable between all three bricks. I also noted curved lines were coming away from the three bricks.

I continued to move brick (C), by a millimetre or so at a time, until the radial lines became reasonably straight in all cases. From brick (A) there were three radial lines, and from bricks (B and C) six radial lines. I did not move brick (C) any further at that stage, but I believe that if I had achieved perfection as regard to the Golden Ratio then there may have been the same number of radials from all bricks.

I then marked on the end of the bricks, in pencil, their centre position - and I measured the distance between them. The measurements found are as shown on the above photograph to the nearest millimetre.

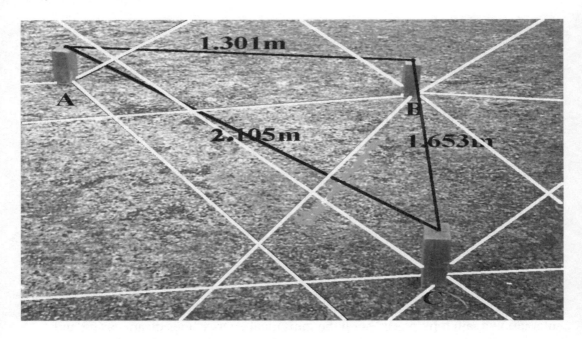

The Golden Mean is a ratio of 1 to 1.618, the square root of which is 1.272. A triangle constructed to this ratio has a base as 1, the perpendicular side as 1.272 times the base, and the hypotenuse as 1.618 times the base.

It is interesting to compare the measurement of a triangle conforming to this ratio with the triangle that I constructed with the three bricks through dowsing.

Base = 1301 mm

	Calculated Values	Measured
	1301 mm x 1.272 = 1654.872 mm	1653 mm
	1301 mm x 1.618 = 2105.018 mm	2105 mm

Side A to C conformed exactly - and side B to C was just under 2 mm out.

I would point out again that the final position of brick C was determined, by dowsing, through observing the disappearance of the individual energy fields, and the formation of radial lines from each of the three bricks.

This shows that when objects are at distances apart that conform with the Golden Mean their energy fields interact with each other. Additionally, the energy generated by this combined field is mainly beneficial, depending on the degree of accuracy of the placement. I am sure that in nature arrangements such as this occur, creating areas of 'good' energy.

The Golden Mean can be expressed in many other geometrical shapes such as rectangles, pentagons etc. Egg-shapes can also comply where the sum of the length of the long and short axes, multiplied by 1.618, is equal to the perimeter length. Some of the egg-shaped stone circles, as well as some of the flattened circles identified by Alexander Thom, closely match this ratio.

The incorporation of the Golden Mean into architecture, and in the construction of buildings and other structures, is therefore likely to create an atmosphere pleasing to those who live in them or use them. Old churches and cathedrals are a good example of this - where the peace within can be felt immediately on entering.'

Appendix F

The Acoustic Qualities of Underground Water

'A few years ago, I went to a Norman castle at Dundrum. It has an unusual circular keep. As I was approaching it, I noticed, by visual dowsing, there was a spring of underground water beneath the keep. When I reached the keep itself, there was a notice bringing visitors' attention to the fact that there was indeed a well in the centre of the floor of the keep. In fact, there was a glass panel over the well, so you could look down into it - so that was immediate confirmation that my initial dowsing was correct!

While I was walking over certain sections of the floor, I became aware that as I was talking to my friend, my voice changed its tone and resonance. It was similar to the effect you get when you put your hands loosely over your ears - and you get a kind of echoing sound. I got my friend to do it too - and we observed the same effect with his voice.

To start with, I wasn't sure if it was the underground water that was causing this effect, or whether it was just the circular nature of the keep echoing back in all directions.

A couple of days later, I tried an experiment by wandering around a field on my farm, talking nonsense to myself whilst continuously walking. I noticed that at certain places the tone of the voice changed in a similar manner - maybe not to the same extent I had experienced at the castle, but enough to be clearly noticeable. When I stopped to dowse at the places where this effect occurred, I found I was always standing above significant flows of underground water.

I found I wasn't able to detect all flows of underground water that way - it seemed to be only streams at particular depths. To find streams at other depths, I had to talk using a higher or a lower pitch of voice.'

Appendix G

Glossary of Dowsing Terms

One of the many contributions that Billy has made to the development of earth energy dowsing has been the first serious attempt to standardise the way in which dowsing concepts are described.

As we have seen, earth energy dowsing is a relatively new discipline and the terminology used is still in the process of crystallising into a stable understanding. In 1995, Billy produced a schedule of terms in common use, together with a description of what he felt they were intended to mean.

Over the years, many new terms have been added, while some on the original list have morphed in meaning. Billy's own work has contributed to the length of the schedule.

Such an undertaking is an unfolding process, as it is with any dictionary, but shown below is how dowsers generally describe the component parts of their work, as at the publication date of this book:

AQUIFER

A rock layer that contains water which may be released in appreciable amounts. The rock contains water-filled spaces, and when the spaces are connected by fissures the water is able to flow through the rock in underground streams.

AREA OF INFLUENCE
The extent of the zone around an object that is influenced by the energy field of that object. This distance can be much greater than the extremities of the energy field related to the object.

AURA
Another name for **energy field** but generally looked upon as the energy field around a living body. It is multi-layered and it reflects the well-being of the person on the physical, emotional and spiritual levels. Where illness is present in the body, a hole or weakness in the aura can be dowsed adjacent to the position in the body where an illness exists. It is considered that weaknesses in the aura will many times occur prior to clinical evidence of an illness; therefore dowsing of the aura can be used to give early diagnosis of a forthcoming health problem.

Sig Lonegren in *Spiritual Dowsing* refers to seven layers of the human aura. They are the Physical, the Astral or Emotional, the Mental, the Spiritual with three outer layers, the Causal, Monadic and Divine. The Divine covers the entire Cosmos and links us with the Creator.

BENEFICIAL ENERGY

A type of energy that is dowsed as being of benefit. This requires further definition to determine to what it may be beneficial. Energies that are dowsed as beneficial to humans can also be subdivided to determine the part or spectrum of our being that is most affected, i.e. the physical, emotional, mental or spiritual. Energies dowsed as beneficial or **detrimental** can usually be verified as such by using **kinesiology.** Beneficial energy is also dowsed as **yang** energy.

BLIND SPRING

A vertical shaft of ascending water that does not rise to the surface of the earth but disperses through several horizontal fissures which can be at various depths. Dowsers identify blind springs as several underground streams radiating from a central point. Some of these may subdivide into smaller streams.

Blind springs are found under many ancient sites and churches but are also to be found elsewhere throughout the countryside. There is an associated **energy field** that is unique to a blind spring as well as the water component. The Blind Spring will have a feeder stream at a greater depth. It is thought that the water is forced to rise up the vertical fissure due to a narrowing of the feeder stream.

CIRCADIAN RHYTHM

An observable rhythm or energy movement that can be measured over a period of twenty-four hours or one day-length. However the term is also loosely used to describe any cyclical movement of energy that corresponds with the phases of the sun, moon or planets and may be more than one day-length.

CONCENTRIC RINGS OR HALOES

These are circular rings of energy which some dowsers find around standing stones, tumuli, etc. There is debate amongst dowsers whether they are real phenomena or thought forms.

CRITICAL RELATIONSHIP

Where two or more objects are situated at specific distances apart so that their energy fields interact with each other and they behave as a single unit.

DETRIMENTAL ENERGY

A type of energy that is dowsed as harmful. This requires further definition to determine to what it may be harmful as certain energies may be harmful to one species of life and be

338

tolerated by others. Energies that are dowsed as detrimental to humans can also be subdivided to determine the part or spectrum of our being that is most affected i.e. the physical, emotional, mental or spiritual. Energies dowsed as detrimental to the physical being can usually be verified as such by using **kinesiology**.

DISTANT DOWSING / REMOTE DOWSING
Remotely dowsing the site or person under investigation; this can be done with the use of a map, photograph or as a purely mental process through visualisation.

DIVINING
(a) In ancient times divination was done by various procedures with no connection to modern dowsing procedures.

(b) The art and practice of discovering unknown things, usually by means of a pendulum, rods etc. or acquiring information by means which do not involve the use of the five senses, is also called divination.

DOME
A term used in the U.S.A. to describe a **Blind Spring**.

DOWN SHOOT (ENERGY)
This is where energy descends vertically into the Earth. It is usually in the form of a **spiral** or **vortex** but can also manifest as a pillar and occurs at some crossing points of underground water veins and grid crossing points. The spiral can rotate in a clockwise or anticlockwise direction.

DOWNSHAFT OR DOWNER (WATER)
This is where water from a horizontal subterranean water course descends vertically down a fissure before flowing onwards, horizontally, usually as a single vein. This is the opposite to a **blind spring** where the water rises. There is a unique **energy field** associated with a downshaft of water which can be identified through dowsing.

DOWSING
The art of discovering the presence of energies, substances, objects or missing persons or things not apparent to the senses, usually by using rods, a pendulum, etc. Dowsing can also be carried out without the use of tools. This is called deviceless dowsing. Dowsing is generally divided into three categories: physical or **site dowsing**, **map or distant dowsing** and **information dowsing**. The word "dowsing" derives from mediaeval German (da sein) which means 'it is there'; its first recorded use was by John Lock in 1692. It is sometimes taken as equivalent to divining, but the two terms are not completely synonymous. In the U.S.A. dowsing for water is known as "water witching" but most dowsers are now trying to get away from using this term.

EARTH ENERGY
A naturally-occurring field of subtle energy relating to or emanating from the earth as a whole.

EARTH ENERGIES
Different from the above in that they include all energies that can be dowsed on the surface of the earth. The source of these energies may be outside the earth or in specific parts of the earth, e.g. solar, lunar, planetary and other cosmic sources as well as topographical features on earth.

EARTH GRIDS
A regular pattern of crossing energy lines which surround the earth. Some of these energies alone or in combination with other energies, it is thought, may cause illness. Several different grids have been dowsed, each with their own characteristics. The best known are the **Hartmann** (N/S, E/W) and **Curry** (diagonal) grids. R. Schneider discovered two others called the 3rd and 4th (diagonal) grids. The distance between lines in a specific grid form appears to vary according to latitude and form a rectangle rather than a square. Each grid form has a different orientation.

The **Hartmann grid** was named after Dr Ernst Hartmann who is believed to be the first to observe earth grids. It is a world wide grid in accordance with the earth's magnetic field, i.e. approximately N/S, E/W. There are considerable variations in the grid spacing dependent on local conditions and the degree of latitude.

The **Curry grid** was named after the German doctor Dr Manfred Curry who was the founder of the Bioclimatic Institute in Bavaria. It is thought to be more biologically damaging than the Hartmann, especially the double lines that occur at approximately every 50 metres. The distance of the grid line spacings vary according to location and can vary from 2.5 x 3.5 m. In England they are approximately at 2.36 x 2.7 m.

EARTH SPIRIT / SPIRIT OF PLACE / GENIUS LOCII.
A manifestation found in a particular place, often a natural setting, such as a grove of trees or a stone circle. It is considered to be the guardian or controlling spirit of that location and it is recommended that proper respect be given to it when visiting the area and its permission gained before entering the site.

ENERGY DOME
A discernible area of energy in the shape of a sphere, half of which is above the surface of the ground and is to be found above some conjunctions of underground water. Quite often a circle of energy as dowsed on the surface of the ground when dowsed on its vertical plane will be found to form a dome.

ENERGY FIELD

An area of energy around an object which is specific to that object and being transmitted by it. This energy can be detected by dowsing or at certain frequencies by instruments. Another term for energy field is **"aura"** although this is generally associated with the human energy field.

ENERGY GRIDS

A series of crossing parallel lines that can be found as a component of the energy field of all objects. The ends of these lines are joined together so that energy can flow from one section of the grid to the other. Each grid type has different spacings and number of lines and the orientation of the lines are different. Each line is part **positive** and part **negative** in nature. The diagram on page 129 shows one typical grid type in two dimensional form. However energy grids display themselves three dimensionally and are therefore cubic in form. (First observed by W. A. Gawn.)

ENERGY LEYS

Lines of dowsable energy which generally run straight, are 6-8 feet wide at their central core, and often have further bands or edges to either side. Influenced both in width and strength by lunar and solar cycles. They are often found at what are called sacred sites. Whilst energy leys are considered to be natural energy phenomena it is also thought that they can be created by the formation of structures and in some cases have been observed to appear after a structure is built and are drawn to the site as the result of human activity of a spiritual nature.

ENERGY LINE

The direction energy takes when moving. It may be straight or curved, in several dimensions and be composed of one or more different types of energies, i.e. negative, positive or neutral. Energy lines can be found at standing stones and ancient sites but are a general feature in all **energy fields**.

ENERGY SOURCE

The object creating the **energy field** within which the particular energy is found. This could be a tree, a mountain, a river, a stone or any other feature on the earth, or the earth as a whole. If the energy is of cosmic origin then the source would be external to the earth. There is a line of opinion that it is the **energy field** that manifests the physical object and not the other way around (Walter Russell).

ENERGY SPRING OR SHAFT

A place where a shaft of energy is dowsed as rising vertically from the surface of the earth. This may have no association with underground water and is not to be confused with a **blind spring**. Generally this energy rises in the form of a vortex where the two dimensional plan view is in the form of a spiral; but it sometimes manifests as a helical cylinder of constant diameter, where the plan view appears as a circle.

FENG SHUI
Literally means "wind and water" and is a form of **geomancy** used by the Chinese that balances earth energies with human energies. It is said to place people between heaven and earth. It is used to determine the siting of dwellings and graves and regulates the flow of ch'i.

FLOW DIRECTION
The direction of movement of energy along a dowsable **energy line**.

FORCE OF ATTRACTION
An attractive force similar to, but different from, gravity that is within all matter and radiates from a hub in the form of lines. (First observed by W. A. Gawn.)

GEOGLYPH
A picture, diagram or shape found in the energy field by dowsing. These are formed by a single convoluted line of subtle earth energy. (First found by C. Bloy and investigated by H. Miller who called them pictograms.) Some more complicated forms that can be observed are similar to those found in rock art and landscape figures throughout the world and have also been termed as archetypal images by W. A. Gawn.

GEOLOGICAL FAULT
Major fractures in the rock structure of the earth's surface that create stress which, when relieved causes earthquakes. These faults emit energies that are generally considered by dowsers to be **detrimental** to most forms of life.

GEOMANCY
The art of placing structures on the landscapes, in such a way as to encourage and enhance beneficial energies, while the structure itself is in harmony with the earth.

GEOPATHIC STRESS
An unfavourable reaction of the biological system as the result of exposure to radiations from the earth that would be dowsed as **detrimental**.

GEOPATHIC ZONE
An area of the earth's surface that emits energy that is detrimental in nature and likely to cause geopathic stress in any life form exposed to it.

GOLDEN MEAN
The basic geometric ratio of 1 : 1.618 is both ancient and sacred . The Golden Mean is often found in nature and has been utilised extensively in the construction of early sacred and religious sites.   1.272 is the square root of the Golden Mean, and this has also been widely used in design and construction. A building constructed incorporating the Golden Mean in its design is unlikely to contain detrimental energy.

INFORMATION DOWSING
Where dowsing is used for gathering information about the subject under study, e.g. the depth or quantity of an underground flow of water.

KINESIOLOGY
A form of muscle resistance testing which can be used to identify whether different types of energy are **detrimental** or **beneficial** to us. One of its uses is to detect allergies and the health of the human body.

LEY
A significant alignment of sacred and secular sites across a landscape, generally inter-visible. The minimum number of aligned sites to qualify as a ley is five. The term was first used by Alfred Watkins in 1921. There is no associated energy line indicated by the term ley as Watkins described it, and therefore it is not to be confused with **Energy Ley.**

LEY LINE
The term used by many British dowsers to describe an **energy ley**, a straight line of energy that links ancient sites. It is easily confused with the term **ley** which is a purely visual alignment and therefore its use is not recommended.

MAGER ROSETTE
A disc divided into eight coloured segments. The colours of the segments, going clockwise, are black, white, purple, blue, green, yellow, red, and grey. It is used in energy dowsing, held between the finger and thumb, to identify differences in energy types so that the dowser can distinguish more accurately between one energy line and another. It is also used in water dowsing to identify the quality of water in an underground source.

MANIFESTATION
A dowsable symmetrical pattern found at the crossing point of two significant earth energy lines. (First mentioned by H. Miller.)

MAP DOWSING
A method of dowsing using a map, or drawing, instead of visiting the site, or beforehand . This can be done using a pendulum in one hand whilst pointing at the map, or drawing, with a pencil in the other hand. When the target is found the pendulum will swing in the affirmative. However, many other techniques are used successfully. Map dowsing undertaken prior to a site visit will reduce the time spent on site.

MEASUREMENT
Any method by which a rule or calibrated instrument on a scale of 1-100 is used to determine the quality, rate or vibration of an object. It can be also be done by counting in whatever measurement is most suitable until a positive dowsing response is felt. In many applications measurement will greatly assist the dowser.

NEGATIVE
A term used to indicate energy of a specific type, i.e. opposite to **positive**. This use of the word negative does not necessarily indicate any similarity in earth energies to the behaviour of electricity or magnetism. Whilst that is so it may be that some energies that are dowsed have electrical and/or magnetic components. Lunar energy is thought to be negative as is **yin** energy. Some negative energy is **detrimental** to various forms of life.

NOXIOUS ENERGY
A type of energy that may be harmful to humans or some other species of life or vegetation. This is generally found in association with underground water and at the crossing points of some types of energy line. It is considered that noxious energy will cause **geopathic stress** in humans and most animals and affect the growth of trees etc. Other forms of life, ants, cats etc. appear to tolerate and continue to thrive in the presence of noxious energy.

PLANETARY GRID
A regular pattern of crossing energy lines detectable on the Earth's surface, similar to Earth Grids, but relating to other planets. Planetary Grid lines are much farther apart than those of Earth Grids. Grids of all the planets as far as Saturn have been detected. (First observed by W. A. Gawn.)

POLARISATION
Polarisation is the preferred direction of light, radio and earth energy waves. All have oscillating and overlapping electric and magnetic fields which travel in planes perpendicular to each other. There can be horizontal, vertical, circular and elliptical polarisation.

POLARITY
Polarity is used to indicate opposites such as **positive** and **negative**, male and female. The relationship between polarity and the dowsing response is not universal, but can be identified by a different action such as a rod turning up or down or a pendulum rotating clockwise or anticlockwise.

POSITIVE
A term used to indicate energy of a specific type, i.e. opposite to **negative**. This use of the word positive does not necessarily indicate any similarity in earth energies to the behaviour of electricity or magnetism. Whilst that is so it may be that some energies that are dowsed have electrical and/or magnetic components. Solar energy is thought to be positive as is **yang** energy. Some positive energy can be **beneficial** to various forms of life.

POWER CENTRE

A place where there is an intensity of **beneficial energy** and a meeting point of **yang** and **yin earth energies**. Power centres are associated with **blind springs** that have at least one **energy ley** crossing them and are found at most ancient sacred sites. However they can also be found elsewhere. Power centres are generally considered to be places suitable for spiritual enlightenment and healing. Dowsers using a sleeved L rod have noted that when directly over a power centre the rod will rotate through 360 degrees.

PRIMARY WATER or VIRGIN WATER

Primary water is formed inside the earth, as opposed to surface water that is formed in the atmosphere as rain, snow, etc. The primary water theory says that steam under great pressure, deep in the earth, is forced upwards, condensing as it gets closer to the surface. This occurs in deep faults and fractures; where these are, vertical **blind springs** or **domes** are formed. At places where primary water is found the energy will be predominately **yin** or **negative** in nature.

RADIAL LINES

A series of **energy lines** radiating out from a source point. These lines terminate some distance from the source point, the larger the source the greater the length of the lines. They usually terminate in a **spiral** and are not of equal length or equal distance apart. They can be of different polarities, i.e. **negative**, **positive** or neutral.

REVERSAL POINT

A location on the earth's surface where if an object is placed it will cause a reversal of the earthing of detrimental energy and allow it to invade our living environment. This can occur naturally due to the topography of the earth or through casual or intentional actions by humans.

SECONDARY WATER

This is water that forms the water table of the earth. It is derived from rain water and other forms of condensation at the surface of the earth. See also **Primary Water**.

SERPENT LINE

Lines of energy found on the surface of the earth by dowsers, and are unlike **energy leys** in that they do not run straight. They can be of any length from a few feet to many miles. The term was coined by Hamish Miller and Paul Broadhurst. The Michael and Mary lines which cross England from Cornwall to the East coast of Norfolk are described in their book *The Sun and the Serpent*, and the Apollo and Athena lines that cross Europe are described in their book *The Dance of The Dragon*.

SITE DOWSING

Dowsing on the expected or desired site for the object or information sought: also called survey dowsing or on site dowsing.

SPIRALS
These may be clockwise or anticlockwise in direction of flow. They are formed by a line spiralling either in towards or out from a point. There can be differing numbers of coils but they are generally of uneven number, the most common being seven. Close examination may show that a spiral is the plan view of an energy cone or vortex. Spirals are often connected to each other by gently curving **energy lines**.

SPRINGS
Springs are the point where water, **primary** or **secondary**, naturally wells out of the ground. The water from some springs is considered to be of benefit and assist in healing. Others due to their location and quality of water are called holy wells.

TELLURIC ENERGY
Another name for **earth energy**.

TOROID
The form taken when a spiralling line rotates in a closed curve lying in its plane. Colloquially known as a 'donut' (doughnut) in the U.S.

TOROIDAL ENERGY
Energy that moves in the form of a **toroid.** This can often be found at the commencement and termination points of a vertical pillar or **vortex** of energy. Often found at ancient sites, particularly henges.

VORTEX
The form that energy can take when either ascending or descending vertically. Usually found in groups of up to seven terminating in a toroid, joined either point to point or base to base. In some cases, at these junctions, the flow of the energy can change from clockwise to anticlockwise or vice-versa. Change in **polarity** can also occur from negative to positive can also occur. Vortices are a feature where **energy lines** intersect.

WAVELENGTH
The characteristics of an energy, indicating its rate of vibration. The wavelength is measured as one complete oscillation of the wave.

YANG
A term used by practitioners of feng shui, and although not exactly the same, is used by western dowsers as an alternative term for positive energy. Yang energy is considered to be masculine and active.

YIN
A term used by practitioners of feng shui, and although not exactly the same, is used by western dowsers as an alternative term for negative energy. Yin energy is considered to be feminine and receptive.

Bibliography

From Genetics to Revelation

W.A. Gawn
Megalithic Structures: Why?, Self published, 2009

W. A. Gawn
A History of Second Donegore Presbyterian Church, Second Donegore
Presbyterian Church, 2008

John Steele and Paul Deveraux
Earth Mind, Destiny, 1992

Francis Hitching
Earth Magic, Morrow, 1977

Terry Ross and Richard Wright
The Divining Mind, Inner Traditions, 1989

Earth Energy Matters (journals)
British Society of Dowsers, 1995-2005

Hidden Heritage (TV programme)
Ulster Television, 2006

Dowsing in Theory and Practice

Christopher Bird
The Divining Hand, Schiffer Press, 1979

Aubrey Burl
A Guide to the Stone Circles of Britain, Ireland and Brittany, Yale University
Press, 1995

Alfred Watkins
The Old Straight Track, Methuen, 1925 and Abacus (reprinted edition), 1974

Guy Underwood
The Pattern of the Past, Abacus, 1969

Rory Macquisten
Dowsing Observations, Self Published, 2011

Tony Hathaway
The Construction of Arigna Circle Earth Energy Matters (Journal), BSD, September 2000

Colin Bloy
Dowsing the Dragon, 2000

Hamish Miller & Paul Broadhurst
The Sun and the Serpent, Pendragon Press, 1990

Alanna Moore
Geomantica (Online Journal), September 2011

New Frontiers

Baron Gustav von Pohl
Earth Currents, Frech Verlag, Germany, 1929 (English translation, 1988)

Professor Philip Callahan
Ancient Mysteries - Modern Visions, Acres (US), 1984

Barbara Brennan
Hands of Light, Bantam, 1988

Neil Turok
The Cyclic Universe, Edge (journal), 2007

Charles Darwin
On the Origin of Species, Murray, 1859

James Lovelock
The Revenge of Gaia, Allen Lane, 2006

John Evans
The Silent Sound, Ross Evans, 2001

Making Sense of the Seriously Spiritual

Lynne McTaggart
The Field, Harper Collins, 2003

Nigel Twinn
Hamish Miller: A Life Divined, Penwith Press, 2010

Jan Spence
Dowsing at Fishbourne Church, Earth Energy Matters (Journal), BSD, 1999

Jan Spence
Dowsing at St David's Catherdral, Earth Energy Matters (Journal), BSD, 2001

Sigmund Freud
The Question of Lay Analysis, 1926

Robert Stone (discussing the work of Cleve Backster)
The Secret Life of Your Cells, Whitford, 1984

Larry Gedney
Do Trees Communicate for Mutual Defence?, Geophysical Institute, University of Alaska, Fairbanks, 1986

Victoria Gill
Plants Can Think and Remember, BBC (website), July 2010

Stanislaw Karpinski
Society of Experimental Biology, Prague (lecture)

Christine Foyer
University of Leeds, BBC (website)

Rupert Sheldrake
The Presence of the Past, Times Books, 1988

Jacques Benveniste
Water Memory, Nature (journal), 1988

Madeline Ennis
Inflammation Research (journal), Queens University Belfast, 2004

Georgius Agricola
De Re Metallica, 1556

J. W. Gough
The Mines of Mendip, David and Charles, 1967

Colonel H. Grattan
A Successful Feat - Practical Dowsing, G. Bell and Sons, 1965

Wayne Dyer
Excuses Begone, Hay House, 2010

Wayne Dyer
The Power of Intention, Hay House, 2010

Wayne Dyer
You'll See It When You Believe It, William Morrow

John Michell
The View Over Atlantis, Harper Collins, 1969

Sir James George Frazer
The Golden Bough, 1890, (reprint of the abridged 1922 edition) Dover, 2002

Alexander Thom
Megalithic Remains in Britain and Brittany, Clarendon Press, 1968

Appendices

Recumbent Stone Circles, Adventures in Archaeology (website)

Tomnaverie, Megaliths - Scotland (website)

Aikey Brae Stone Circle, Undiscovered Scotland (website)

Nine Stanes, Ancient Scotland (website)

Easter Aquhorthies, Aberdeenshire Council (website)

Sig Lonegren
Spiritual Dowsing, Gothic Image, 1986

Hamish Miller and Paul Broadhurst
The Dance of the Dragon, Pendragon Press, 2000